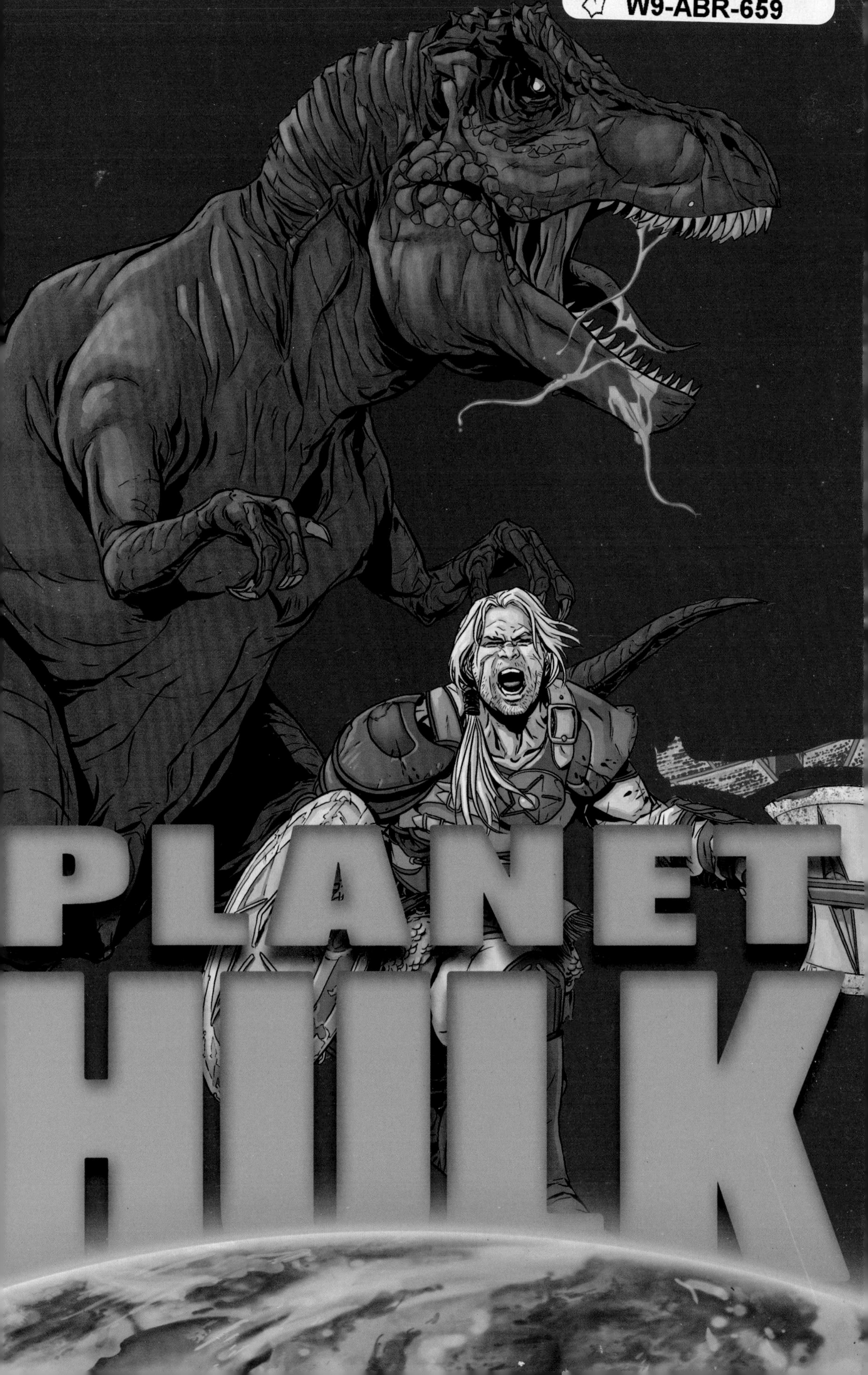
PLANET
HULK

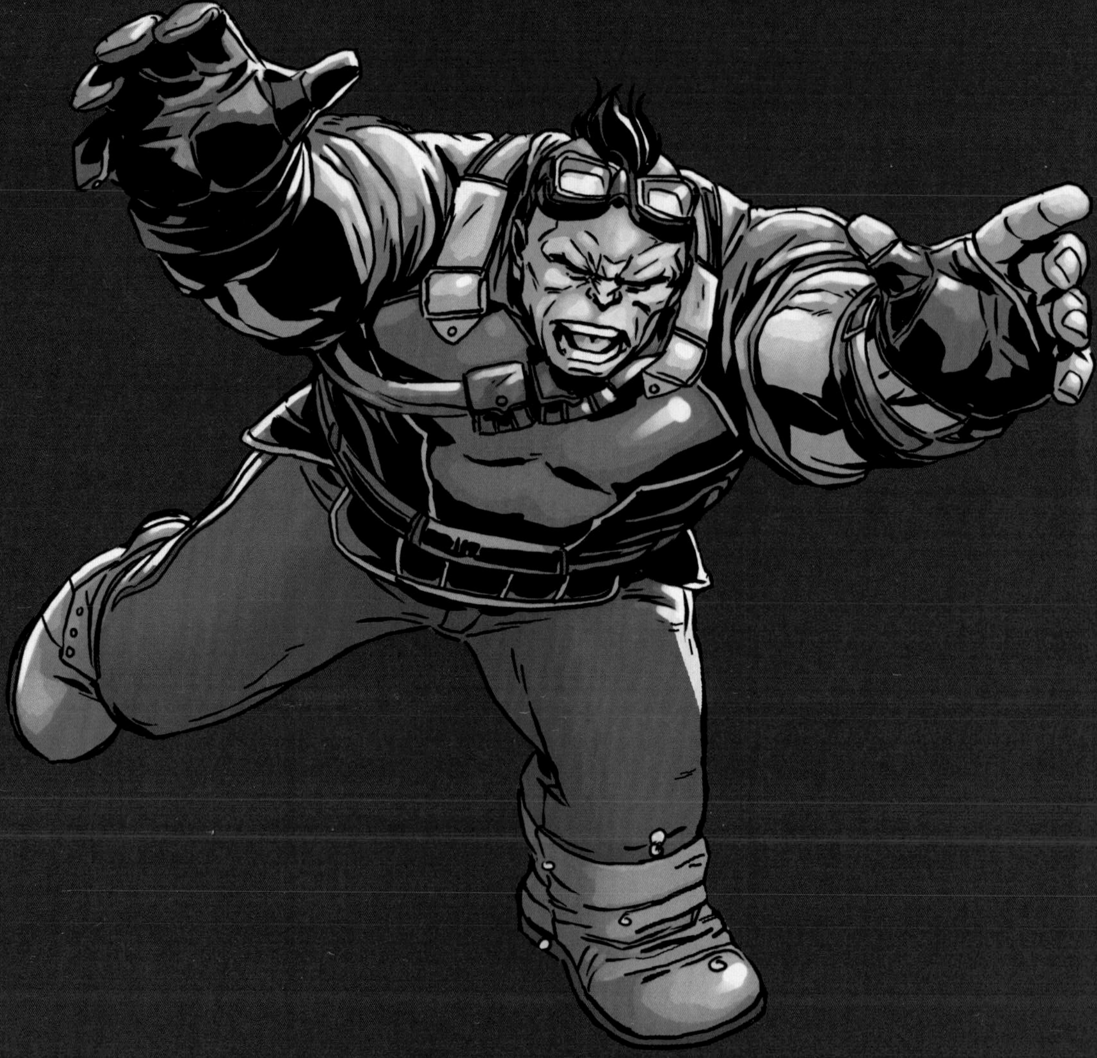

COLLECTION EDITOR: SARAH BRUNSTAD
ASSOCIATE MANAGING EDITOR: ALEX STARBUCK
EDITORS, SPECIAL PROJECTS: JENNIFER GRÜNWALD & MARK D. BEAZLEY
SENIOR EDITOR, SPECIAL PROJECTS: JEFF YOUNGQUIST
SVP PRINT, SALES & MARKETING: DAVID GABRIEL

EDITOR IN CHIEF: AXEL ALONSO
CHIEF CREATIVE OFFICER: JOE QUESADA
PUBLISHER: DAN BUCKLEY
EXECUTIVE PRODUCER: ALAN FINE

PLANET HULK: WARZONES! Contains material originally published in magazine form as PLANET HULK #1-5. First printing 2015. ISBN# 978-0-7851-9881-9. Published by MARVEL WORLDWIDE, INC., a subsidiary of MARVEL ENTERTAINMENT, LLC. OFFICE OF PUBLICATION: 135 West 50th Street, New York, NY 10020. **Printed in Canada.** ALAN FINE, President, Marvel Entertainment; DAN BUCKLEY, President, TV, Publishing and Brand Management; JOE QUESADA, Chief Creative Officer; TOM BREVOORT, SVP of Publishing; DAVID BOGART, SVP of Operations & Procurement, Publishing; C.B. CEBULSKI, VP of International Development & Brand Management; DAVID GABRIEL, SVP Print, Sales & Marketing; JIM O'KEEFE, VP of Operations & Logistics; DAN CARR, Executive Director of Publishing Technology; SUSAN CRESPI, Editorial Operations Manager; ALEX MORALES, Publishing Operations Manager; STAN LEE, Chairman Emeritus. For information regarding advertising in Marvel Comics or on Marvel.com, please contact Jonathan Rheingold, VP of Custom Solutions & Ad Sales, at jrheingold@marvel.com. For Marvel subscription inquiries, please call 800-217-9158. **Manufactured between 11/6/2015 and 12/14/2015 by SOLISCO PRINTERS, SCOTT, QC, CANADA.**

10 9 8 7 6 5 4 3 2 1

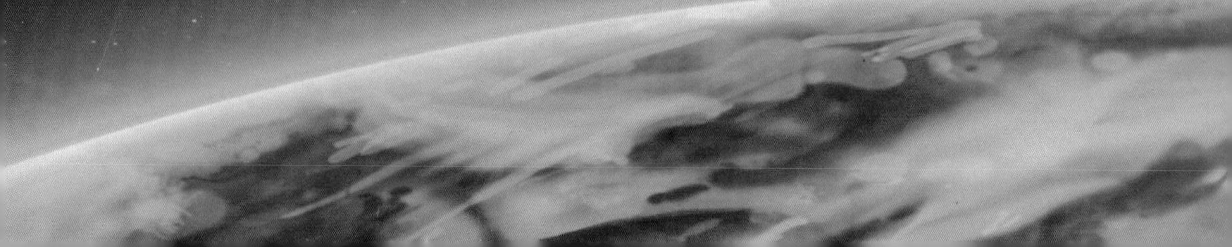

PLANET HULK

WARZONES!

WRITER
SAM HUMPHRIES

ARTIST
MARC LAMING

COLORIST
JORDAN BOYD

WRITER
VC's TRAVIS LANHAM

COVER ART
MIKE DEL MUNDO

"PHOENIX BURNING"

WRITER
GREG PAK

ARTIST
TAKESHI MIYAZAWA

COLORS
RACHELLE ROSENBERG

LETTERER
TRAIS LANHAM

"AMAZING SCIENCE" ART
LEONARD KIRK & TAMRA BONVILLAIN

ASSISTANT EDITORS
CHRIS ROBINSON & EMILY SHAW

EDITOR
MARK PANICCIA

HULK CREATED BY **STAN LEE** & **JACK KIRBY**

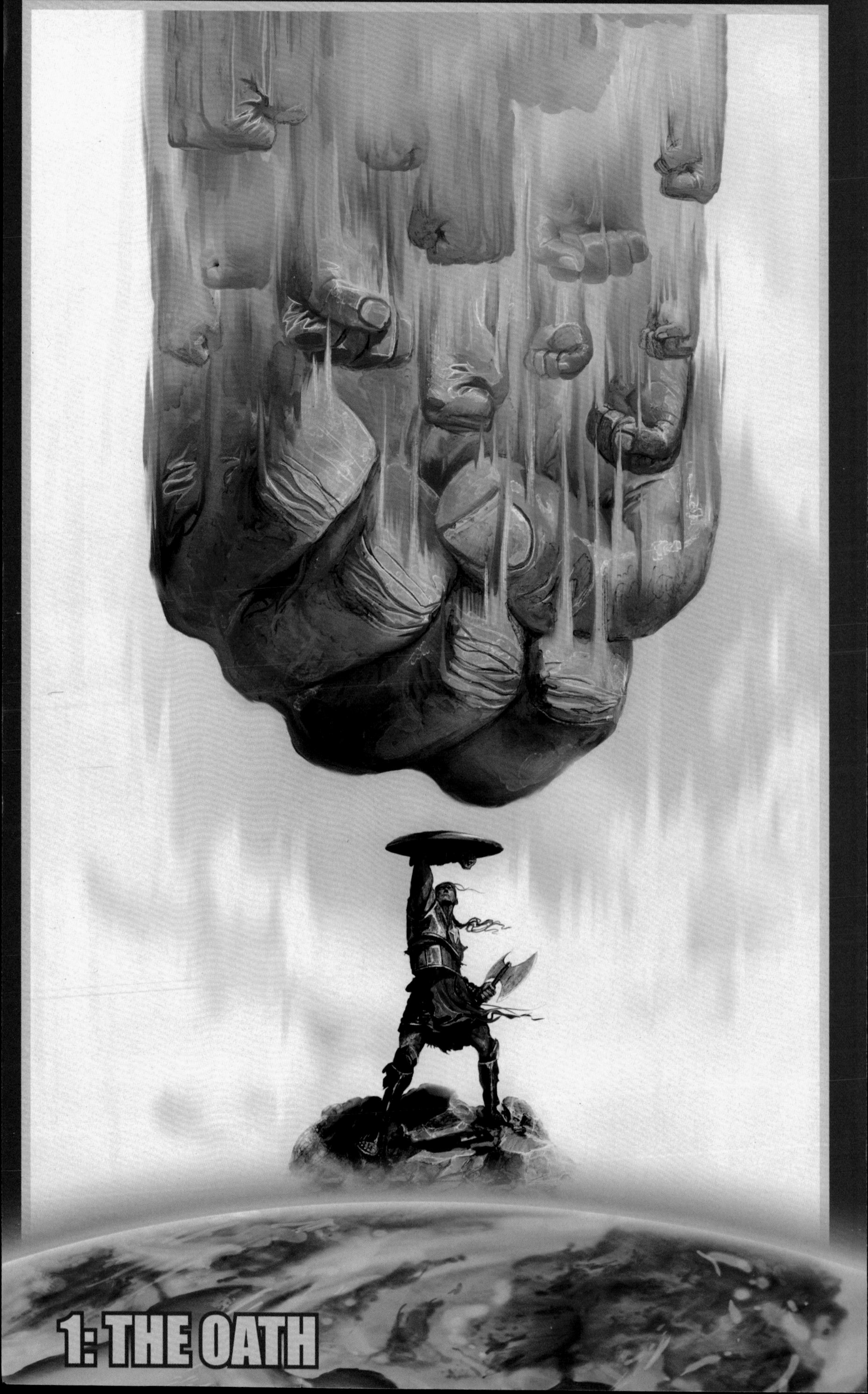

1: THE OATH

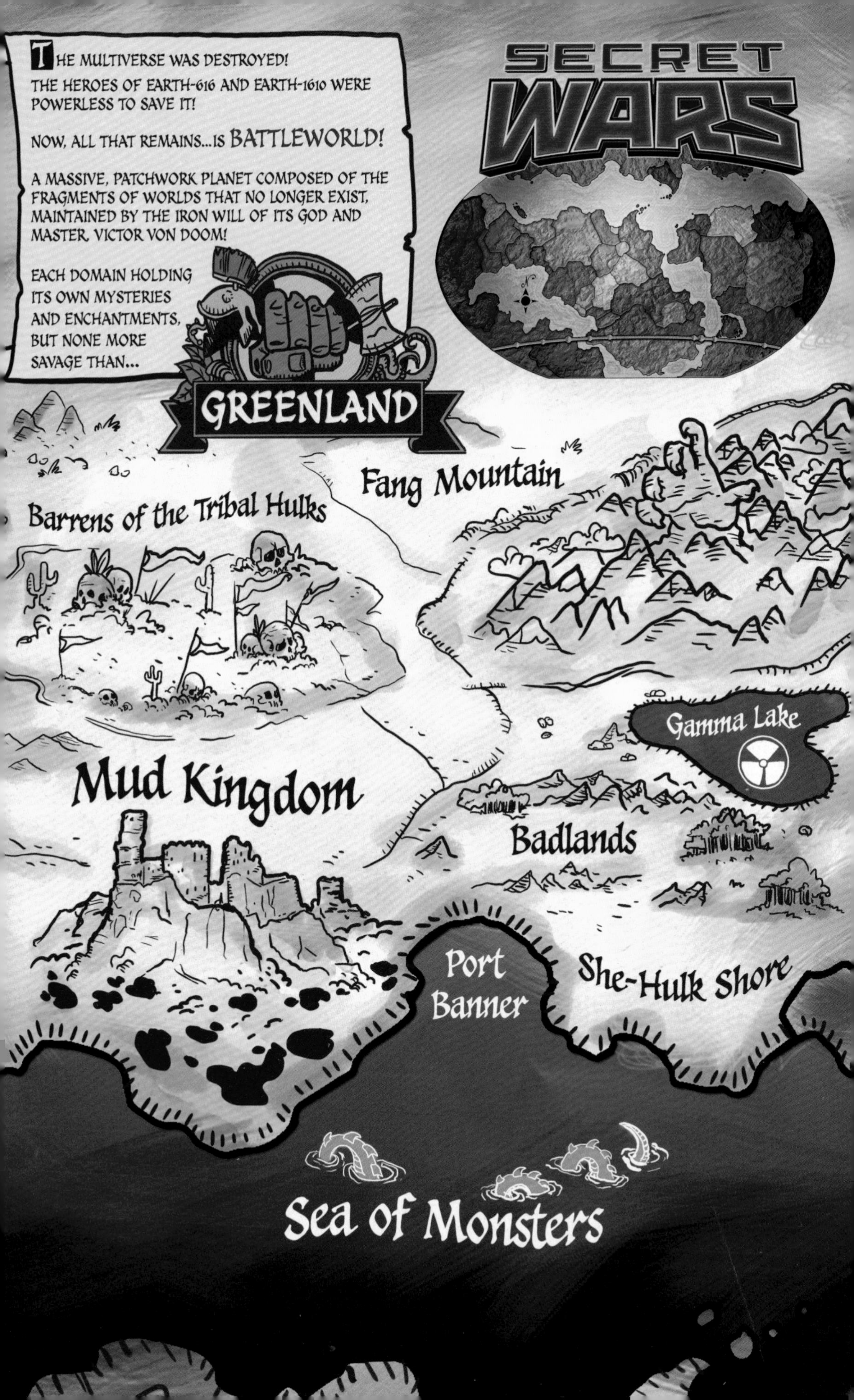
THE MULTIVERSE WAS DESTROYED!
THE HEROES OF EARTH-616 AND EARTH-1610 WERE POWERLESS TO SAVE IT!
NOW, ALL THAT REMAINS...IS BATTLEWORLD!
A MASSIVE, PATCHWORK PLANET COMPOSED OF THE FRAGMENTS OF WORLDS THAT NO LONGER EXIST, MAINTAINED BY THE IRON WILL OF ITS GOD AND MASTER, VICTOR VON DOOM!
EACH DOMAIN HOLDING ITS OWN MYSTERIES AND ENCHANTMENTS, BUT NONE MORE SAVAGE THAN...
SECRET WARS
GREENLAND
Fang Mountain
Barrens of the Tribal Hulks
Gamma Lake
Mud Kingdom
Badlands
Port Banner
She-Hulk Shore
Sea of Monsters

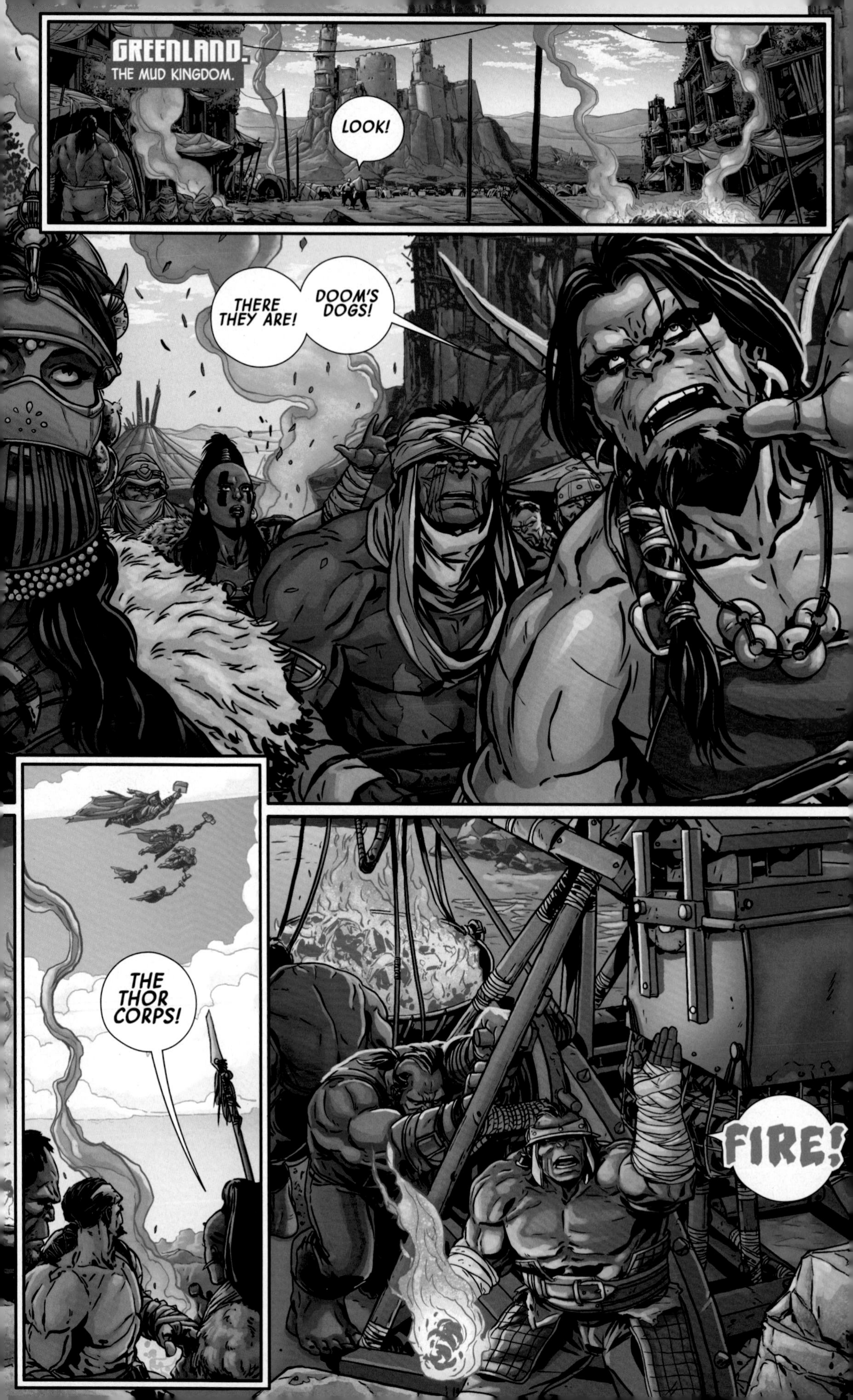
GREENLAND.
THE MUD KINGDOM.
LOOK!
THERE THEY ARE!
DOOM'S DOGS!
THE THOR CORPS!
FIRE!

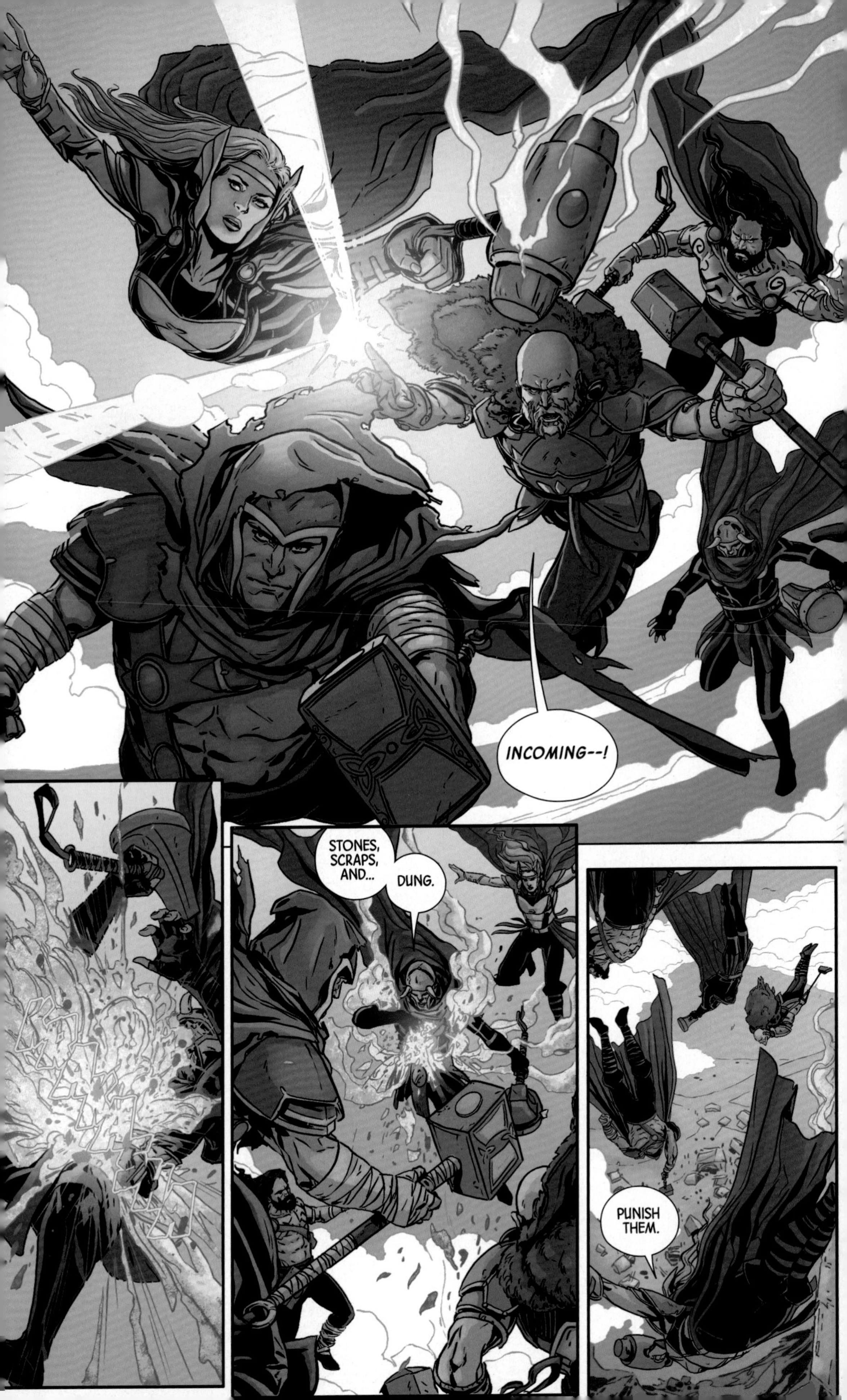
INCOMING--!
STONES, SCRAPS, AND...
DUNG.
PUNISH THEM.

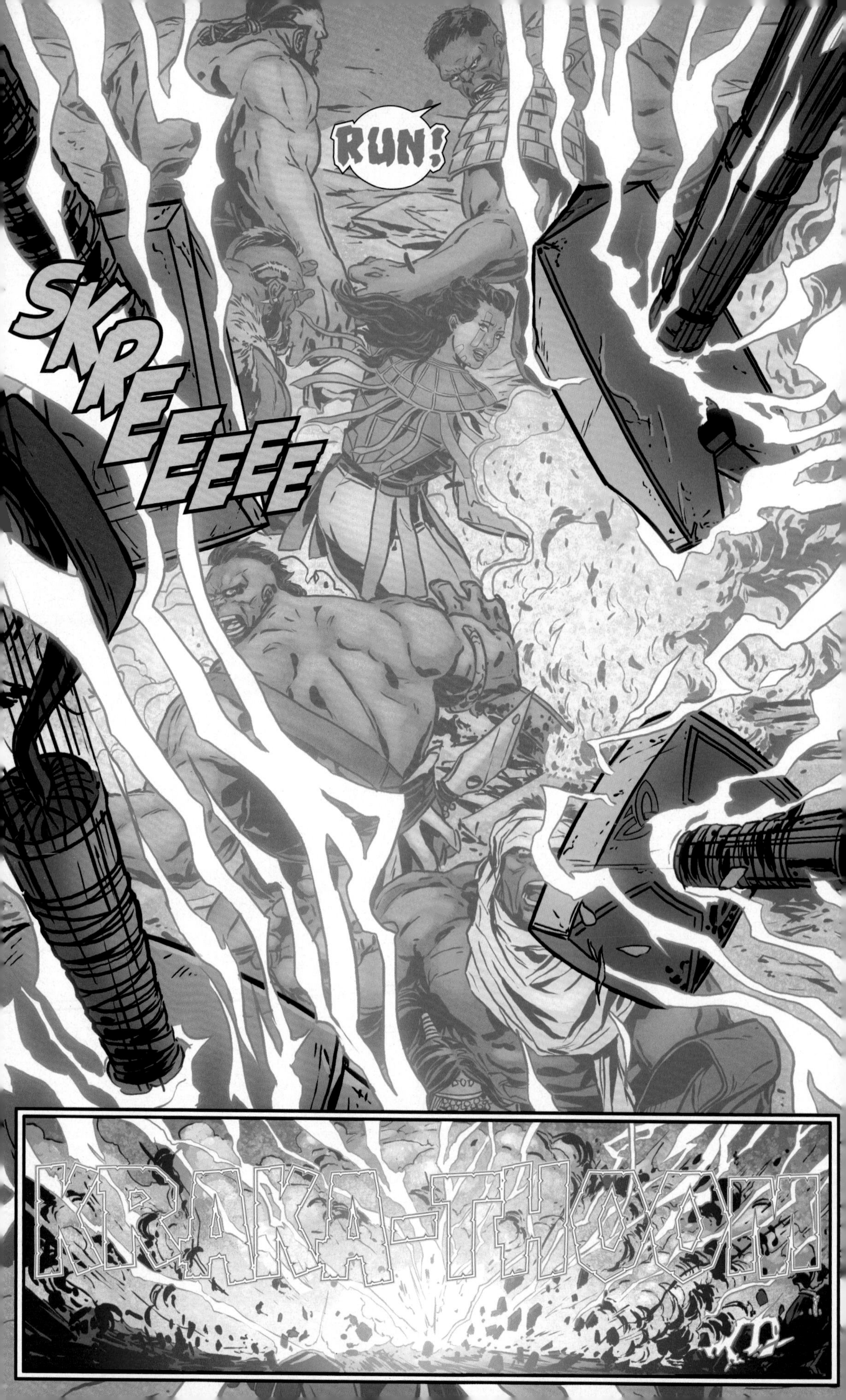
RUN!
SKREEEEEE
KRAKA-THOOM

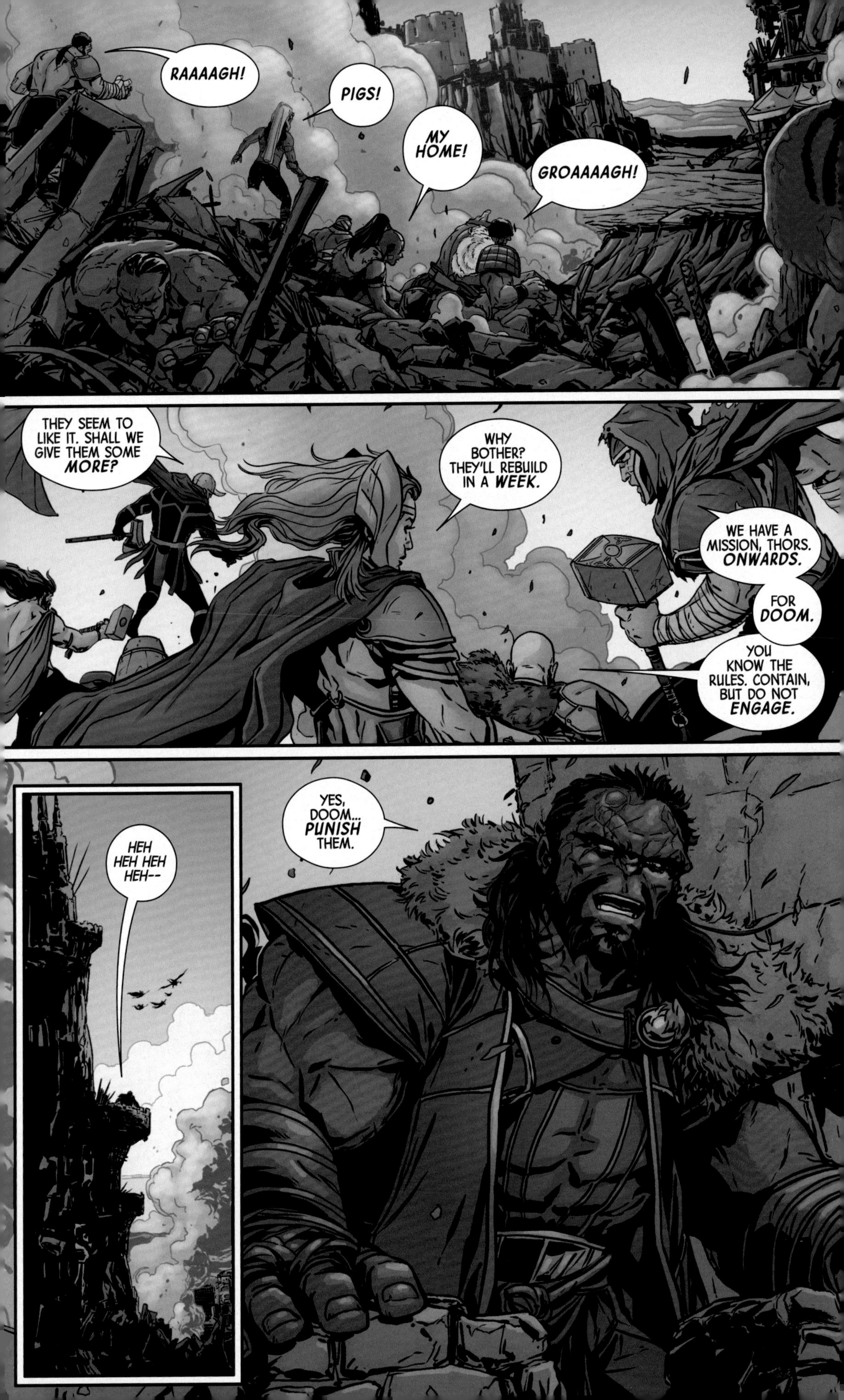
RAAAAGH!
PIGS!
MY HOME!
GROAAAAGH!
THEY SEEM TO LIKE IT. SHALL WE GIVE THEM SOME MORE?
WHY BOTHER? THEY'LL REBUILD IN A WEEK.
WE HAVE A MISSION, THORS. ONWARDS.
FOR DOOM.
YOU KNOW THE RULES. CONTAIN, BUT DO NOT ENGAGE.
HEH HEH HEH HEH--
YES, DOOM... PUNISH THEM.

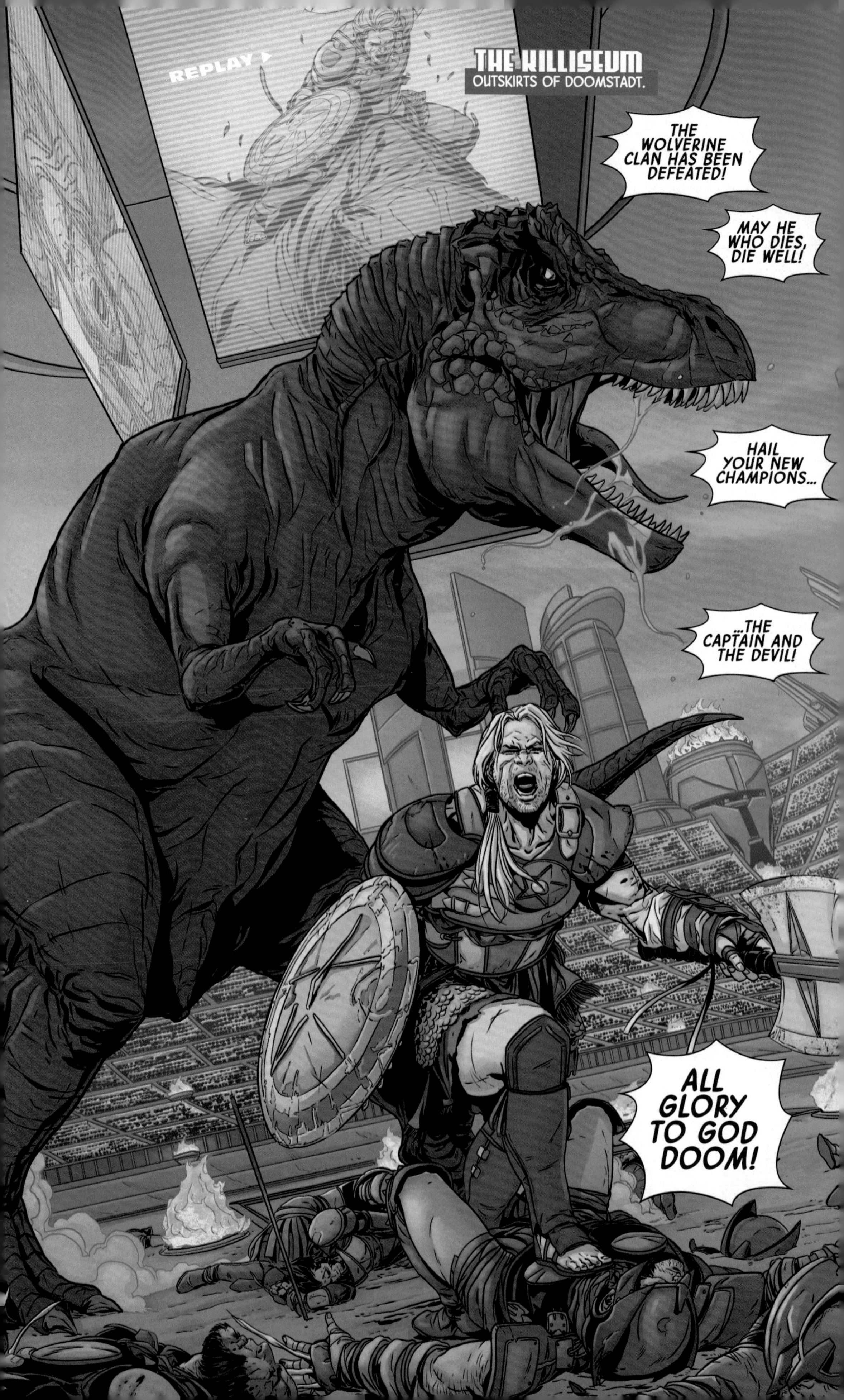
REPLAY
THE KILLISEUM
OUTSKIRTS OF DOOMSTADT.
THE WOLVERINE CLAN HAS BEEN DEFEATED!
MAY HE WHO DIES, DIE WELL!
HAIL YOUR NEW CHAMPIONS...
...THE CAPTAIN AND THE DEVIL!
ALL GLORY TO GOD DOOM!

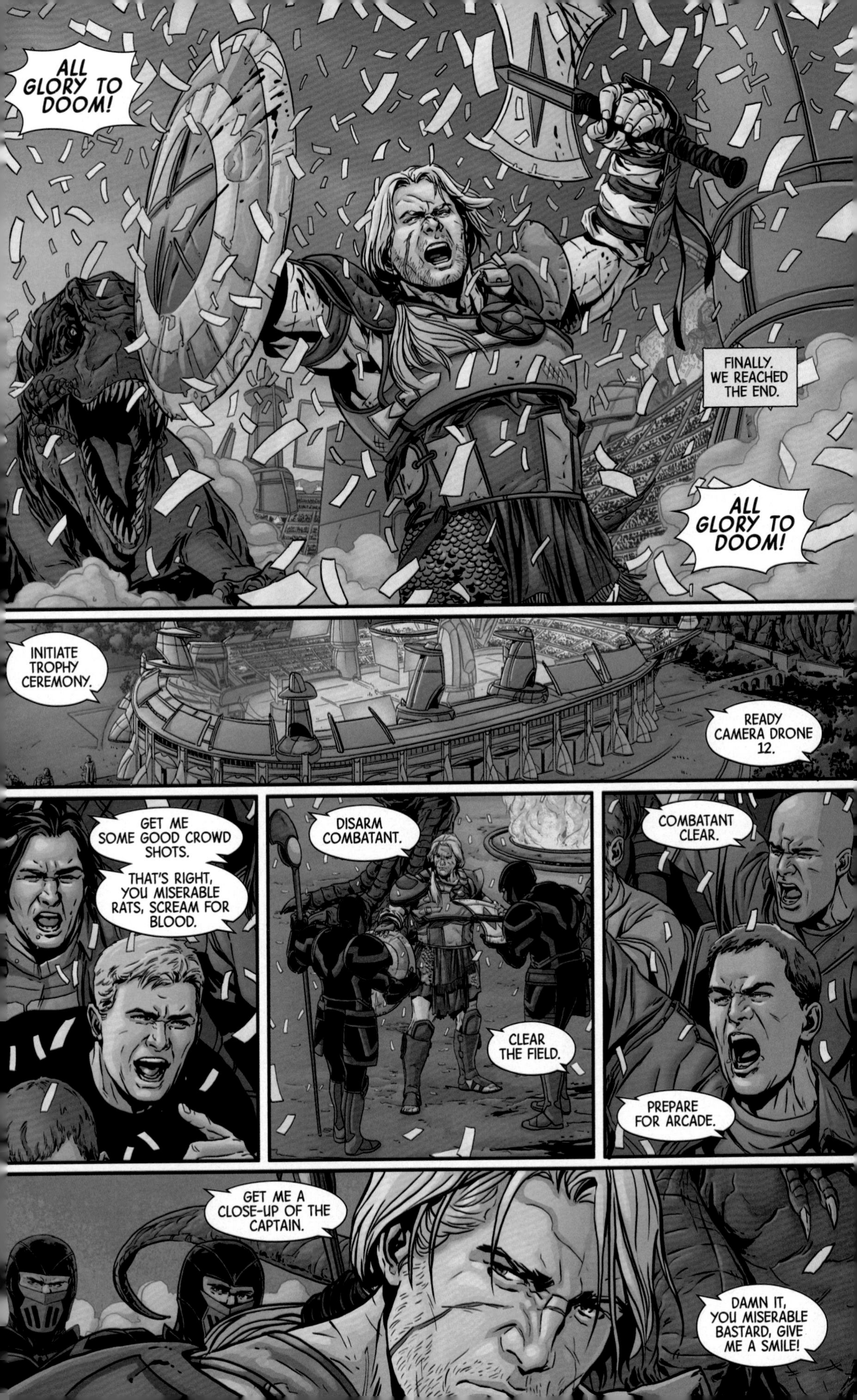
ALL GLORY TO DOOM!
FINALLY. WE REACHED THE END.
ALL GLORY TO DOOM!
INITIATE TROPHY CEREMONY.
READY CAMERA DRONE 12.
GET ME SOME GOOD CROWD SHOTS.
THAT'S RIGHT, YOU MISERABLE RATS, SCREAM FOR BLOOD.
DISARM COMBATANT.
CLEAR THE FIELD.
COMBATANT CLEAR.
PREPARE FOR ARCADE.
GET ME A CLOSE-UP OF THE CAPTAIN.
DAMN IT, YOU MISERABLE BASTARD, GIVE ME A SMILE!

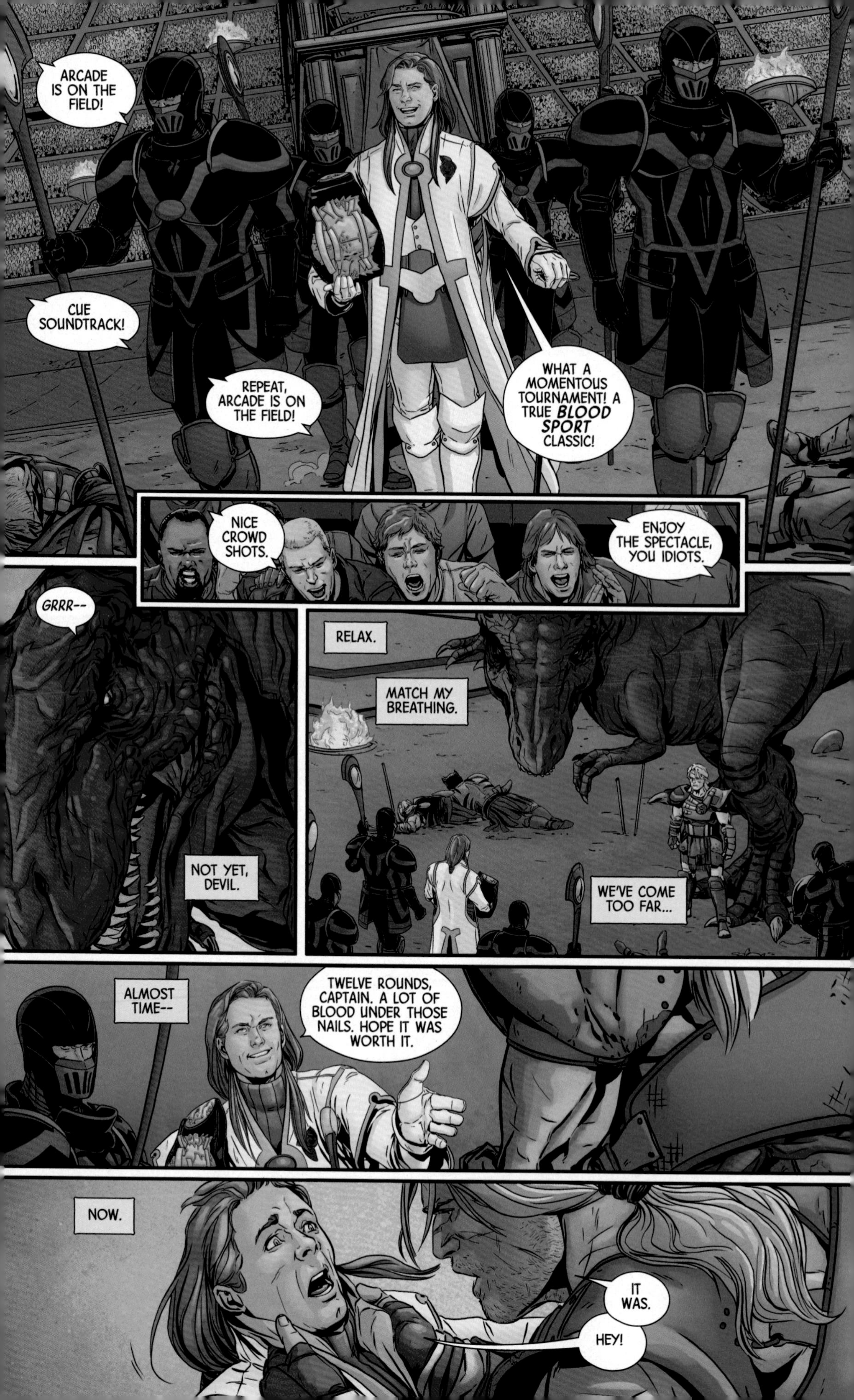
ARCADE IS ON THE FIELD!
CUE SOUNDTRACK!
REPEAT, ARCADE IS ON THE FIELD!
WHAT A MOMENTOUS TOURNAMENT! A TRUE BLOOD SPORT CLASSIC!
NICE CROWD SHOTS.
ENJOY THE SPECTACLE, YOU IDIOTS.
GRRR--
NOT YET, DEVIL.
RELAX.
MATCH MY BREATHING.
WE'VE COME TOO FAR...
ALMOST TIME--
TWELVE ROUNDS, CAPTAIN. A LOT OF BLOOD UNDER THOSE NAILS. HOPE IT WAS WORTH IT.
NOW.
IT WAS.
HEY!

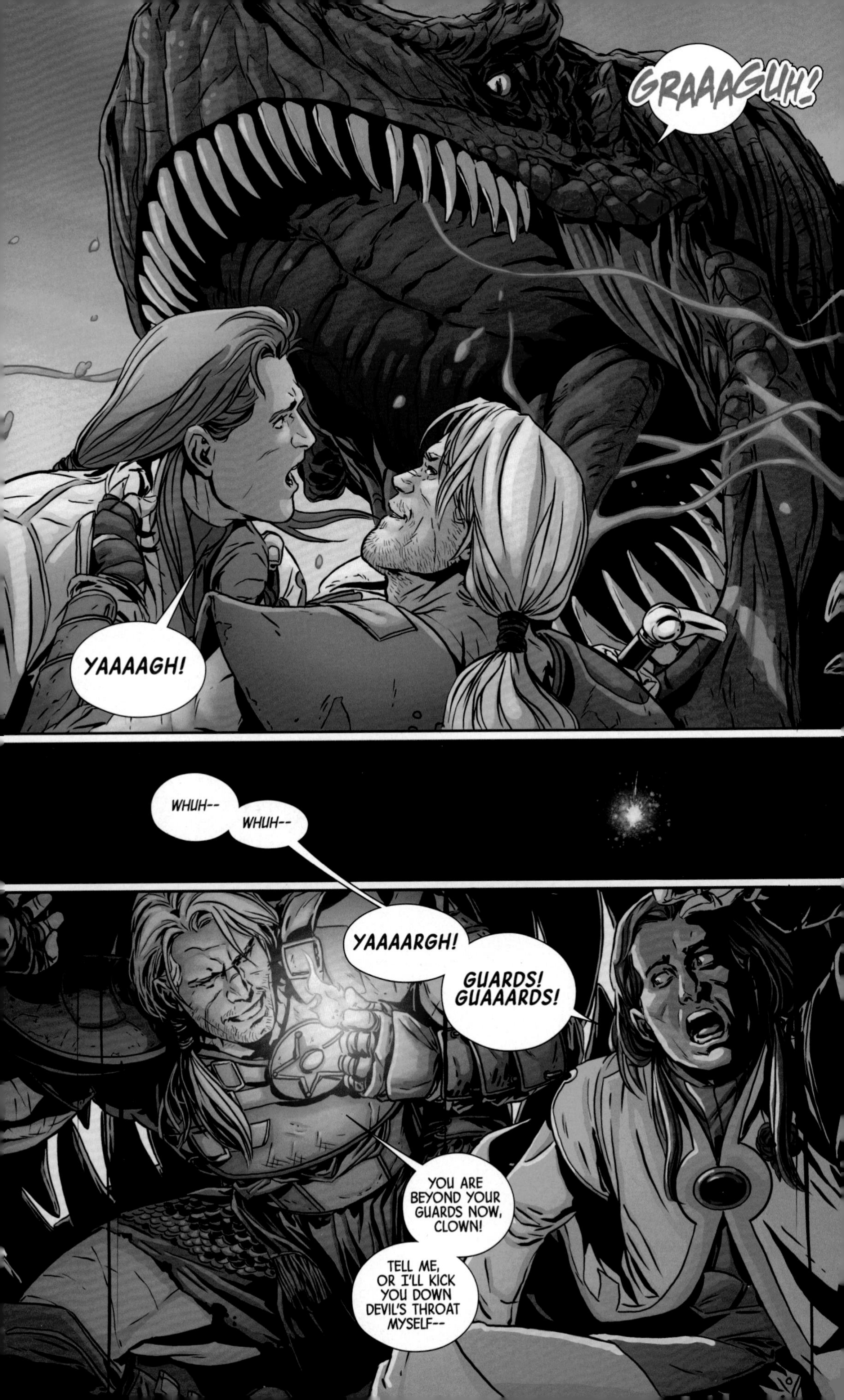
GRAAAGUH!
YAAAAGH!
WHUH--
WHUH--
YAAAARGH!
GUARDS! GUAAARDS!
YOU ARE BEYOND YOUR GUARDS NOW, CLOWN!
TELL ME, OR I'LL KICK YOU DOWN DEVIL'S THROAT MYSELF--

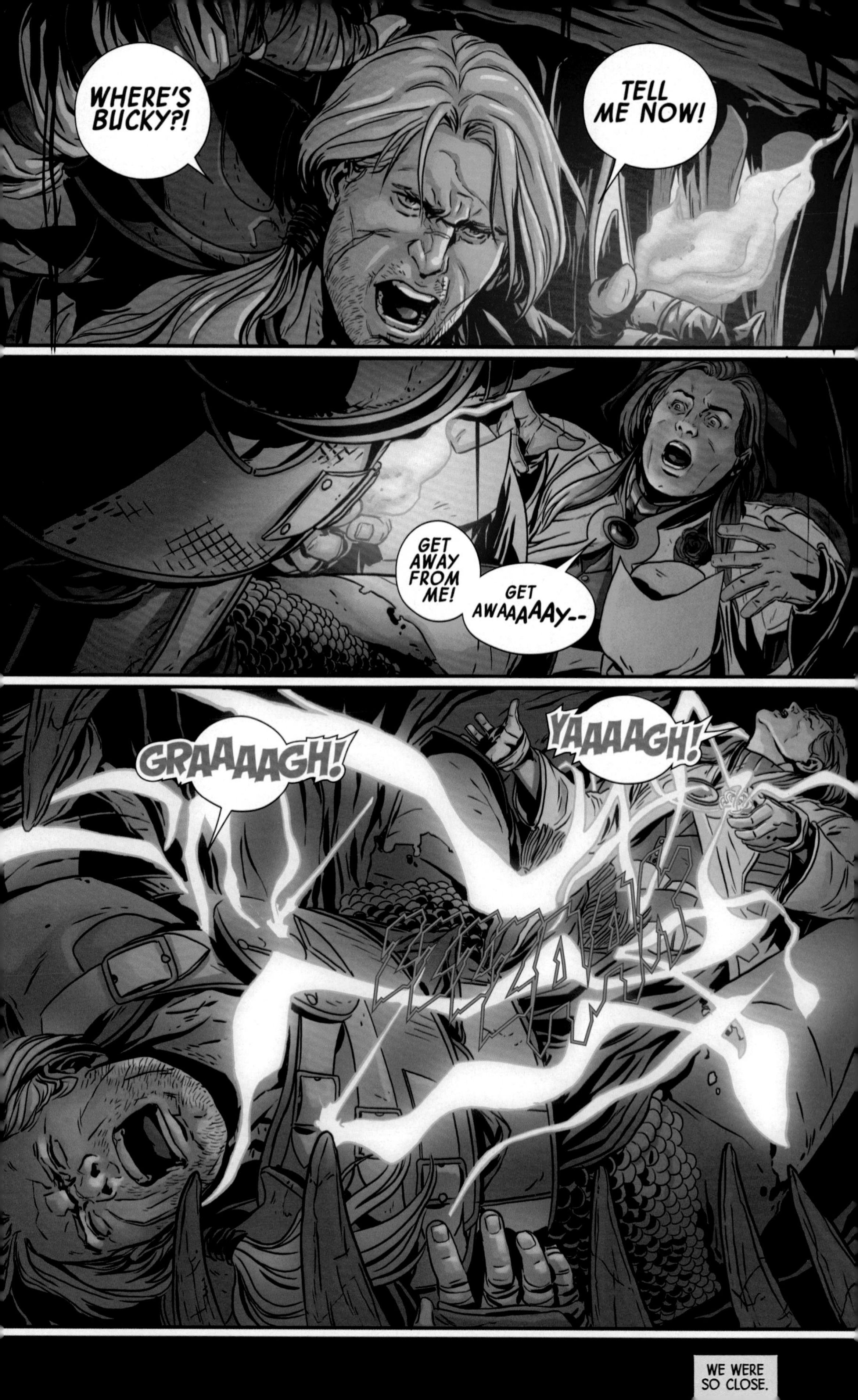
WHERE'S BUCKY?!
TELL ME NOW!
GET AWAY FROM ME!
GET AWAAAAAY--
GRAAAAGH!
YAAAAGH!
WE WERE SO CLOSE.

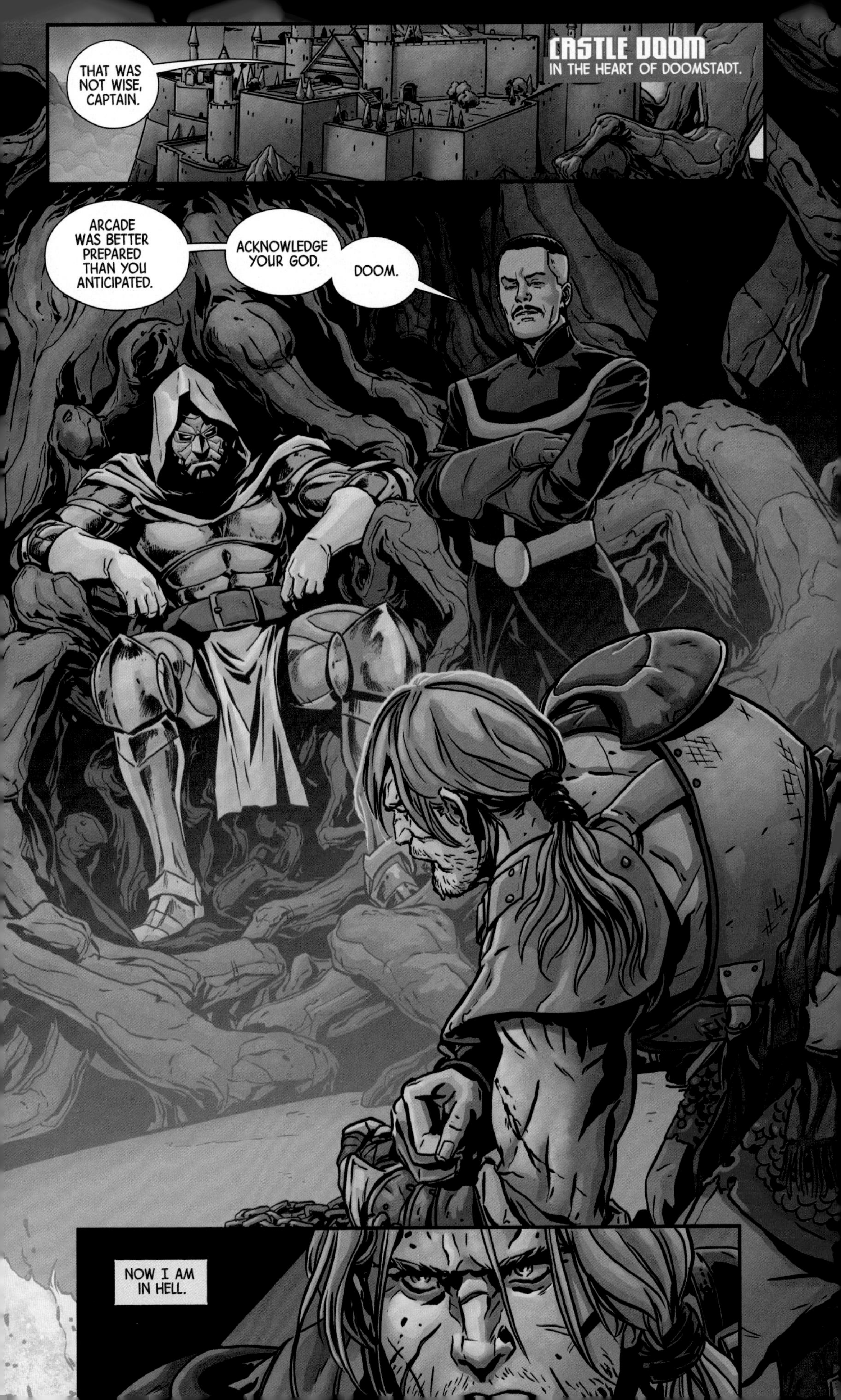

CASTLE DOOM
IN THE HEART OF DOOMSTADT.
THAT WAS NOT WISE, CAPTAIN.
ARCADE WAS BETTER PREPARED THAN YOU ANTICIPATED.
ACKNOWLEDGE YOUR GOD.
DOOM.
NOW I AM IN HELL.

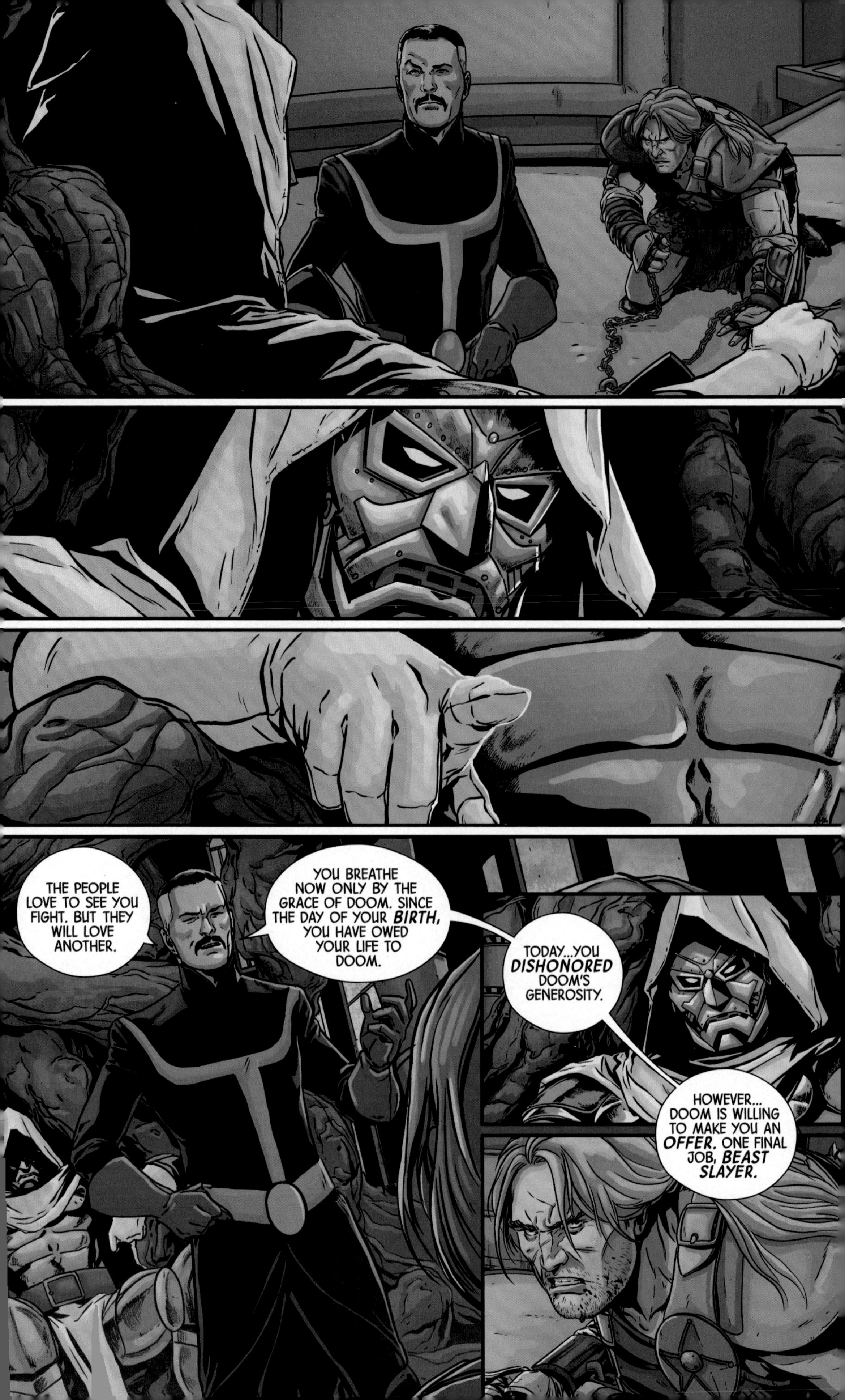
THE PEOPLE LOVE TO SEE YOU FIGHT. BUT THEY WILL LOVE ANOTHER.
YOU BREATHE NOW ONLY BY THE GRACE OF DOOM. SINCE THE DAY OF YOUR *BIRTH*, YOU HAVE OWED YOUR LIFE TO DOOM.
TODAY...YOU *DISHONORED* DOOM'S GENEROSITY.
HOWEVER... DOOM IS WILLING TO MAKE YOU AN *OFFER*. ONE FINAL JOB, *BEAST SLAYER.*

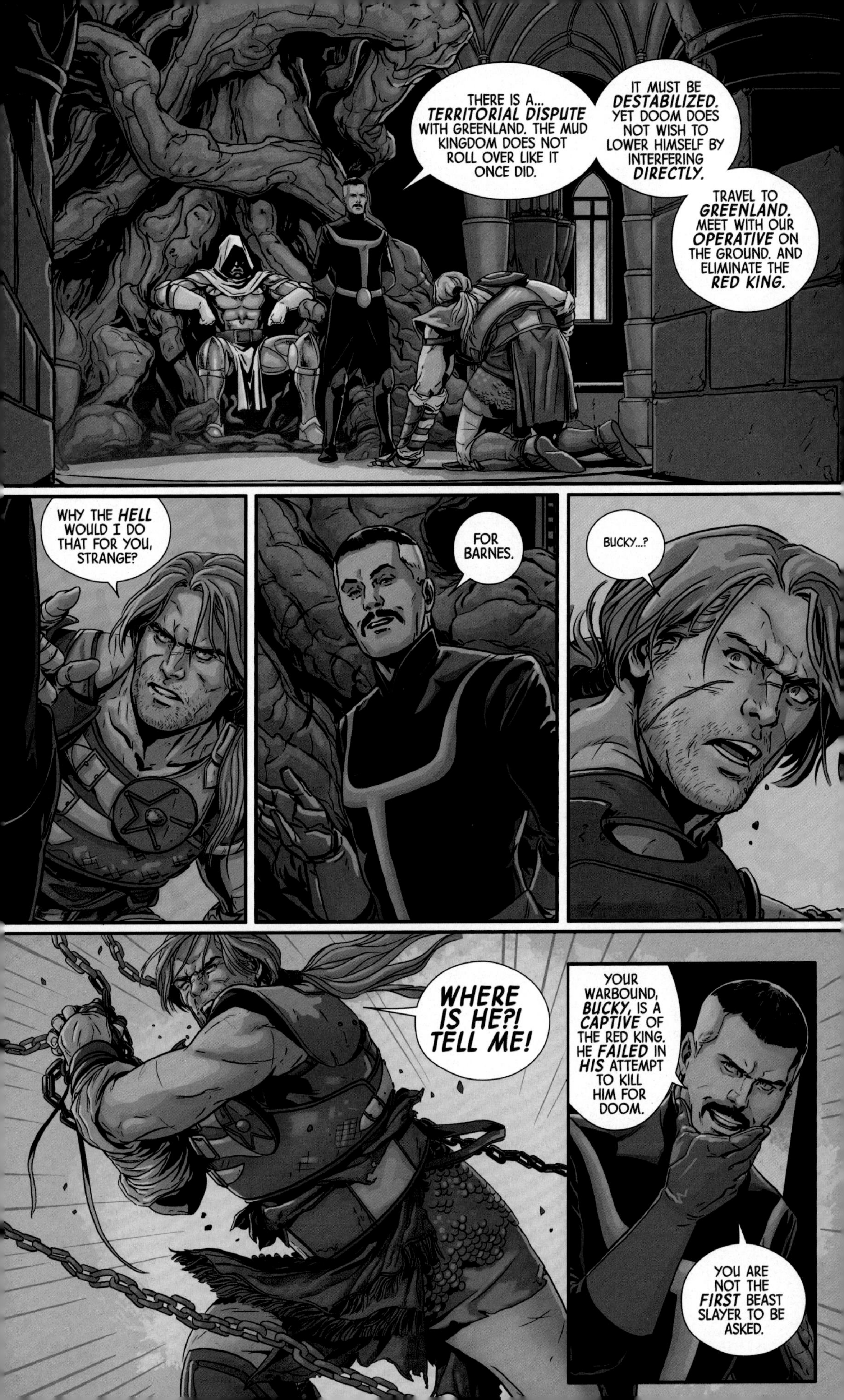
THERE IS A... TERRITORIAL DISPUTE WITH GREENLAND. THE MUD KINGDOM DOES NOT ROLL OVER LIKE IT ONCE DID.
IT MUST BE DESTABILIZED. YET DOOM DOES NOT WISH TO LOWER HIMSELF BY INTERFERING DIRECTLY.
TRAVEL TO GREENLAND. MEET WITH OUR OPERATIVE ON THE GROUND. AND ELIMINATE THE RED KING.
WHY THE HELL WOULD I DO THAT FOR YOU, STRANGE?
FOR BARNES.
BUCKY...?
WHERE IS HE?! TELL ME!
YOUR WARBOUND, BUCKY, IS A CAPTIVE OF THE RED KING. HE FAILED IN HIS ATTEMPT TO KILL HIM FOR DOOM.
YOU ARE NOT THE FIRST BEAST SLAYER TO BE ASKED.

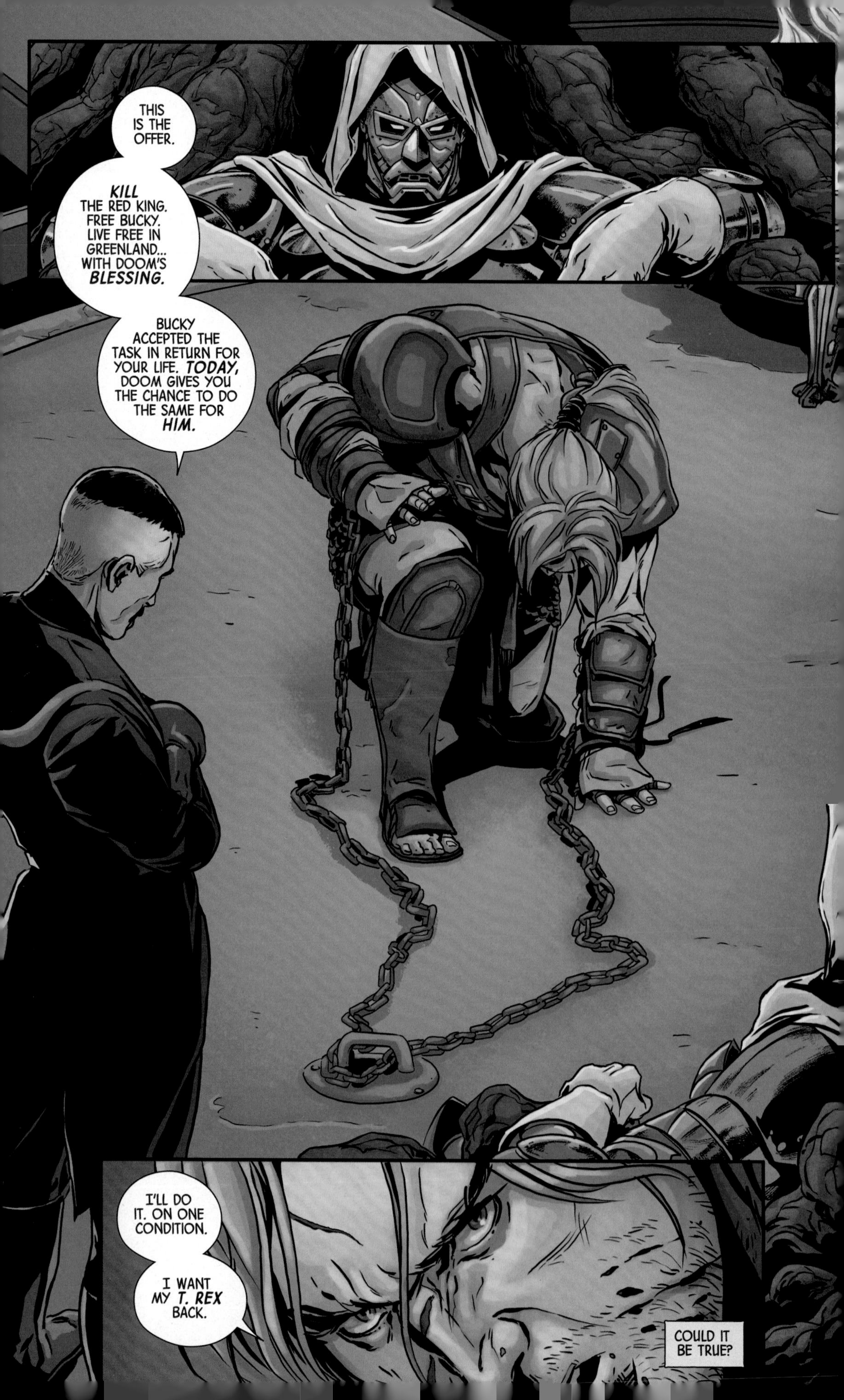
THIS IS THE OFFER.
KILL THE RED KING. FREE BUCKY. LIVE FREE IN GREENLAND... WITH DOOM'S *BLESSING.*
BUCKY ACCEPTED THE TASK IN RETURN FOR YOUR LIFE. *TODAY,* DOOM GIVES YOU THE CHANCE TO DO THE SAME FOR *HIM.*
I'LL DO IT. ON ONE CONDITION.
I WANT MY *T. REX* BACK.
COULD IT BE TRUE?

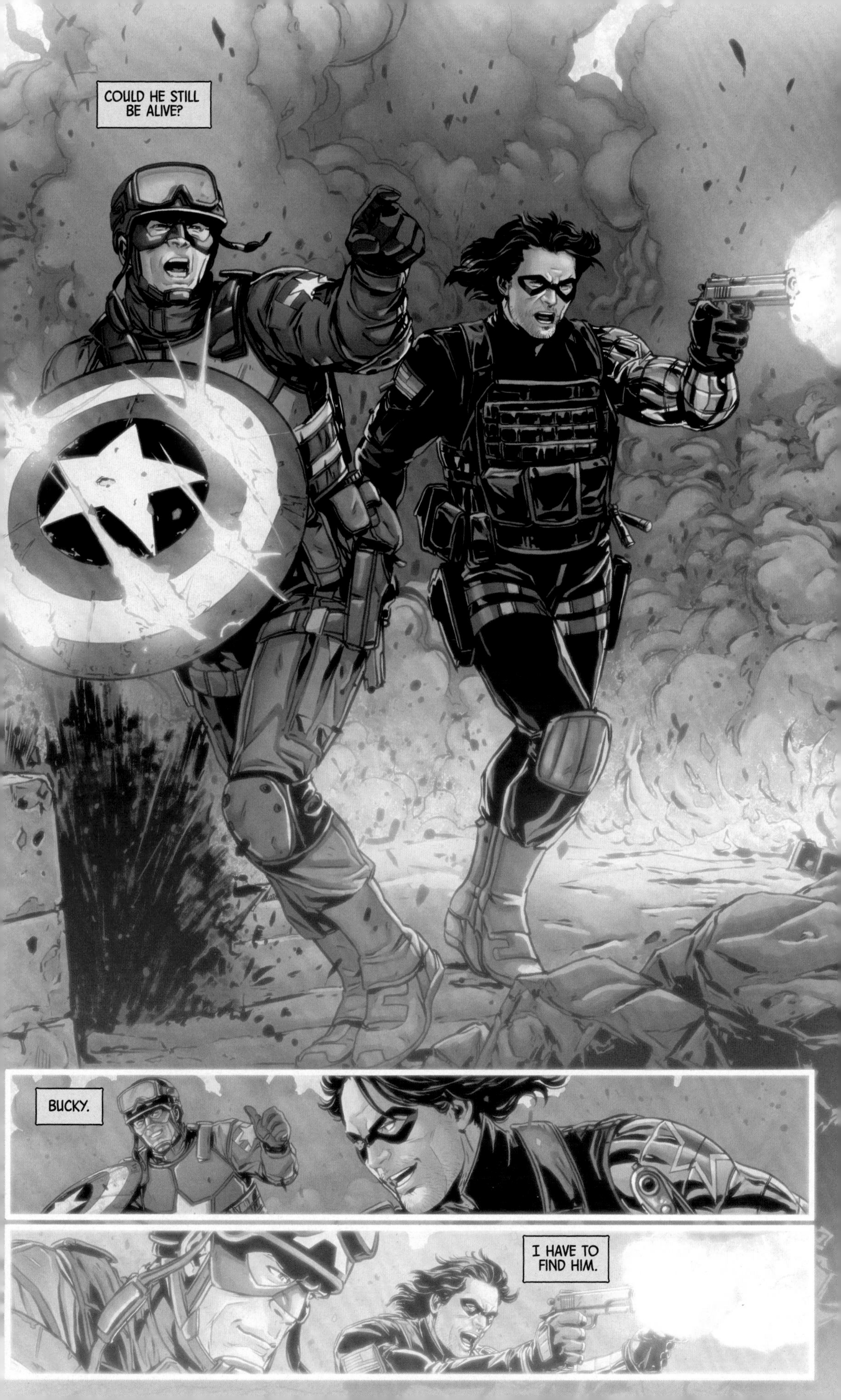
COULD HE STILL BE ALIVE?
BUCKY.
I HAVE TO FIND HIM.

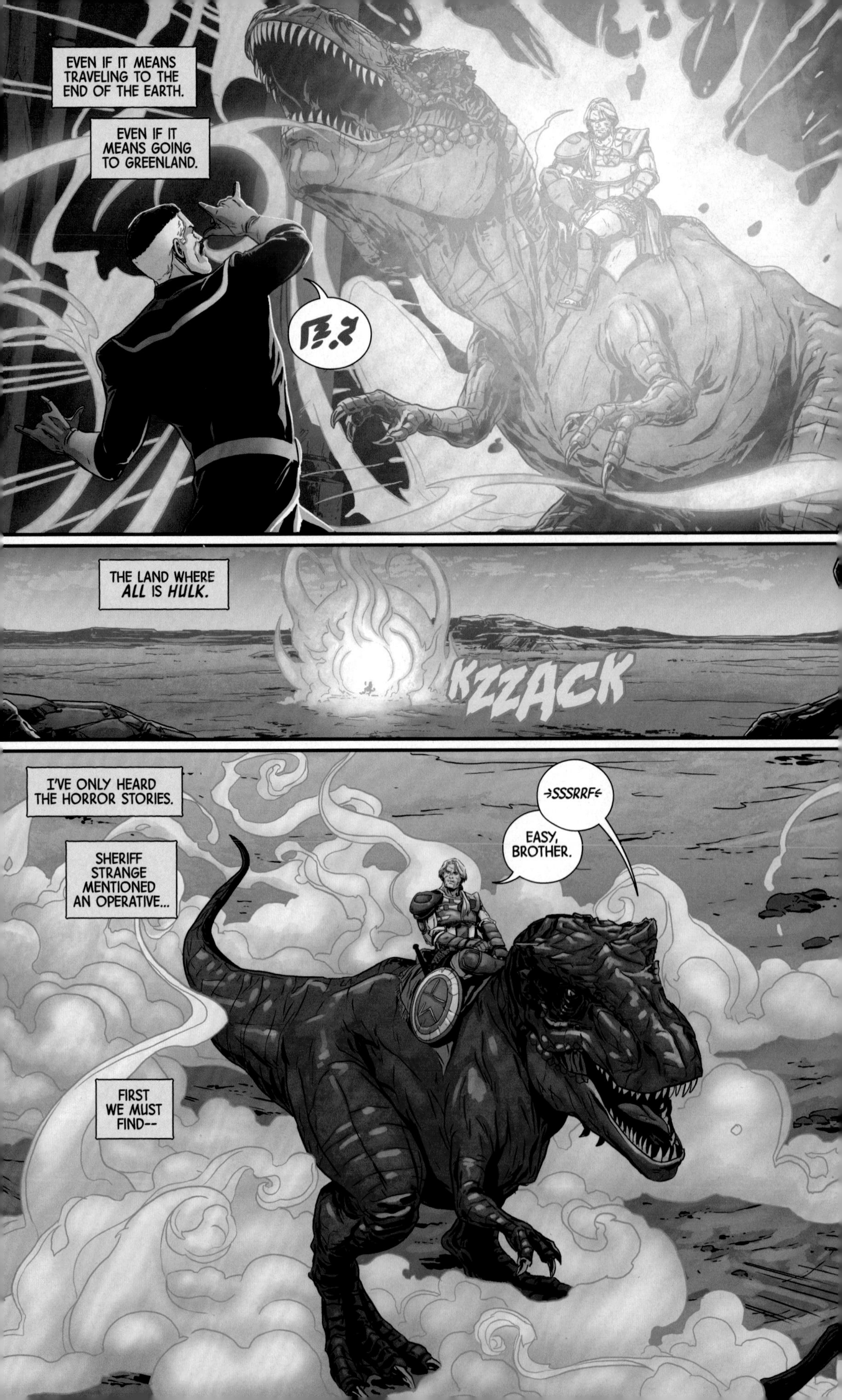

EVEN IF IT MEANS TRAVELING TO THE END OF THE EARTH.
EVEN IF IT MEANS GOING TO GREENLAND.
THE LAND WHERE ALL IS HULK.
KZZACK
I'VE ONLY HEARD THE HORROR STORIES.
SHERIFF STRANGE MENTIONED AN OPERATIVE...
SSSRRF
EASY, BROTHER.
FIRST WE MUST FIND--

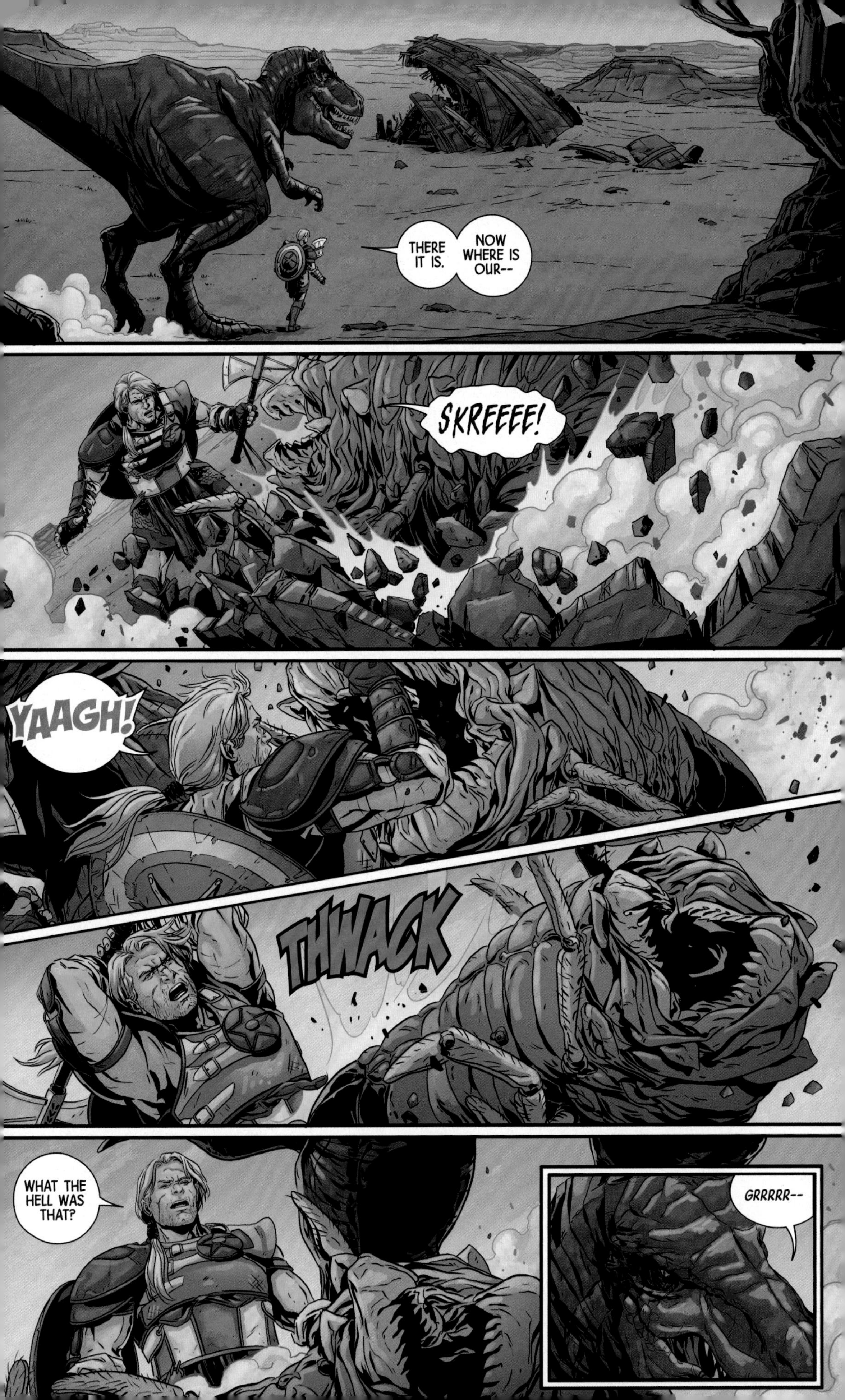
THERE IT IS.
NOW WHERE IS OUR--
SKREEEE!
YAAGH!
THWACK
WHAT THE HELL WAS THAT?
GRRRRR--

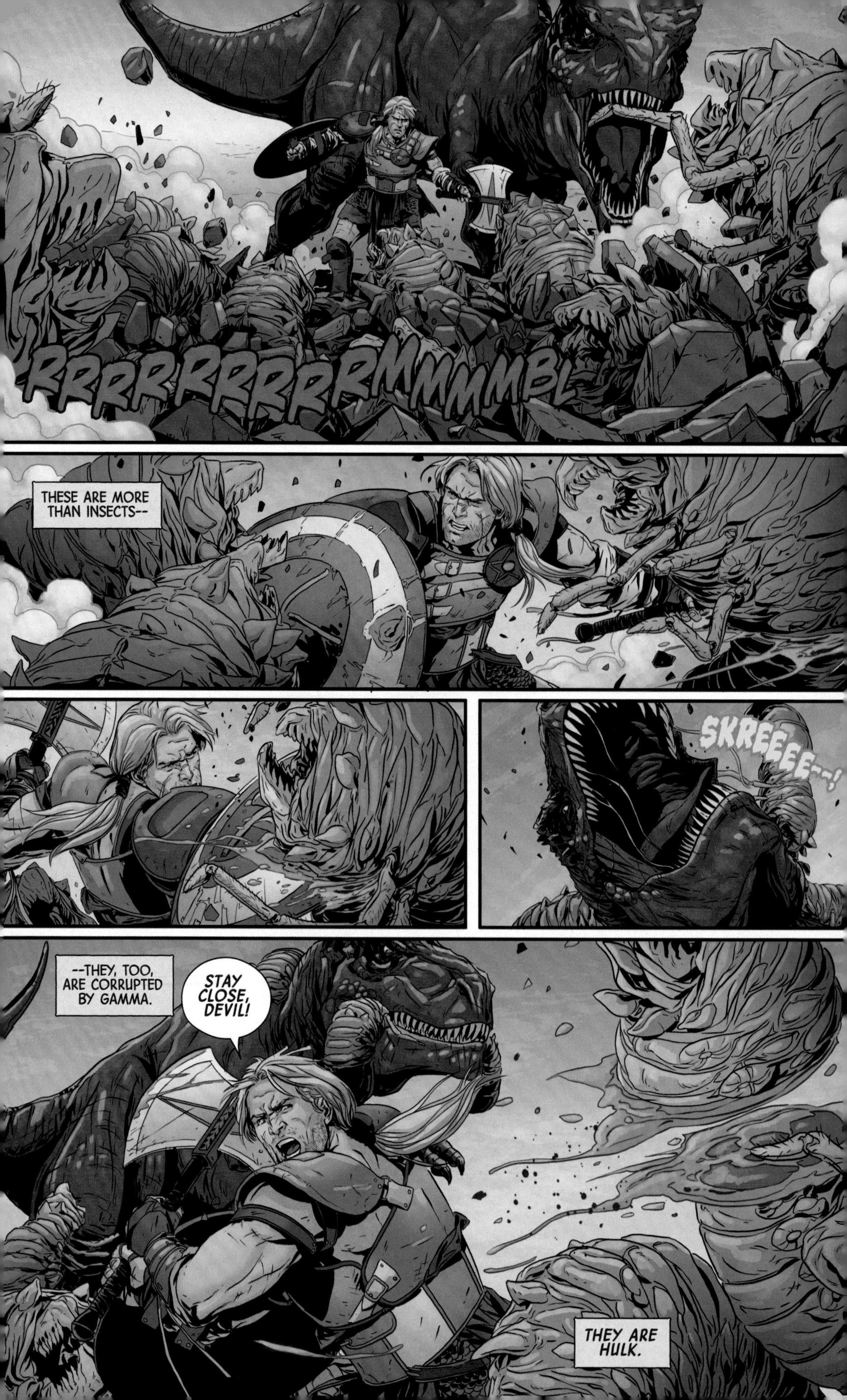
RRRRRRRRRRMMMMMBL
THESE ARE MORE THAN INSECTS--
SKREEEE--!
--THEY, TOO, ARE CORRUPTED BY GAMMA.
STAY CLOSE, DEVIL!
THEY ARE HULK.

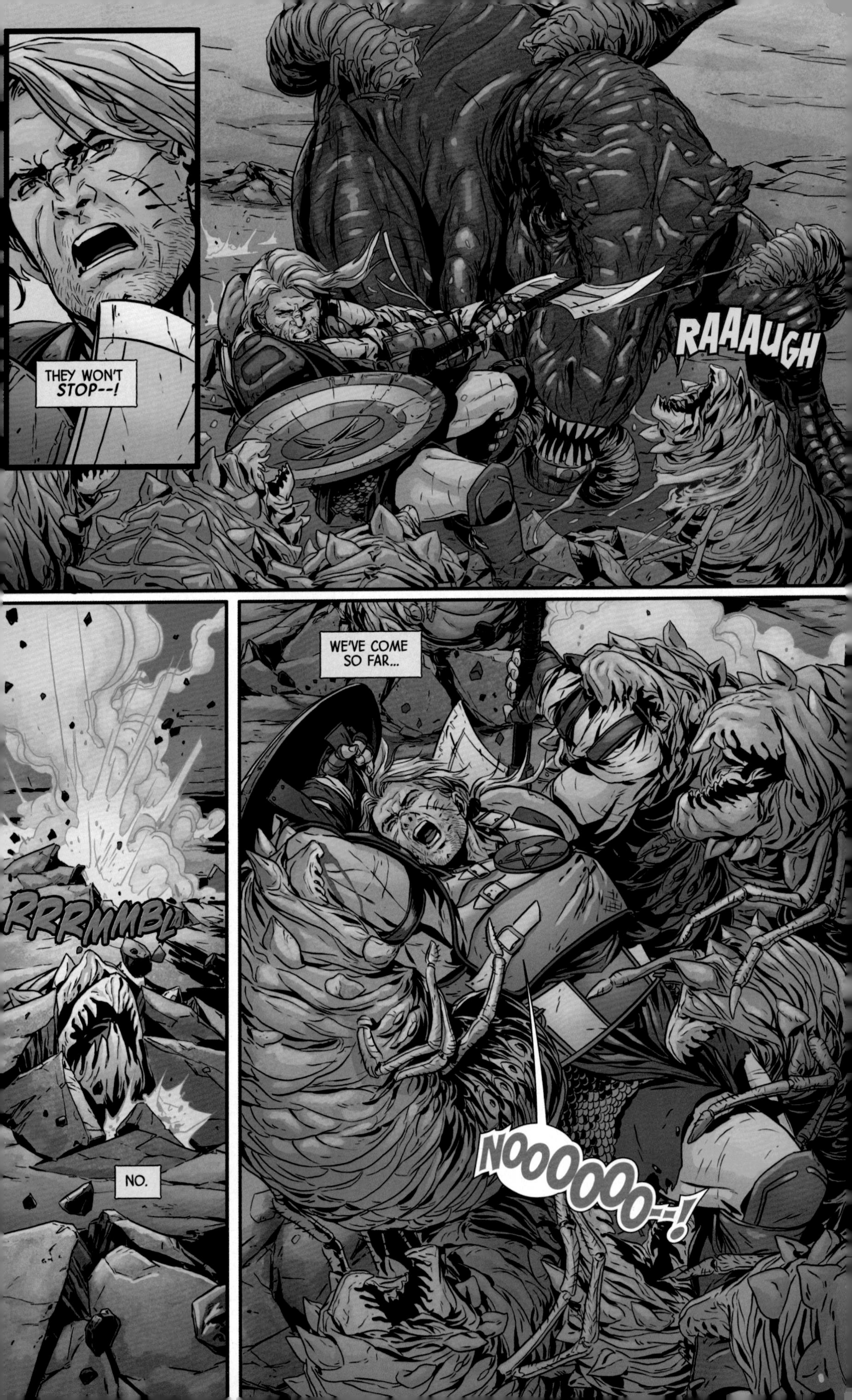
THEY WON'T STOP--!
RAAAUGH
RRRMMBL
NO.
WE'VE COME SO FAR...
NOOOOOO--!

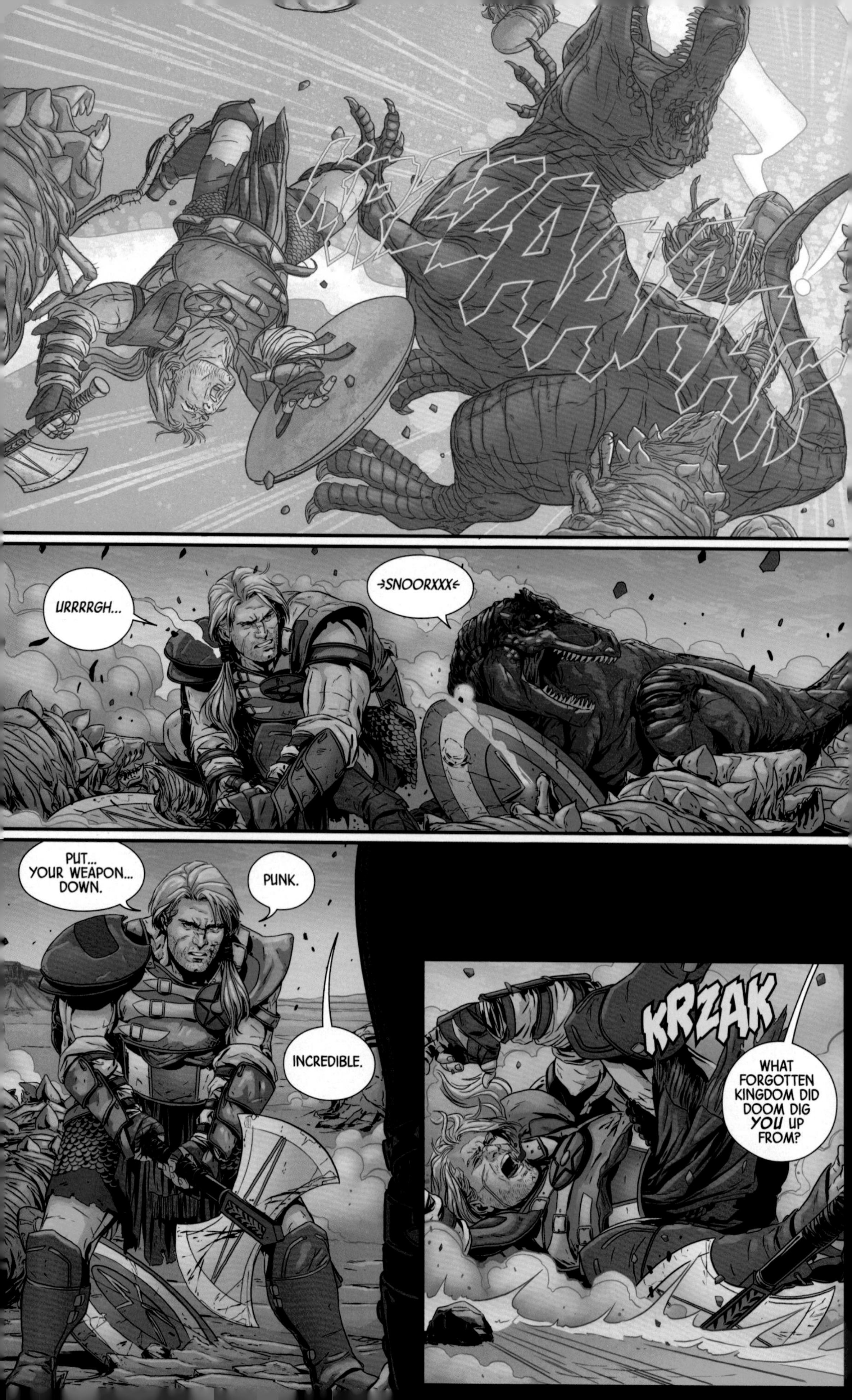
URRRRGH...
SNOORXXX
PUT... YOUR WEAPON... DOWN.
PUNK.
INCREDIBLE.
KRZAK
WHAT FORGOTTEN KINGDOM DID DOOM DIG YOU UP FROM?

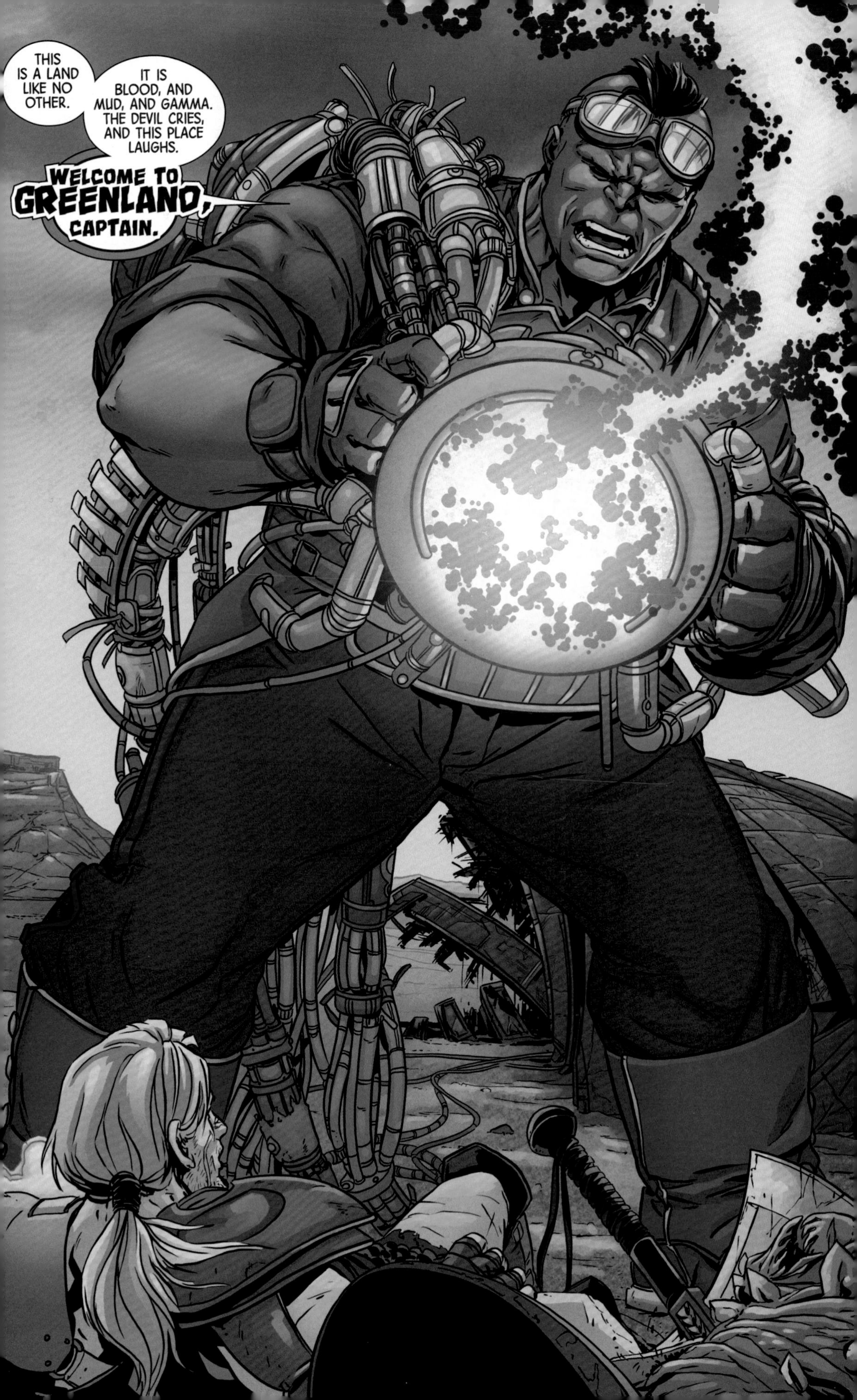
THIS IS A LAND LIKE NO OTHER.
IT IS BLOOD, AND MUD, AND GAMMA. THE DEVIL CRIES, AND THIS PLACE LAUGHS.
WELCOME TO GREENLAND, CAPTAIN.

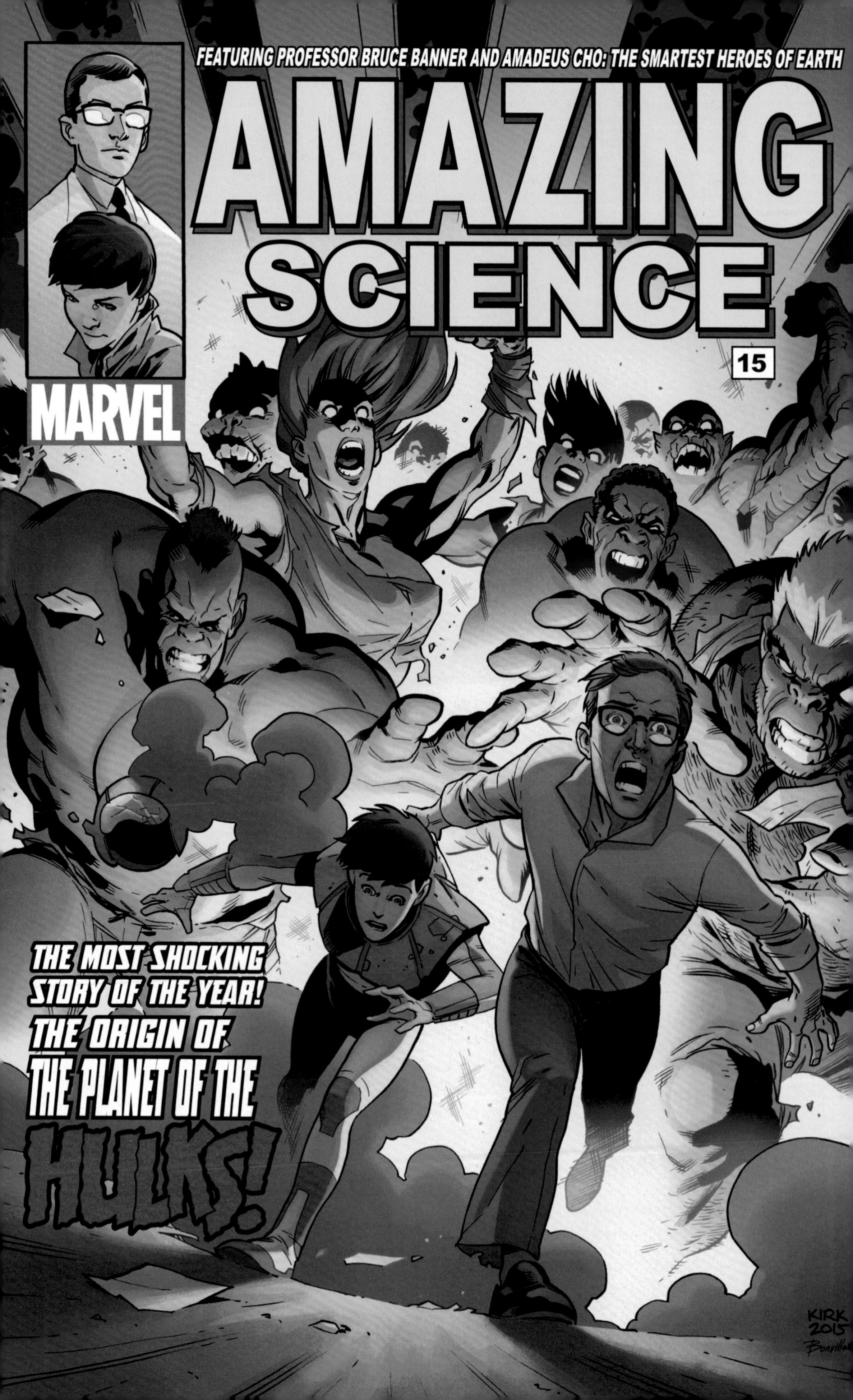
FEATURING PROFESSOR BRUCE BANNER AND AMADEUS CHO: THE SMARTEST HEROES OF EARTH
AMAZING SCIENCE
15
MARVEL
THE MOST SHOCKING STORY OF THE YEAR!
THE ORIGIN OF THE PLANET OF THE HULKS!
KIRK 2015

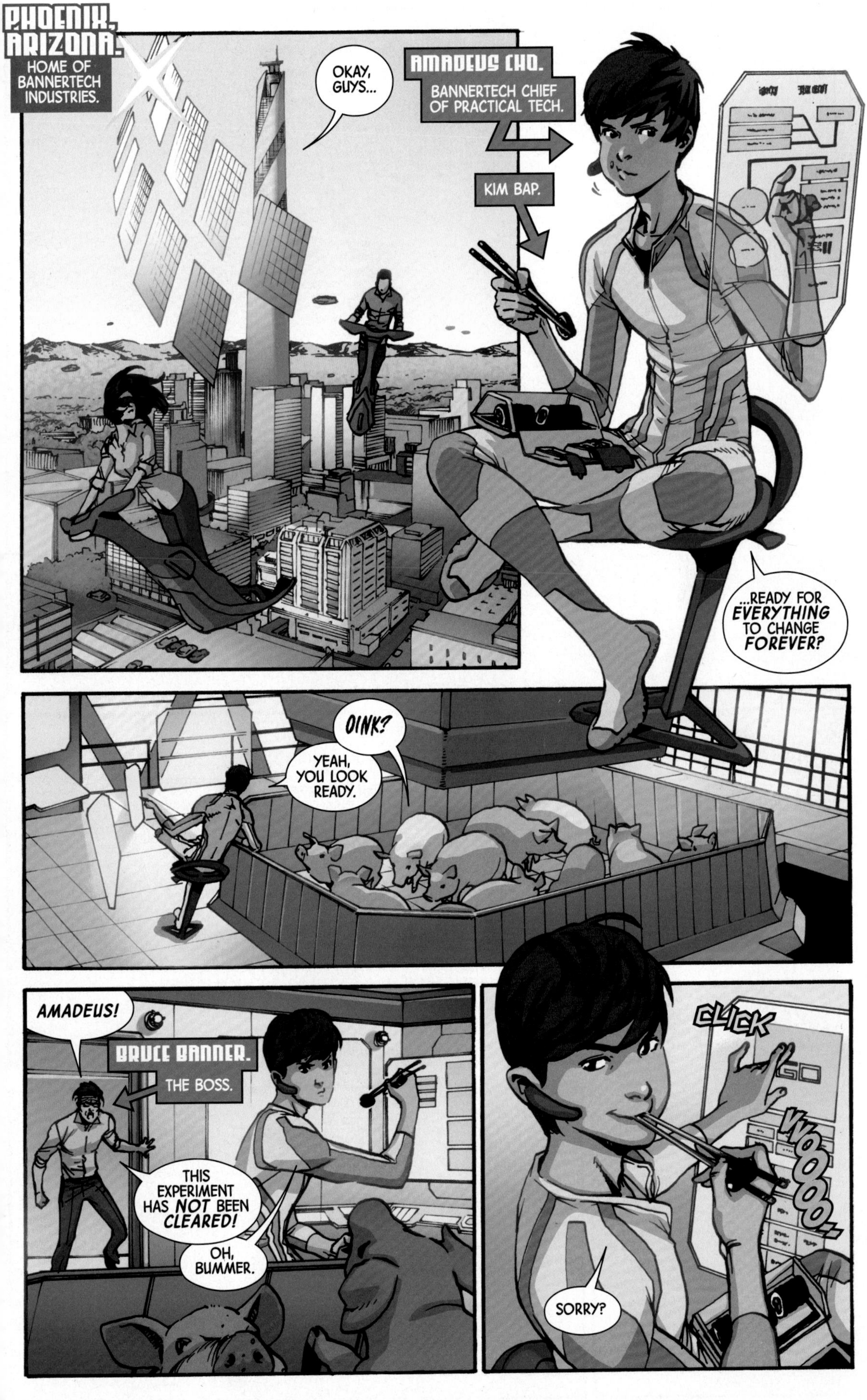
PHOENIX, ARIZONA.
HOME OF BANNERTECH INDUSTRIES.
OKAY, GUYS...
AMADEUS CHO.
BANNERTECH CHIEF OF PRACTICAL TECH.
KIM BAP.
...READY FOR EVERYTHING TO CHANGE FOREVER?
OINK?
YEAH, YOU LOOK READY.
AMADEUS!
BRUCE BANNER.
THE BOSS.
THIS EXPERIMENT HAS NOT BEEN CLEARED!
OH, BUMMER.
CLICK
GO
VVOOOO
SORRY?

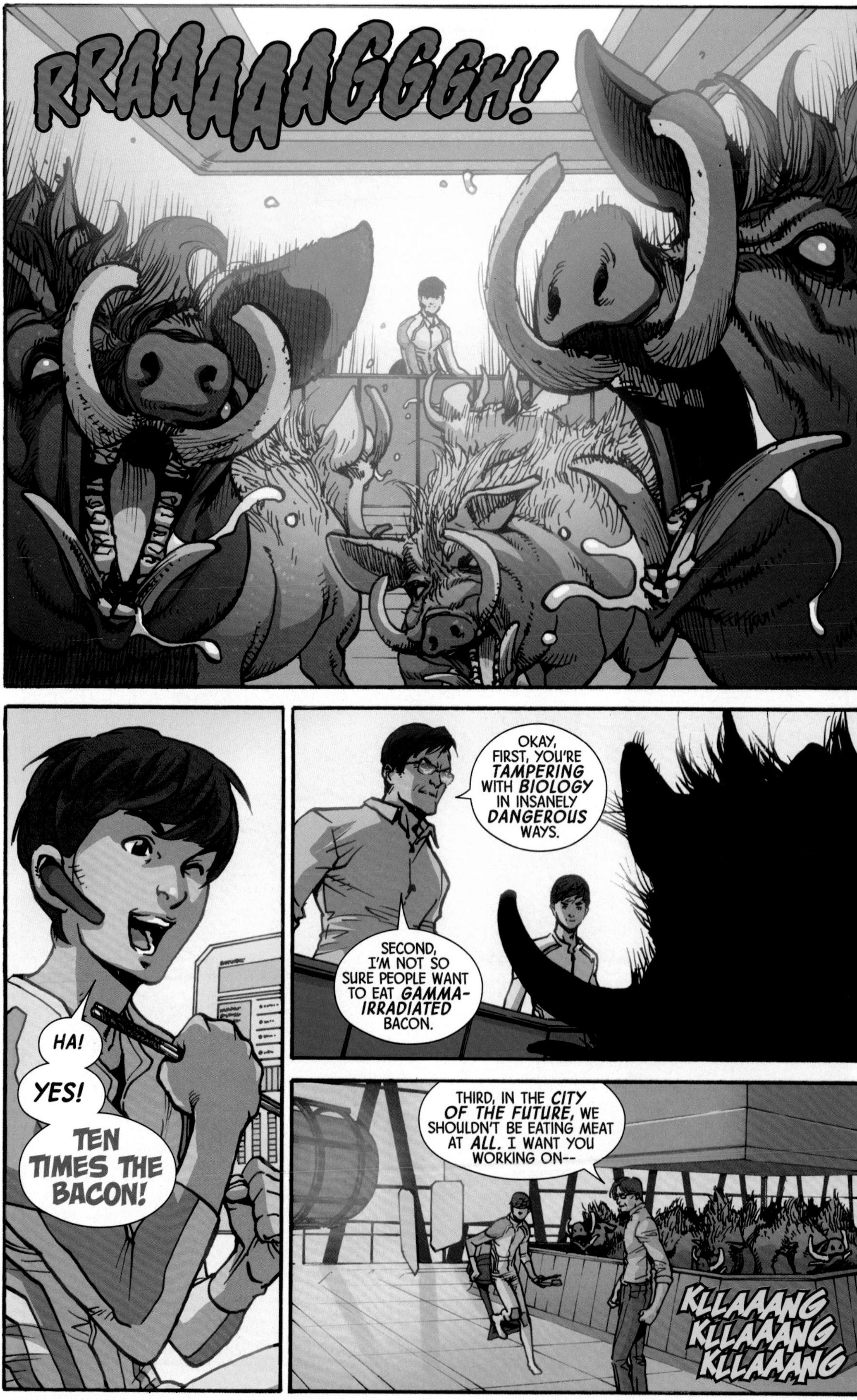
RRAAAAAAGGGGH!
HA!
YES!
TEN TIMES THE BACON!
OKAY, FIRST, YOU'RE TAMPERING WITH BIOLOGY IN INSANELY DANGEROUS WAYS.
SECOND, I'M NOT SO SURE PEOPLE WANT TO EAT GAMMA-IRRADIATED BACON.
THIRD, IN THE CITY OF THE FUTURE, WE SHOULDN'T BE EATING MEAT AT ALL. I WANT YOU WORKING ON--
KLLAAANG KLLAAANG KLLAAANG

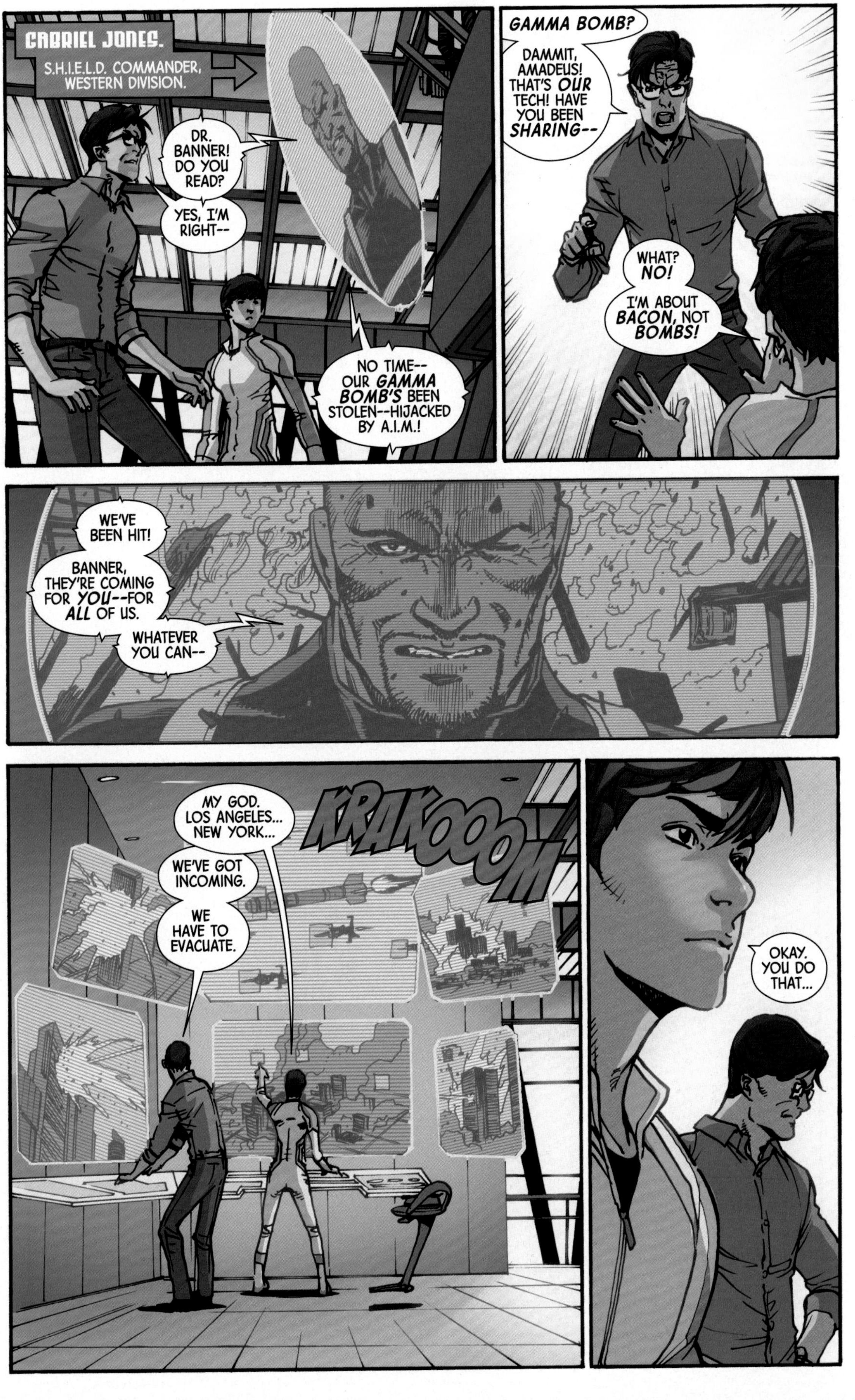
GABRIEL JONES.
S.H.I.E.L.D. COMMANDER, WESTERN DIVISION.
DR. BANNER! DO YOU READ?
YES, I'M RIGHT--
NO TIME-- OUR GAMMA BOMB'S BEEN STOLEN--HIJACKED BY A.I.M.!
GAMMA BOMB?
DAMMIT, AMADEUS! THAT'S OUR TECH! HAVE YOU BEEN SHARING--
WHAT? NO!
I'M ABOUT BACON, NOT BOMBS!
WE'VE BEEN HIT!
BANNER, THEY'RE COMING FOR YOU--FOR ALL OF US.
WHATEVER YOU CAN--
MY GOD. LOS ANGELES... NEW YORK...
WE'VE GOT INCOMING.
WE HAVE TO EVACUATE.
KRAKOOOOM
OKAY. YOU DO THAT...

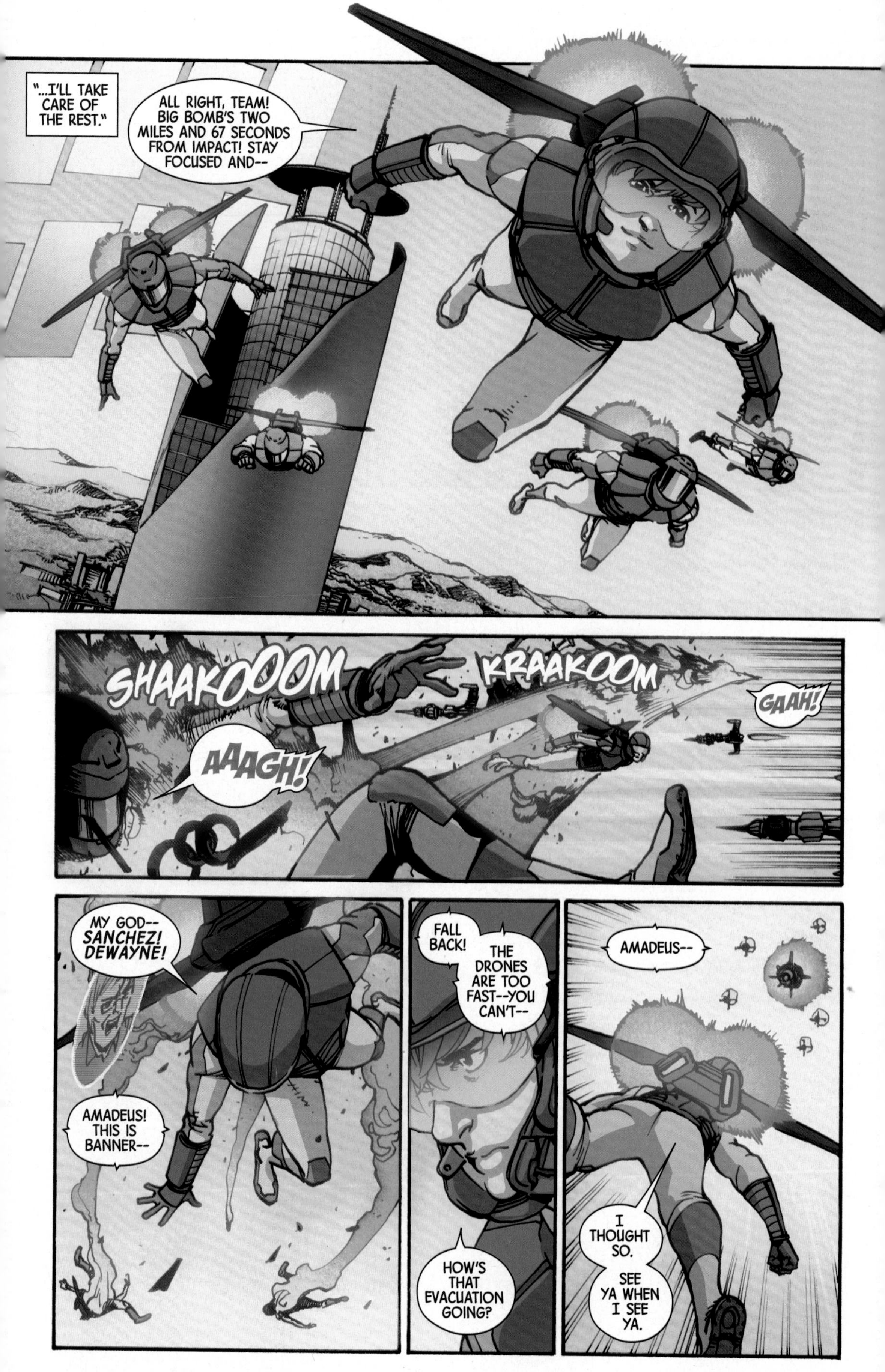
"...I'LL TAKE CARE OF THE REST."
ALL RIGHT, TEAM! BIG BOMB'S TWO MILES AND 67 SECONDS FROM IMPACT! STAY FOCUSED AND--
SHAAKOOOM
KRAAKOOM
GAAH!
AAAGH!
MY GOD-- SANCHEZ! DEWAYNE!
AMADEUS! THIS IS BANNER--
FALL BACK!
THE DRONES ARE TOO FAST--YOU CAN'T--
HOW'S THAT EVACUATION GOING?
AMADEUS--
I THOUGHT SO.
SEE YA WHEN I SEE YA.

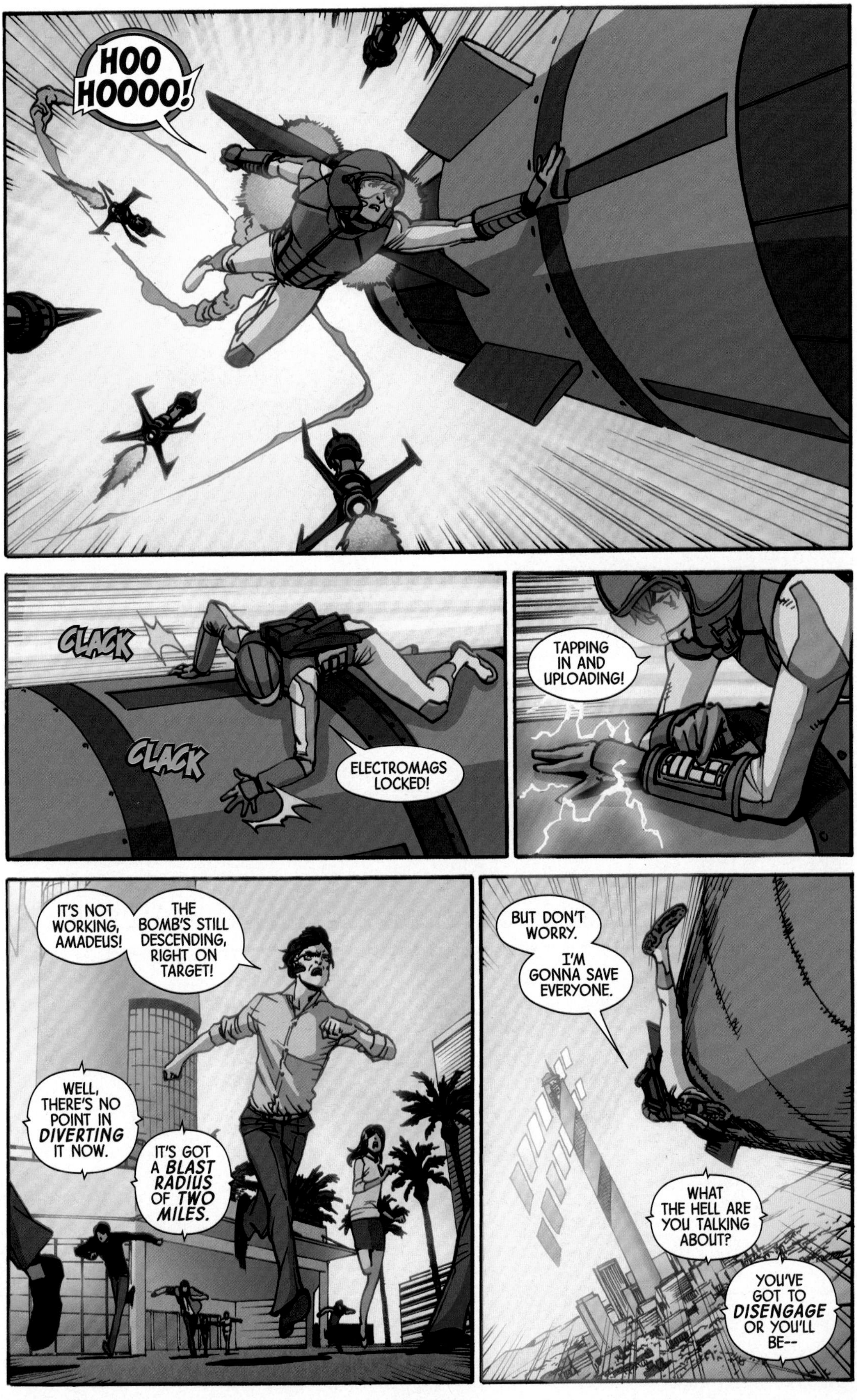
HOO HOOOO!
CLACK
CLACK
ELECTROMAGS LOCKED!
TAPPING IN AND UPLOADING!
IT'S NOT WORKING, AMADEUS!
THE BOMB'S STILL DESCENDING, RIGHT ON TARGET!
WELL, THERE'S NO POINT IN DIVERTING IT NOW.
IT'S GOT A BLAST RADIUS OF TWO MILES.
BUT DON'T WORRY.
I'M GONNA SAVE EVERYONE.
WHAT THE HELL ARE YOU TALKING ABOUT?
YOU'VE GOT TO DISENGAGE OR YOU'LL BE--

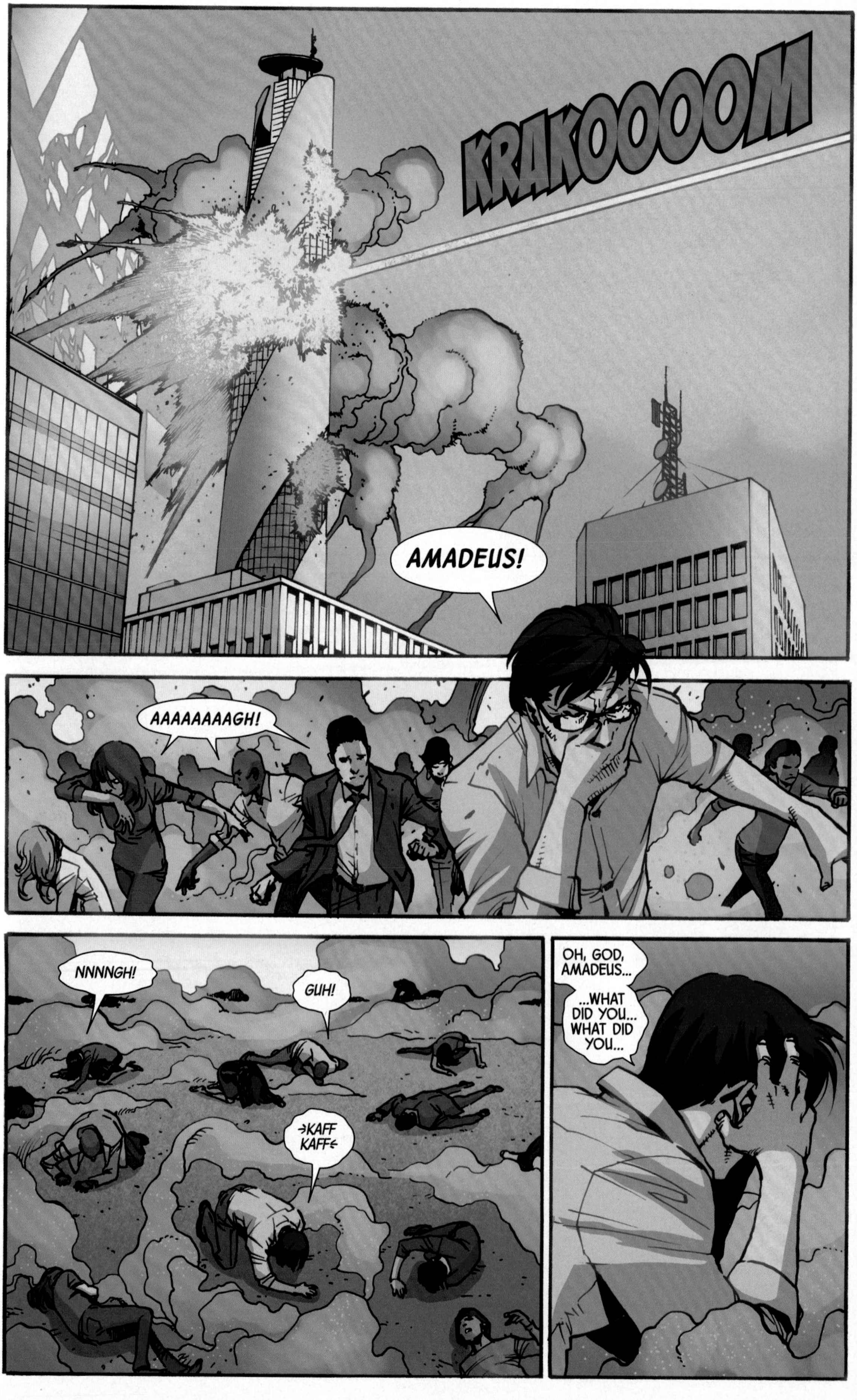
KRAKOOOOM
AMADEUS!
AAAAAAAAGH!
NNNNGH!
GUH!
KAFF KAFF
OH, GOD, AMADEUS...
...WHAT DID YOU... WHAT DID YOU...

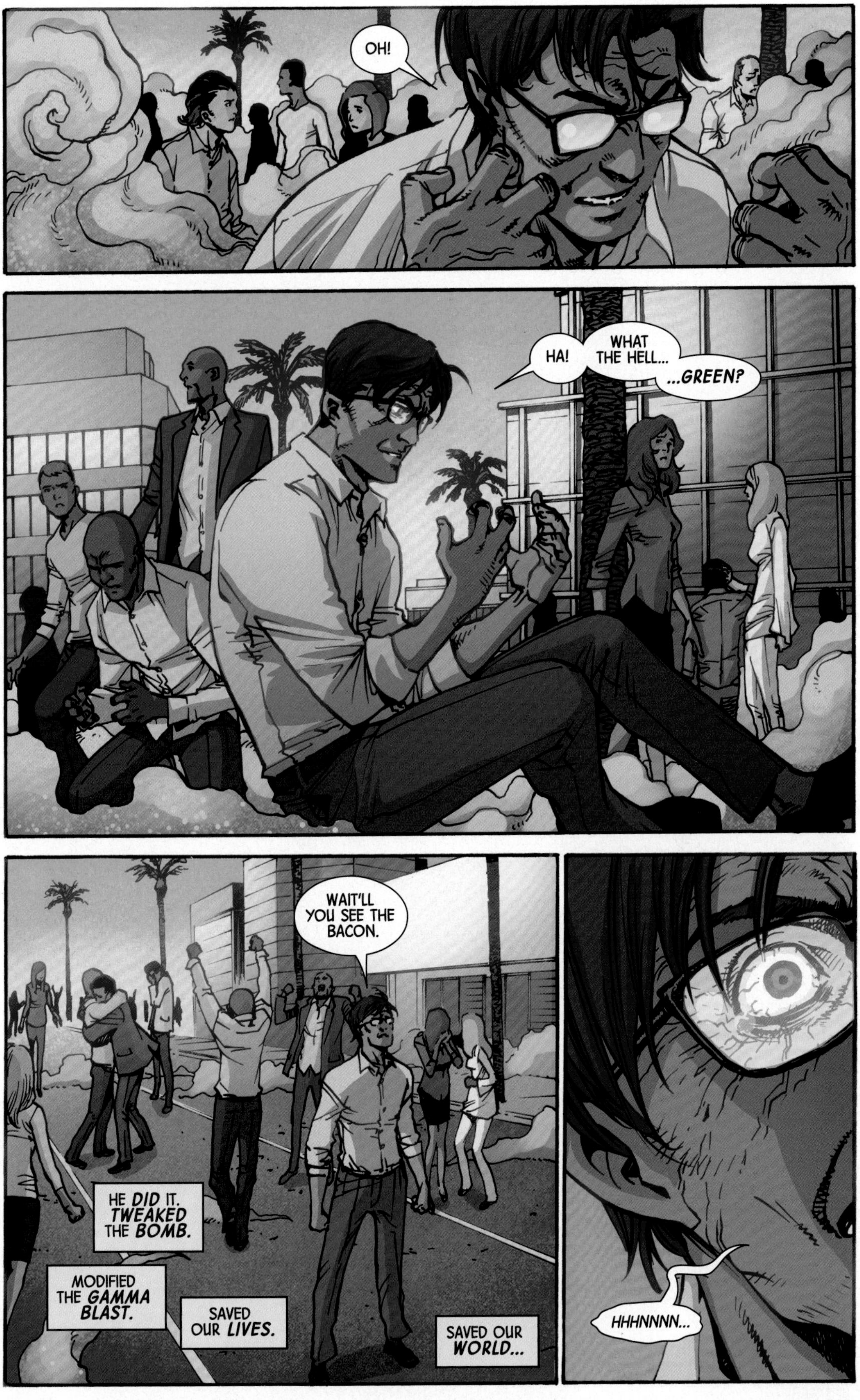
OH!
HA!
WHAT THE HELL...
...GREEN?
WAIT'LL YOU SEE THE BACON.
HE DID IT. TWEAKED THE BOMB.
MODIFIED THE GAMMA BLAST.
SAVED OUR LIVES.
SAVED OUR WORLD...
HHHNNNN...

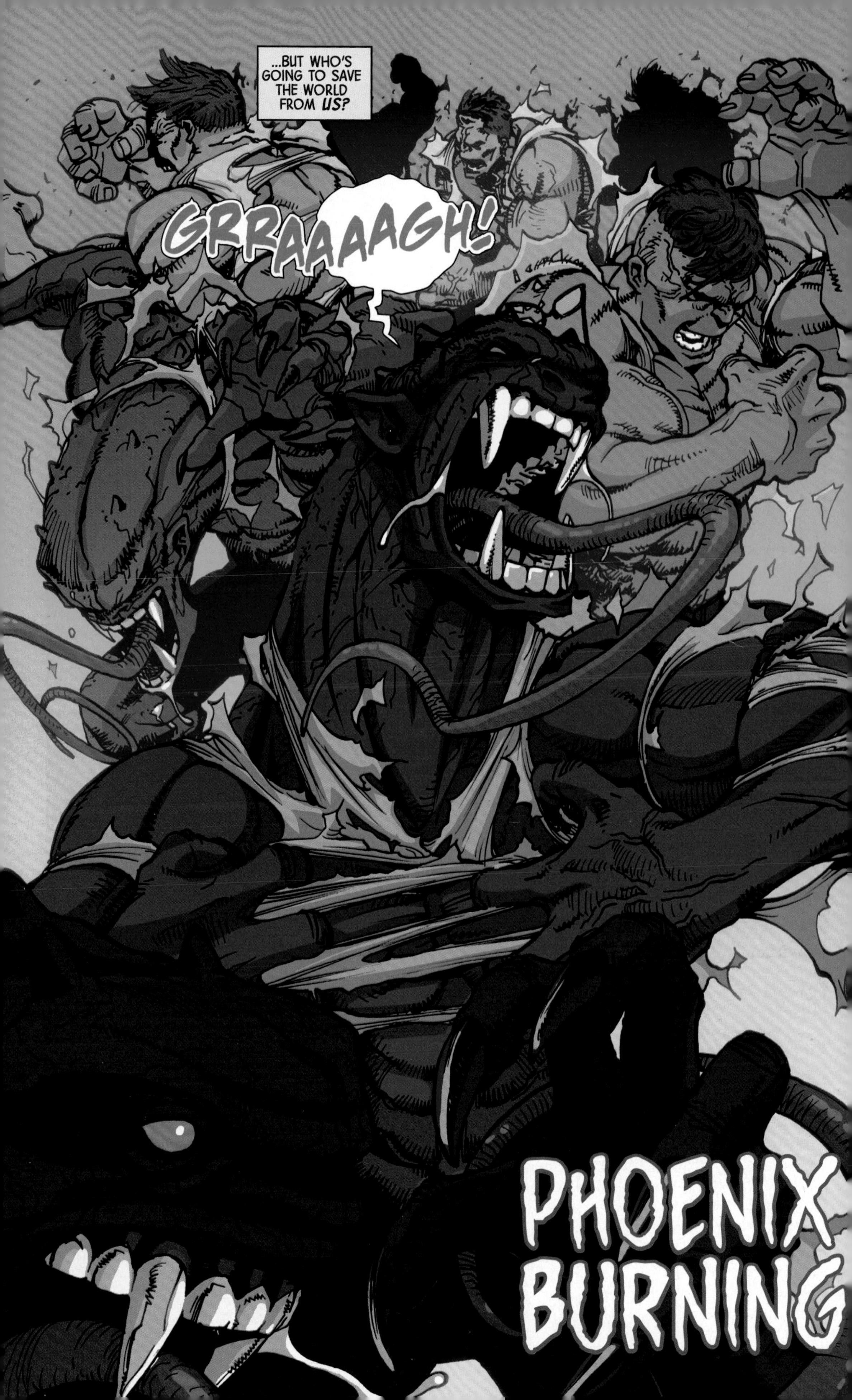

...BUT WHO'S GOING TO SAVE THE WORLD FROM US?
GRRAAAAGH!
PHOENIX BURNING

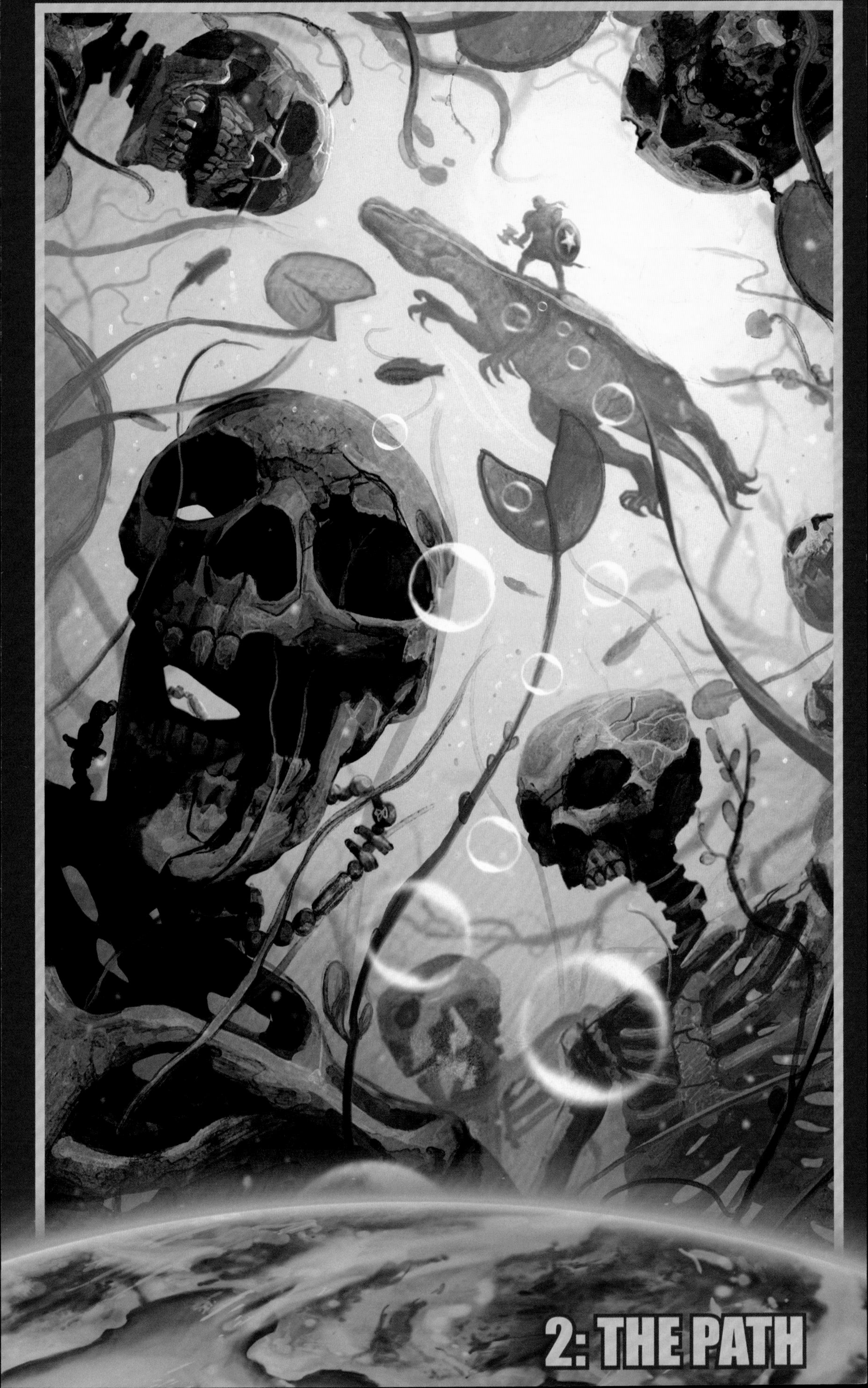
2: THE PATH

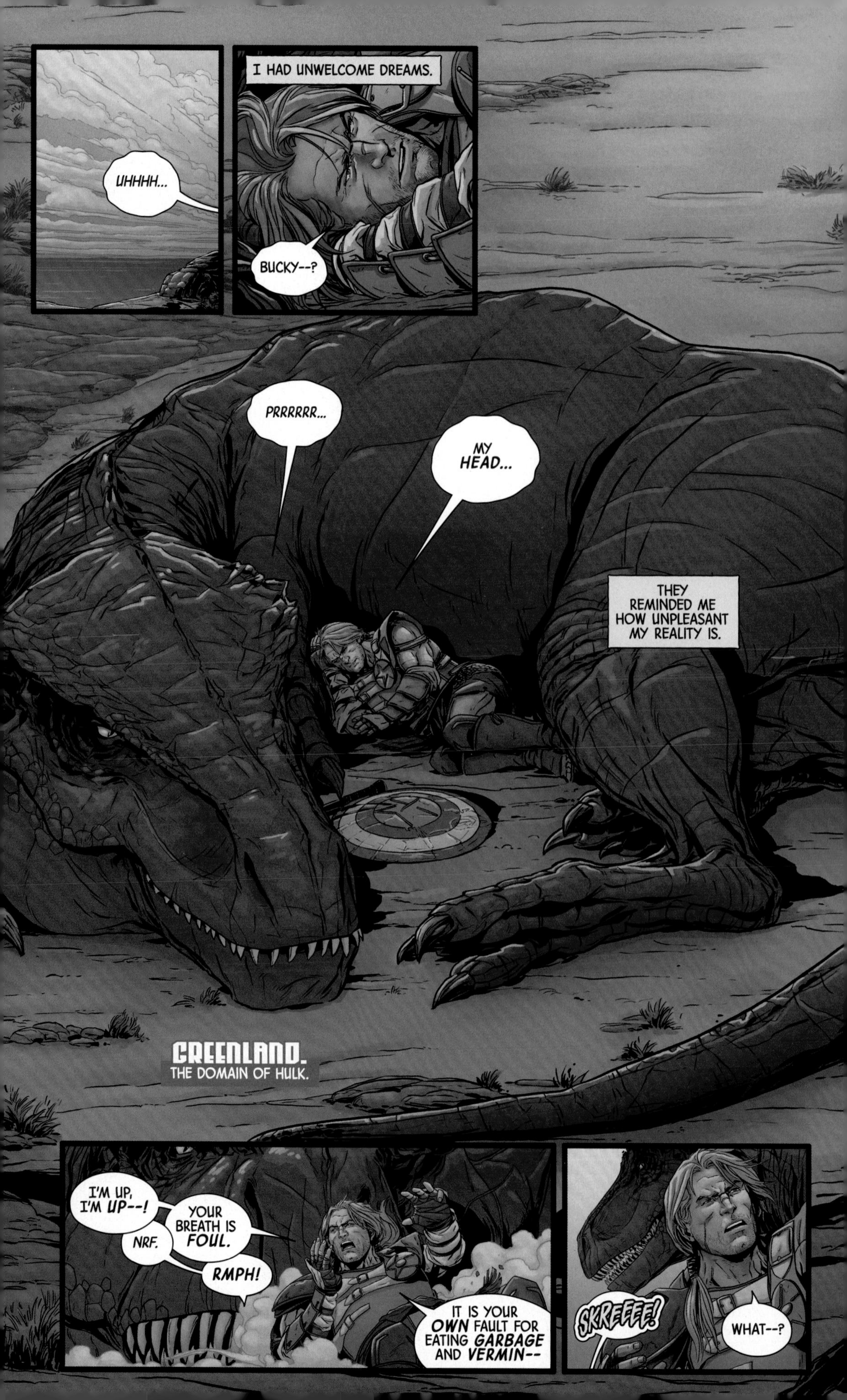
UHHHH...
I HAD UNWELCOME DREAMS.
BUCKY--?
PRRRRRR...
MY HEAD...
THEY REMINDED ME HOW UNPLEASANT MY REALITY IS.
GREENLAND.
THE DOMAIN OF HULK.
I'M UP, I'M UP--!
YOUR BREATH IS FOUL.
NRF.
RMPH!
IT IS YOUR OWN FAULT FOR EATING GARBAGE AND VERMIN--
SKREEEEE!
WHAT--?

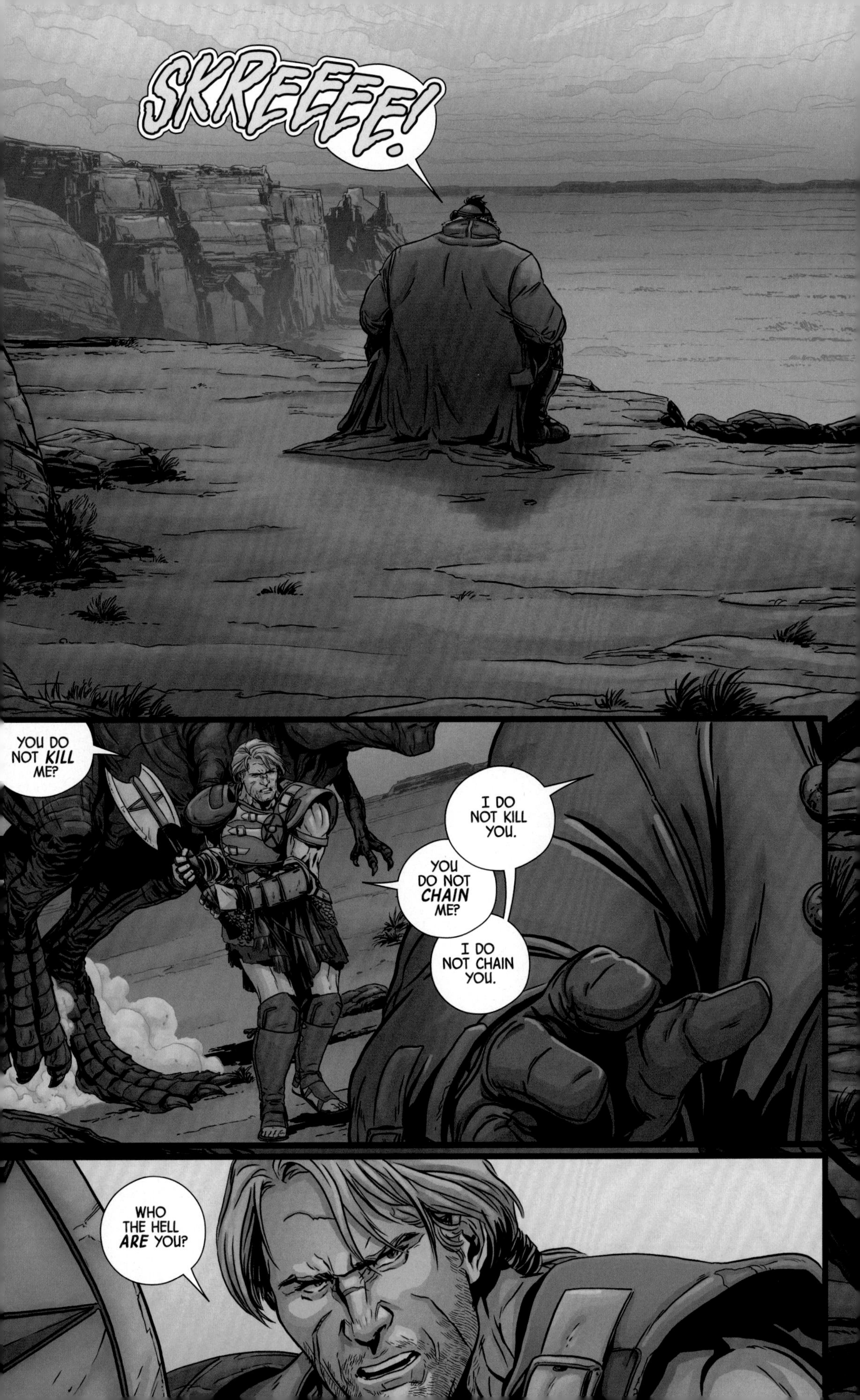
SKREEEEE!
YOU DO NOT *KILL* ME?
I DO NOT KILL YOU.
YOU DO NOT *CHAIN* ME?
I DO NOT CHAIN YOU.
WHO THE HELL *ARE* YOU?

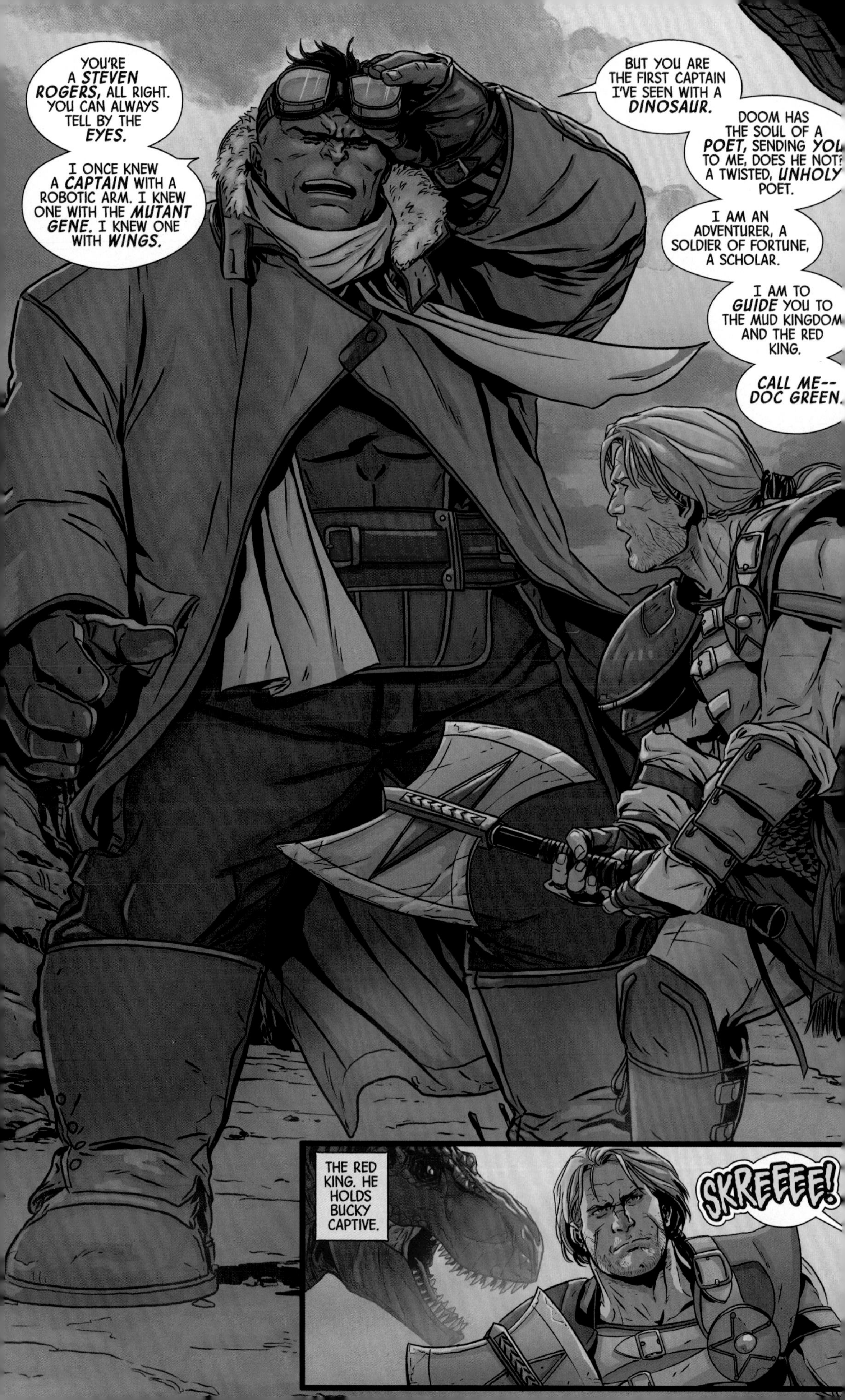
YOU'RE A STEVEN ROGERS, ALL RIGHT. YOU CAN ALWAYS TELL BY THE EYES.
I ONCE KNEW A CAPTAIN WITH A ROBOTIC ARM. I KNEW ONE WITH THE MUTANT GENE. I KNEW ONE WITH WINGS.
BUT YOU ARE THE FIRST CAPTAIN I'VE SEEN WITH A DINOSAUR.
DOOM HAS THE SOUL OF A POET, SENDING YOU TO ME, DOES HE NOT? A TWISTED, UNHOLY POET.
I AM AN ADVENTURER, A SOLDIER OF FORTUNE, A SCHOLAR.
I AM TO GUIDE YOU TO THE MUD KINGDOM AND THE RED KING.
CALL ME-- DOC GREEN.
THE RED KING. HE HOLDS BUCKY CAPTIVE.
SKREEEEE!

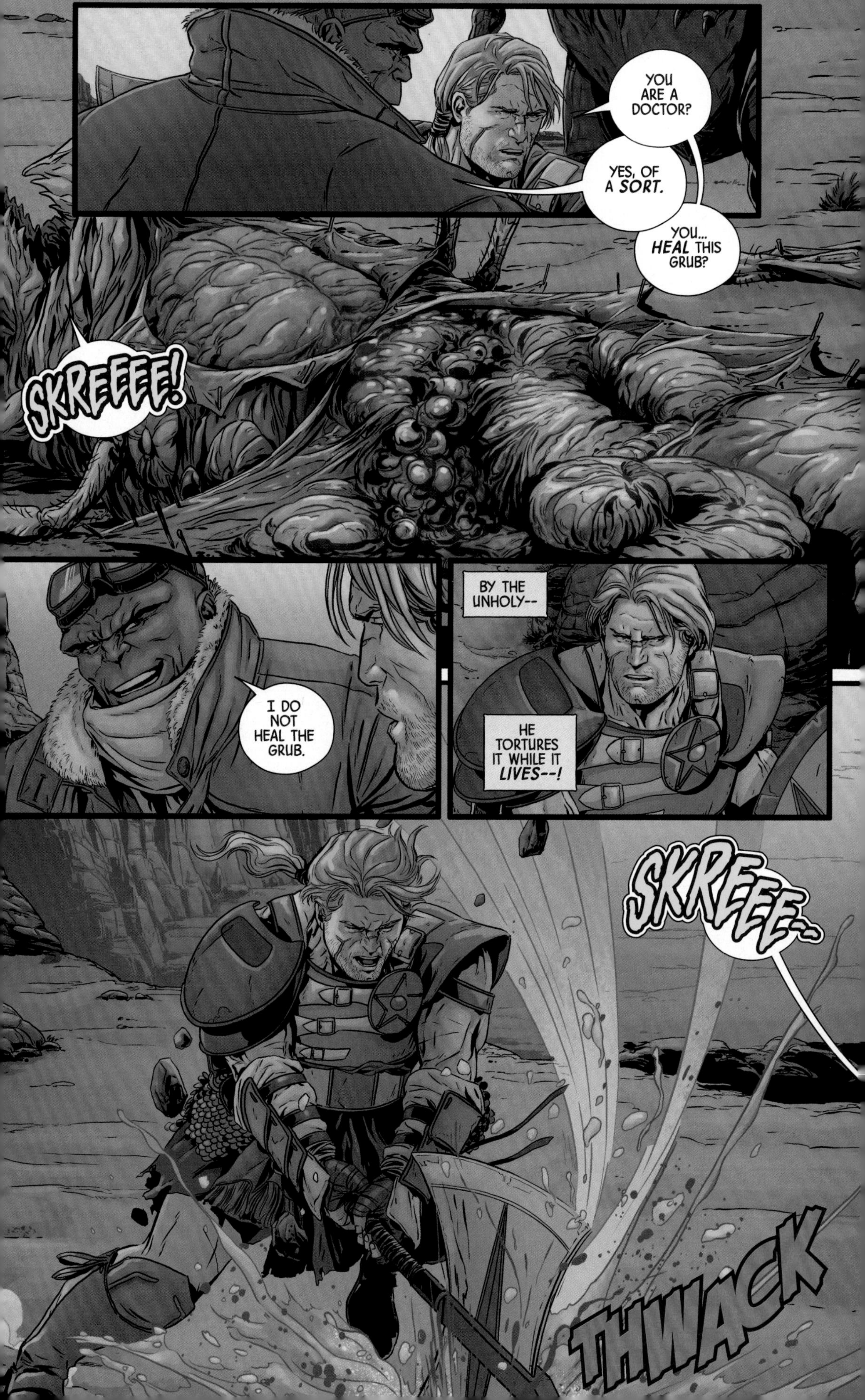
YOU ARE A DOCTOR?
YES, OF A SORT.
YOU... HEAL THIS GRUB?
SKREEEEE!
I DO NOT HEAL THE GRUB.
BY THE UNHOLY--
HE TORTURES IT WHILE IT LIVES--!
SKREEE--
THWACK

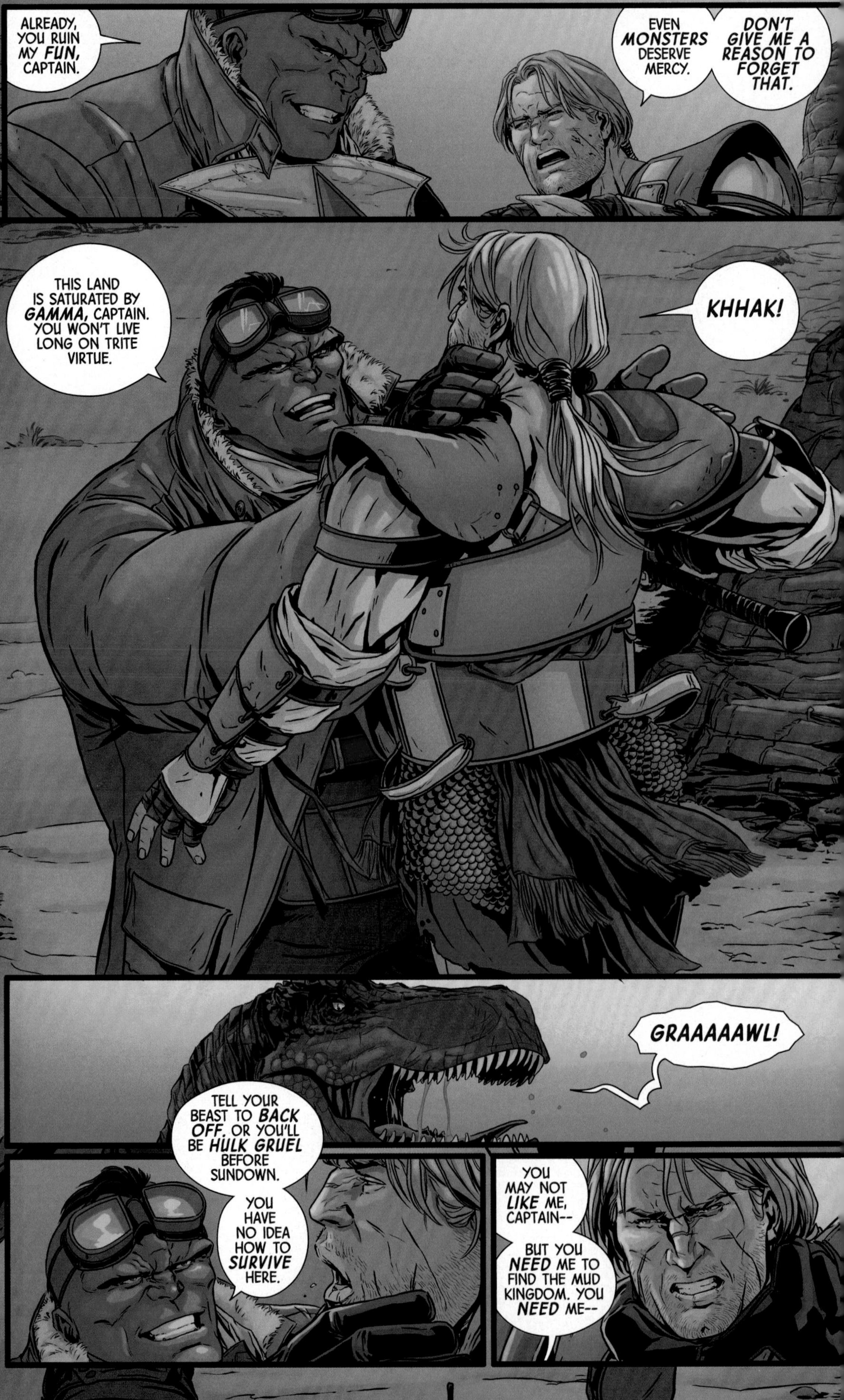
ALREADY, YOU RUIN MY FUN, CAPTAIN.
EVEN MONSTERS DESERVE MERCY.
DON'T GIVE ME A REASON TO FORGET THAT.
THIS LAND IS SATURATED BY GAMMA, CAPTAIN. YOU WON'T LIVE LONG ON TRITE VIRTUE.
KHHAK!
GRAAAAAWL!
TELL YOUR BEAST TO BACK OFF. OR YOU'LL BE HULK GRUEL BEFORE SUNDOWN.
YOU HAVE NO IDEA HOW TO SURVIVE HERE.
YOU MAY NOT LIKE ME, CAPTAIN--
BUT YOU NEED ME TO FIND THE MUD KINGDOM. YOU NEED ME--

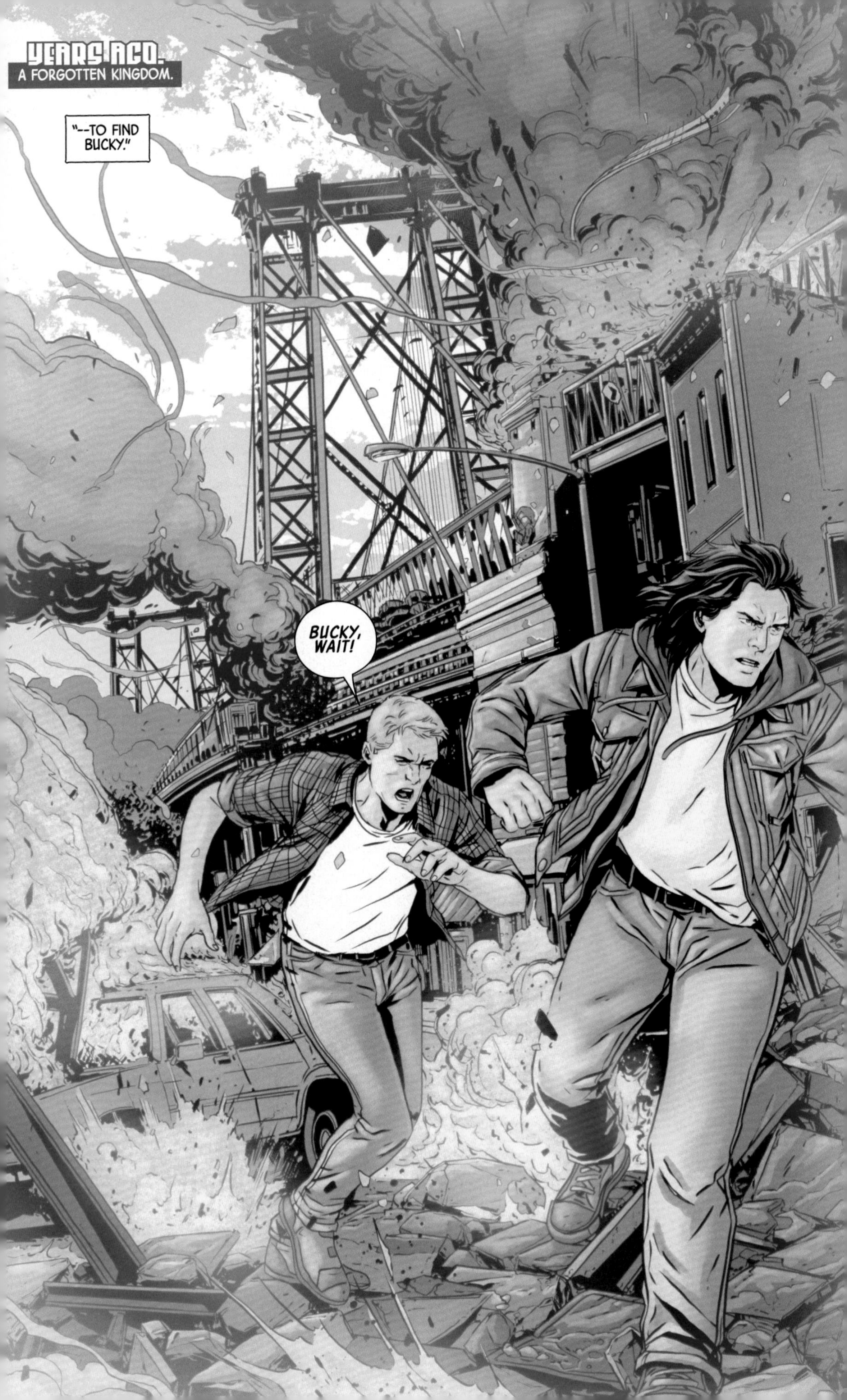
YEARS AGO.
A FORGOTTEN KINGDOM.
"--TO FIND BUCKY."
BUCKY, WAIT!

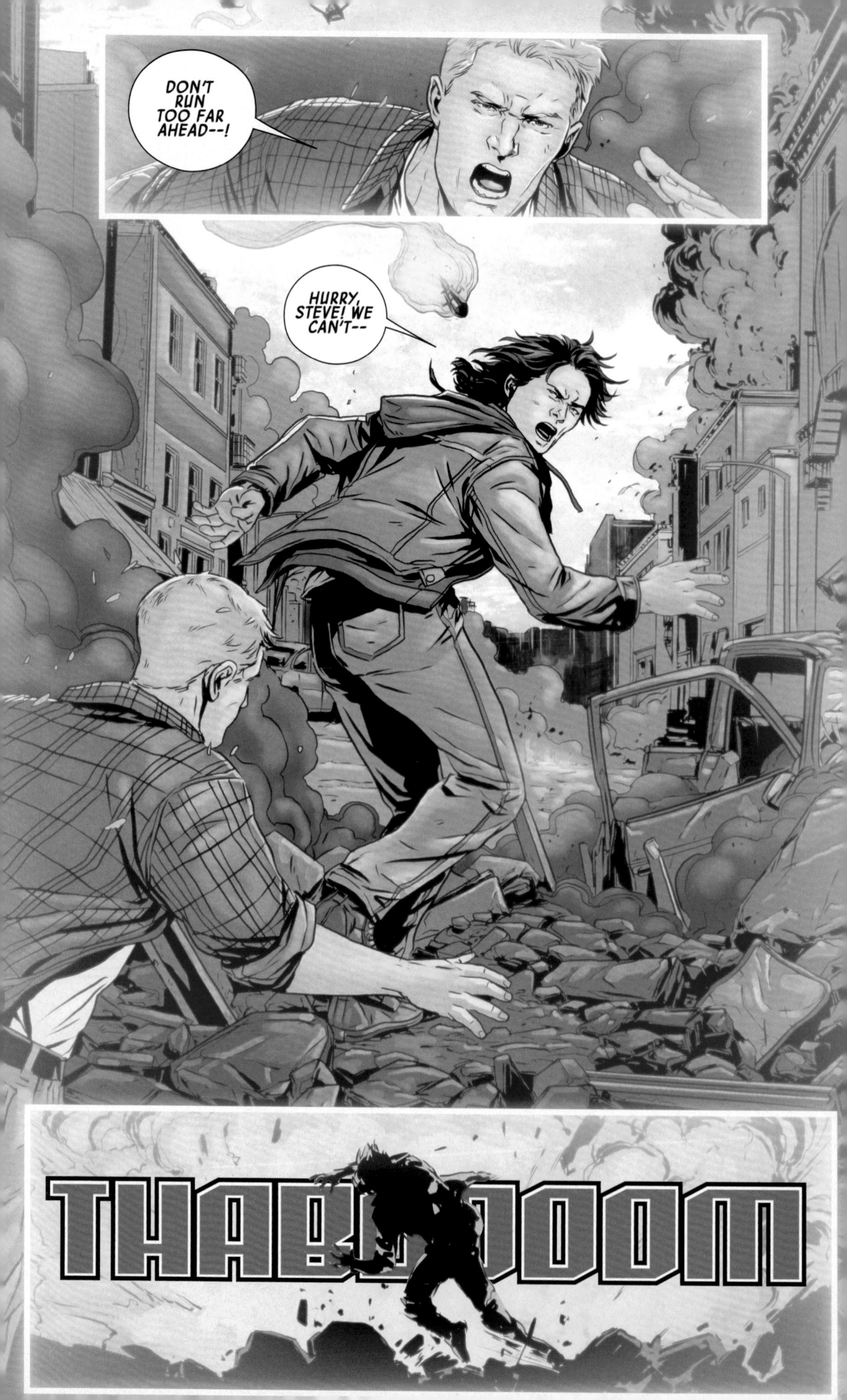
DON'T RUN TOO FAR AHEAD--!
HURRY, STEVE! WE CAN'T--
THABOOOM

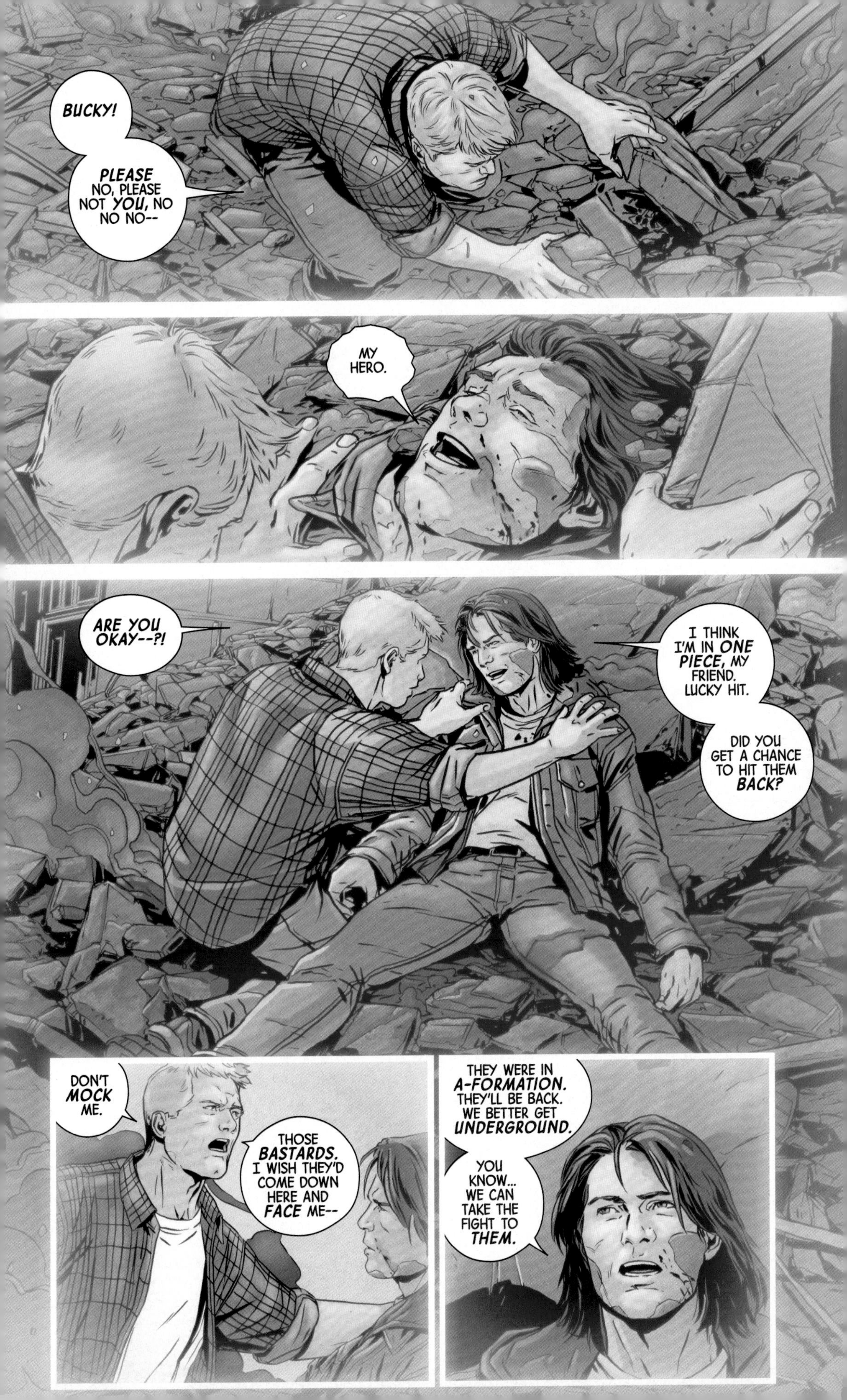
BUCKY!
PLEASE NO, PLEASE NOT YOU, NO NO NO--
MY HERO.
ARE YOU OKAY--?!
I THINK I'M IN ONE PIECE, MY FRIEND. LUCKY HIT.
DID YOU GET A CHANCE TO HIT THEM BACK?
DON'T MOCK ME.
THOSE BASTARDS. I WISH THEY'D COME DOWN HERE AND FACE ME--
THEY WERE IN A-FORMATION. THEY'LL BE BACK. WE BETTER GET UNDERGROUND.
YOU KNOW... WE CAN TAKE THE FIGHT TO THEM.

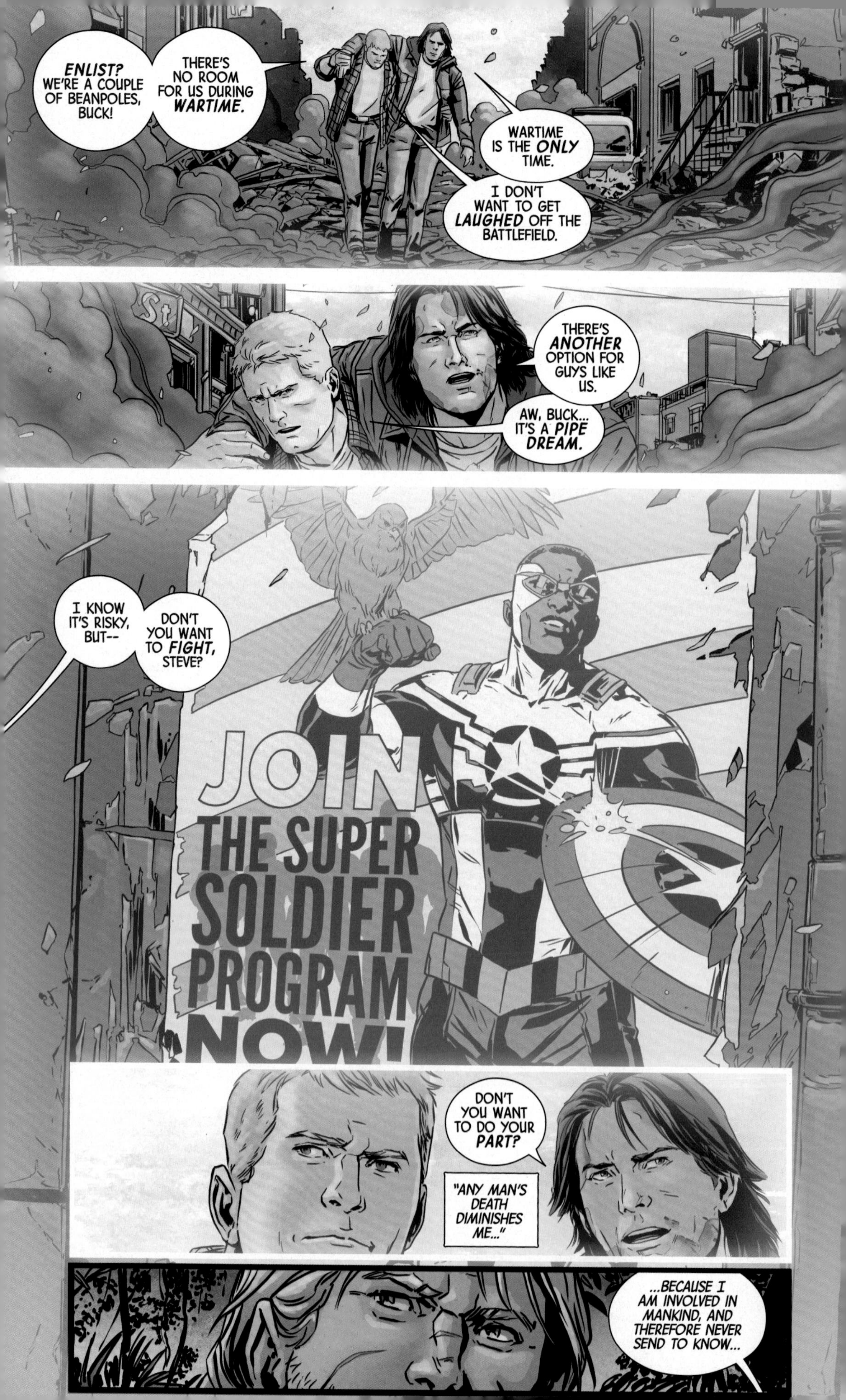
ENLIST? WE'RE A COUPLE OF BEANPOLES, BUCK!
THERE'S NO ROOM FOR US DURING WARTIME.
WARTIME IS THE ONLY TIME.
I DON'T WANT TO GET LAUGHED OFF THE BATTLEFIELD.
THERE'S ANOTHER OPTION FOR GUYS LIKE US.
AW, BUCK... IT'S A PIPE DREAM.
I KNOW IT'S RISKY, BUT--
DON'T YOU WANT TO FIGHT, STEVE?
JOIN THE SUPER SOLDIER PROGRAM NOW!
DON'T YOU WANT TO DO YOUR PART?
"ANY MAN'S DEATH DIMINISHES ME..."
...BECAUSE I AM INVOLVED IN MANKIND, AND THEREFORE NEVER SEND TO KNOW...

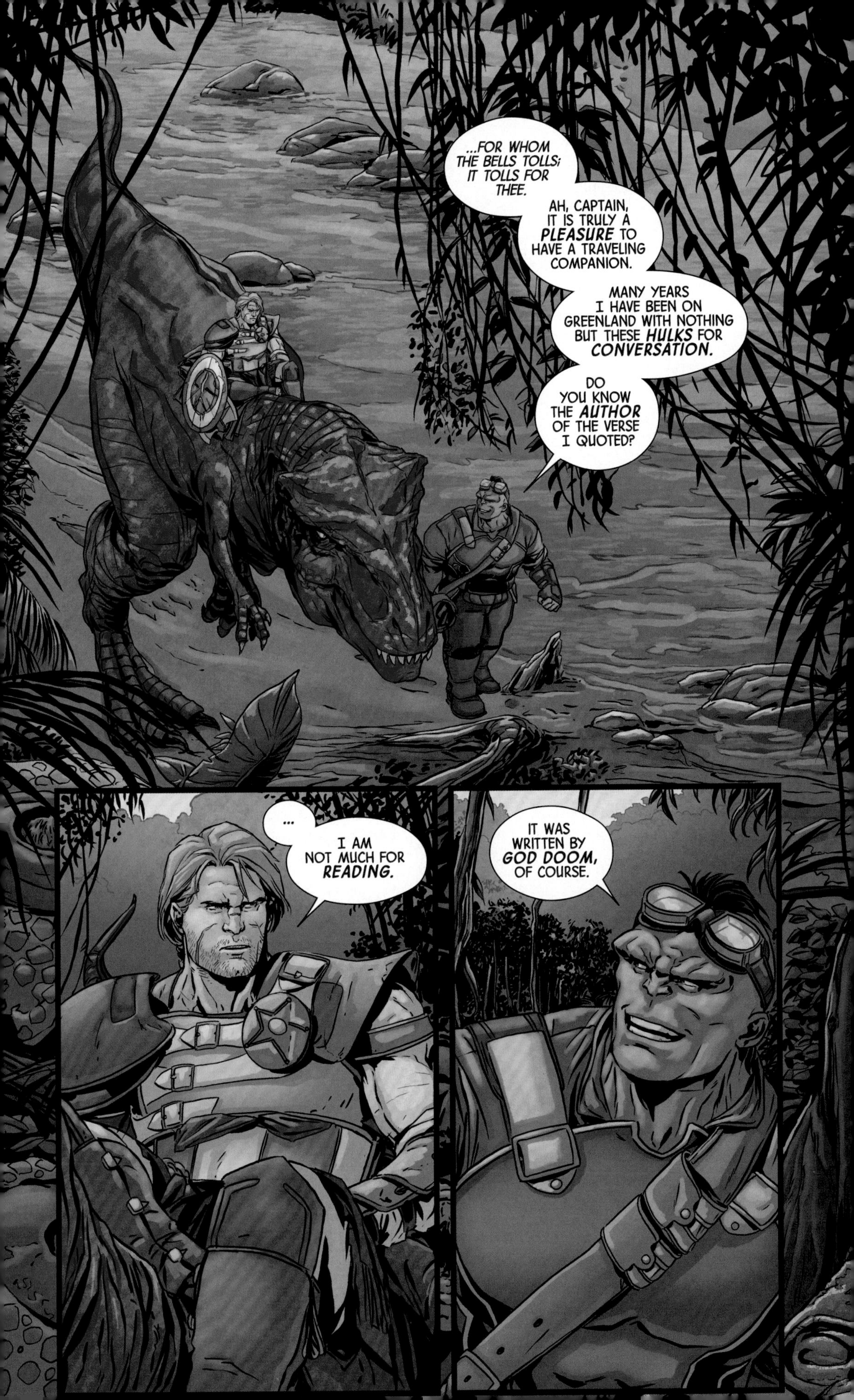
...FOR WHOM THE BELLS TOLLS; IT TOLLS FOR THEE.
AH, CAPTAIN, IT IS TRULY A PLEASURE TO HAVE A TRAVELING COMPANION.
MANY YEARS I HAVE BEEN ON GREENLAND WITH NOTHING BUT THESE HULKS FOR CONVERSATION.
DO YOU KNOW THE AUTHOR OF THE VERSE I QUOTED?
...
I AM NOT MUCH FOR READING.
IT WAS WRITTEN BY GOD DOOM, OF COURSE.

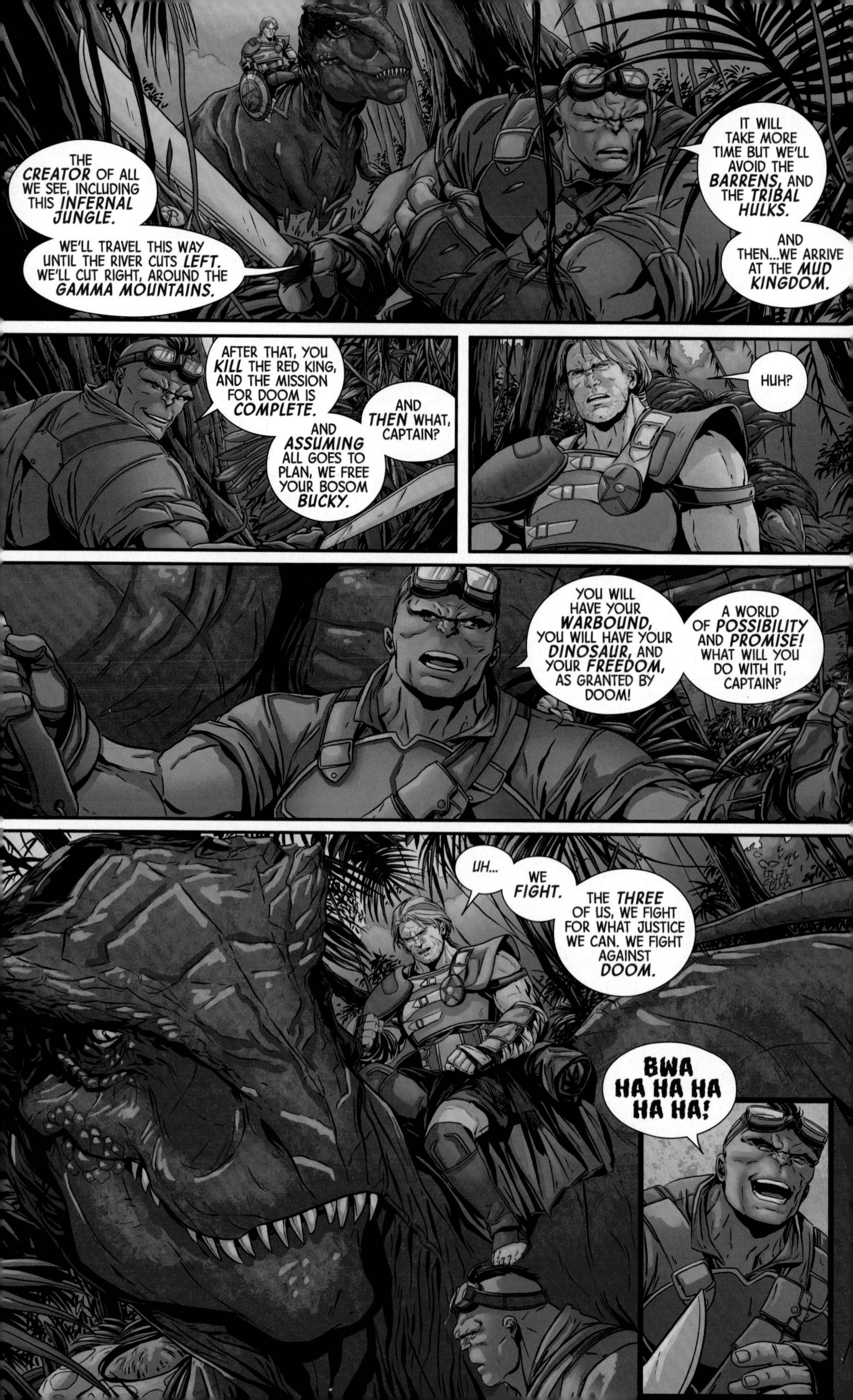

THE CREATOR OF ALL WE SEE, INCLUDING THIS INFERNAL JUNGLE.
WE'LL TRAVEL THIS WAY UNTIL THE RIVER CUTS LEFT. WE'LL CUT RIGHT, AROUND THE GAMMA MOUNTAINS.
IT WILL TAKE MORE TIME BUT WE'LL AVOID THE BARRENS, AND THE TRIBAL HULKS.
AND THEN...WE ARRIVE AT THE MUD KINGDOM.
AFTER THAT, YOU KILL THE RED KING, AND THE MISSION FOR DOOM IS COMPLETE.
AND ASSUMING ALL GOES TO PLAN, WE FREE YOUR BOSOM BUCKY.
AND THEN WHAT, CAPTAIN?
HUH?
YOU WILL HAVE YOUR WARBOUND, YOU WILL HAVE YOUR DINOSAUR, AND YOUR FREEDOM, AS GRANTED BY DOOM!
A WORLD OF POSSIBILITY AND PROMISE! WHAT WILL YOU DO WITH IT, CAPTAIN?
UH...
WE FIGHT.
THE THREE OF US, WE FIGHT FOR WHAT JUSTICE WE CAN. WE FIGHT AGAINST DOOM.
BWA HA HA HA HA HA!

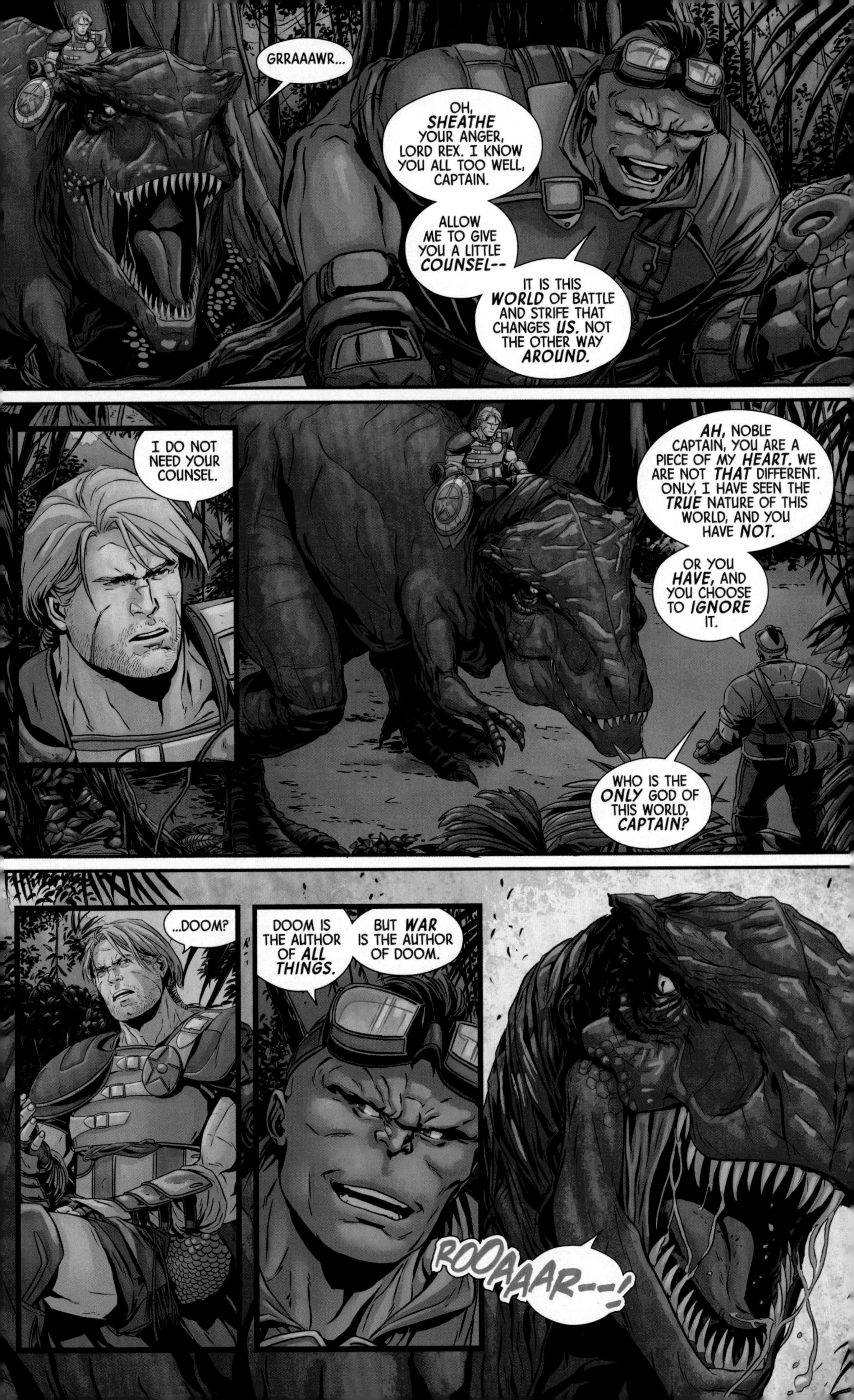
GRRAAAWR...
OH, SHEATHE YOUR ANGER, LORD REX. I KNOW YOU ALL TOO WELL, CAPTAIN.
ALLOW ME TO GIVE YOU A LITTLE COUNSEL--
IT IS THIS WORLD OF BATTLE AND STRIFE THAT CHANGES US. NOT THE OTHER WAY AROUND.
I DO NOT NEED YOUR COUNSEL.
AH, NOBLE CAPTAIN, YOU ARE A PIECE OF MY HEART. WE ARE NOT THAT DIFFERENT. ONLY, I HAVE SEEN THE TRUE NATURE OF THIS WORLD, AND YOU HAVE NOT.
OR YOU HAVE, AND YOU CHOOSE TO IGNORE IT.
WHO IS THE ONLY GOD OF THIS WORLD, CAPTAIN?
...DOOM?
DOOM IS THE AUTHOR OF ALL THINGS.
BUT WAR IS THE AUTHOR OF DOOM.
ROOAAAR--!

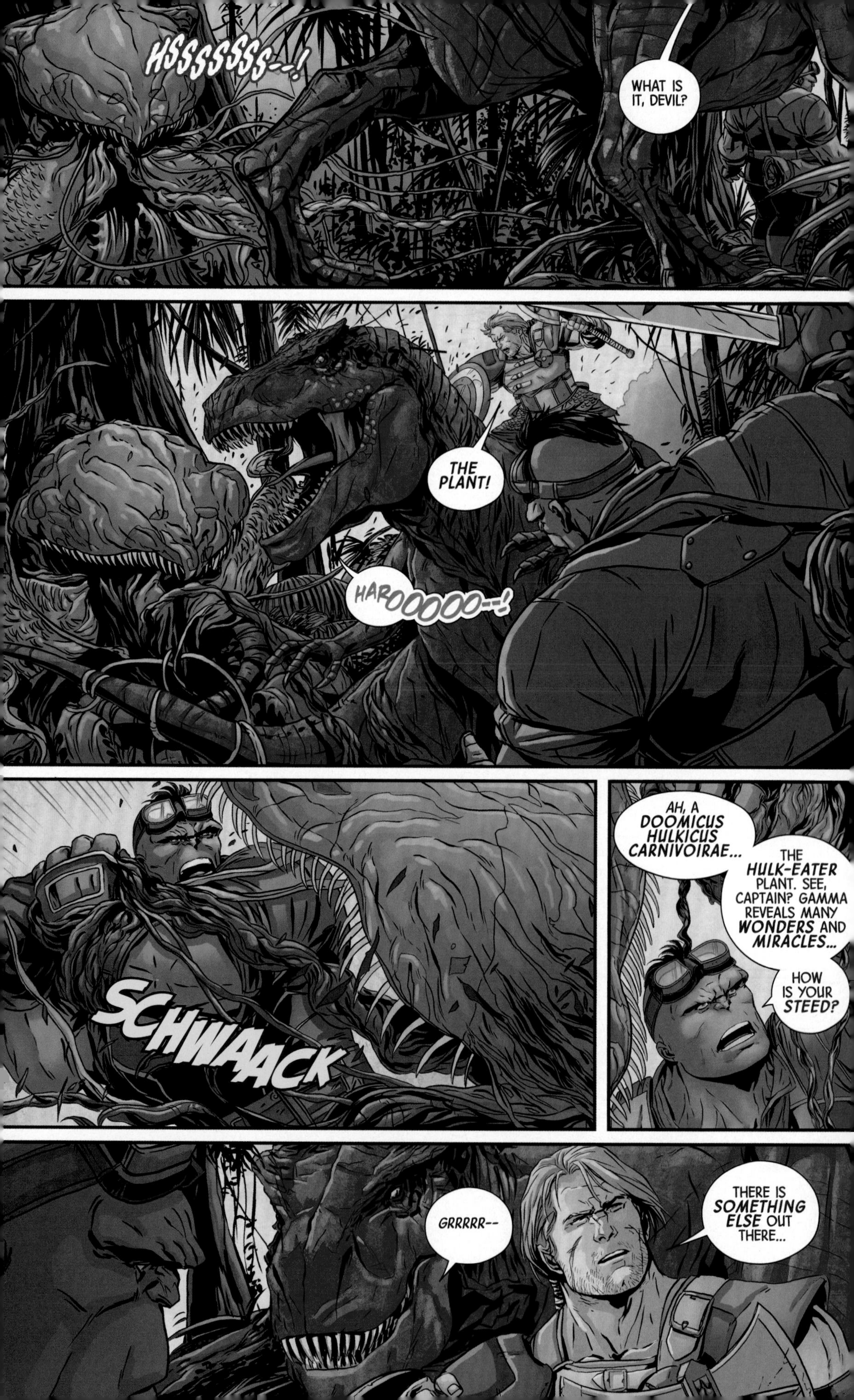
HSSSSSSS--!
WHAT IS IT, DEVIL?
THE PLANT!
HAROOOOO--!
SCHWAACK
AH, A DOOMICUS HULKICUS CARNIVOIRAE...
THE HULK-EATER PLANT. SEE, CAPTAIN? GAMMA REVEALS MANY WONDERS AND MIRACLES...
HOW IS YOUR STEED?
GRRRRR--
THERE IS SOMETHING ELSE OUT THERE...

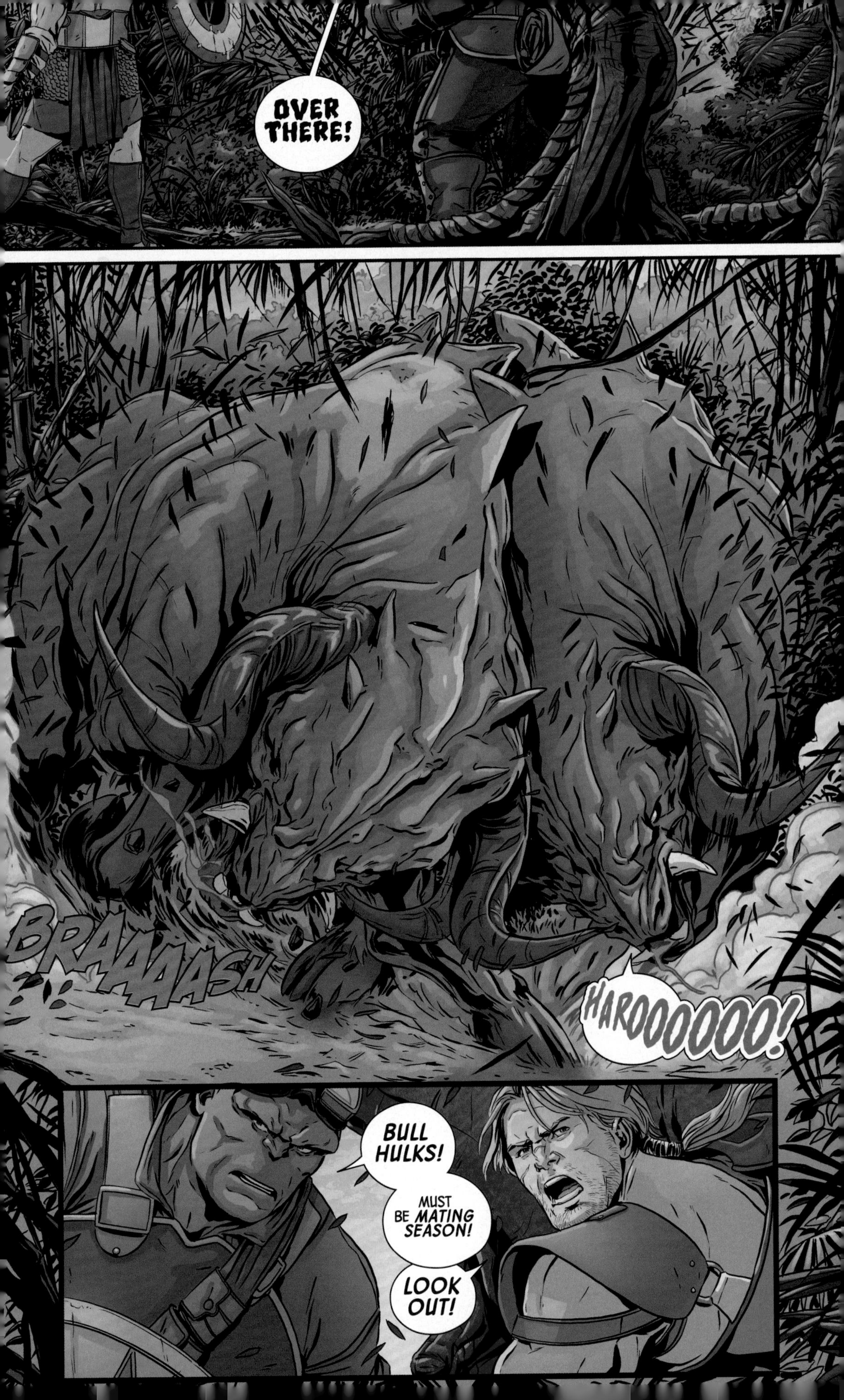
OVER THERE!
BRAAAAASH
HAROOOOOOO!
BULL HULKS!
MUST BE MATING SEASON!
LOOK OUT!

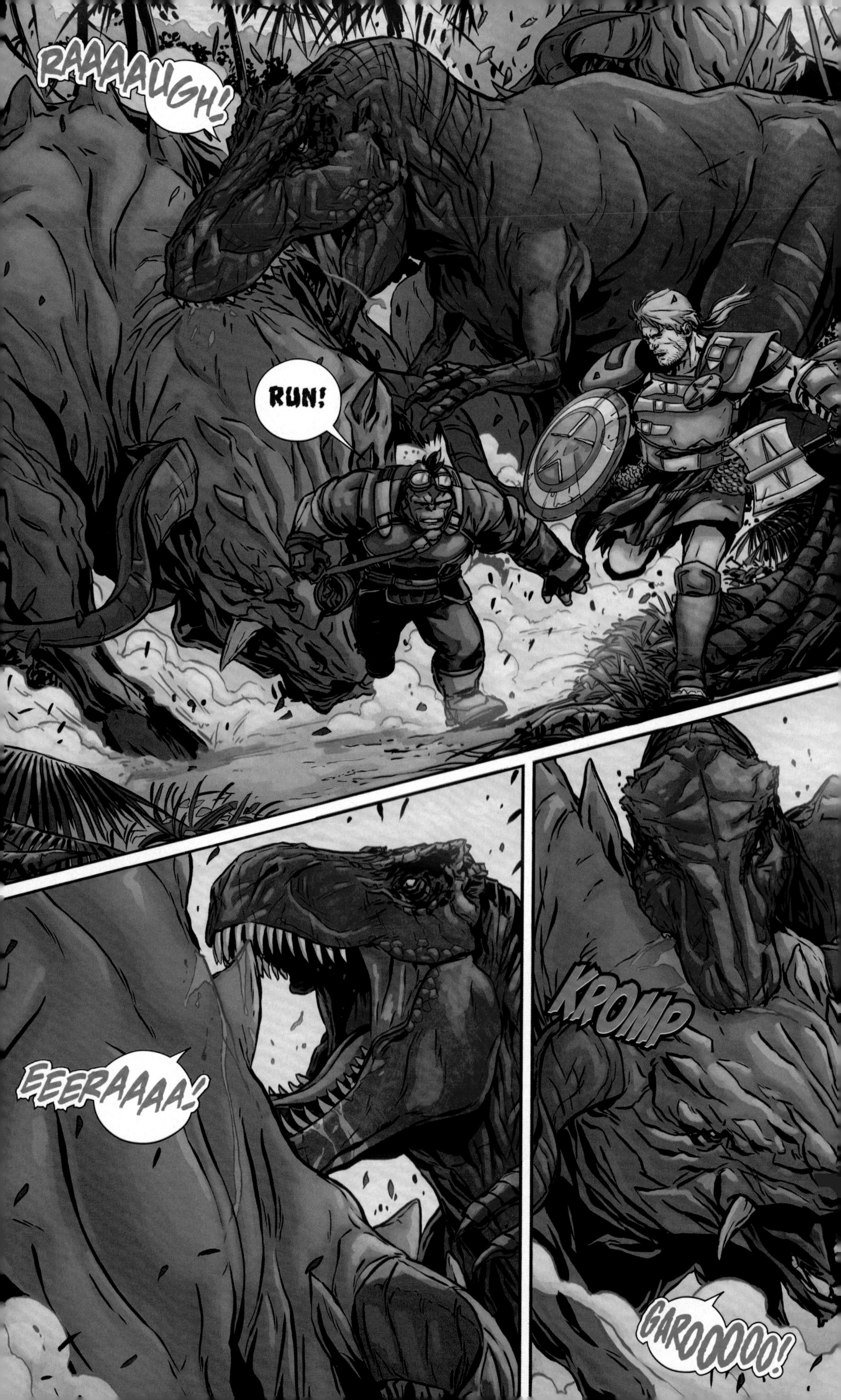
RAAAAAUGH!
RUN!
EEERAAAA!
KROMP
GAROOOOOO!

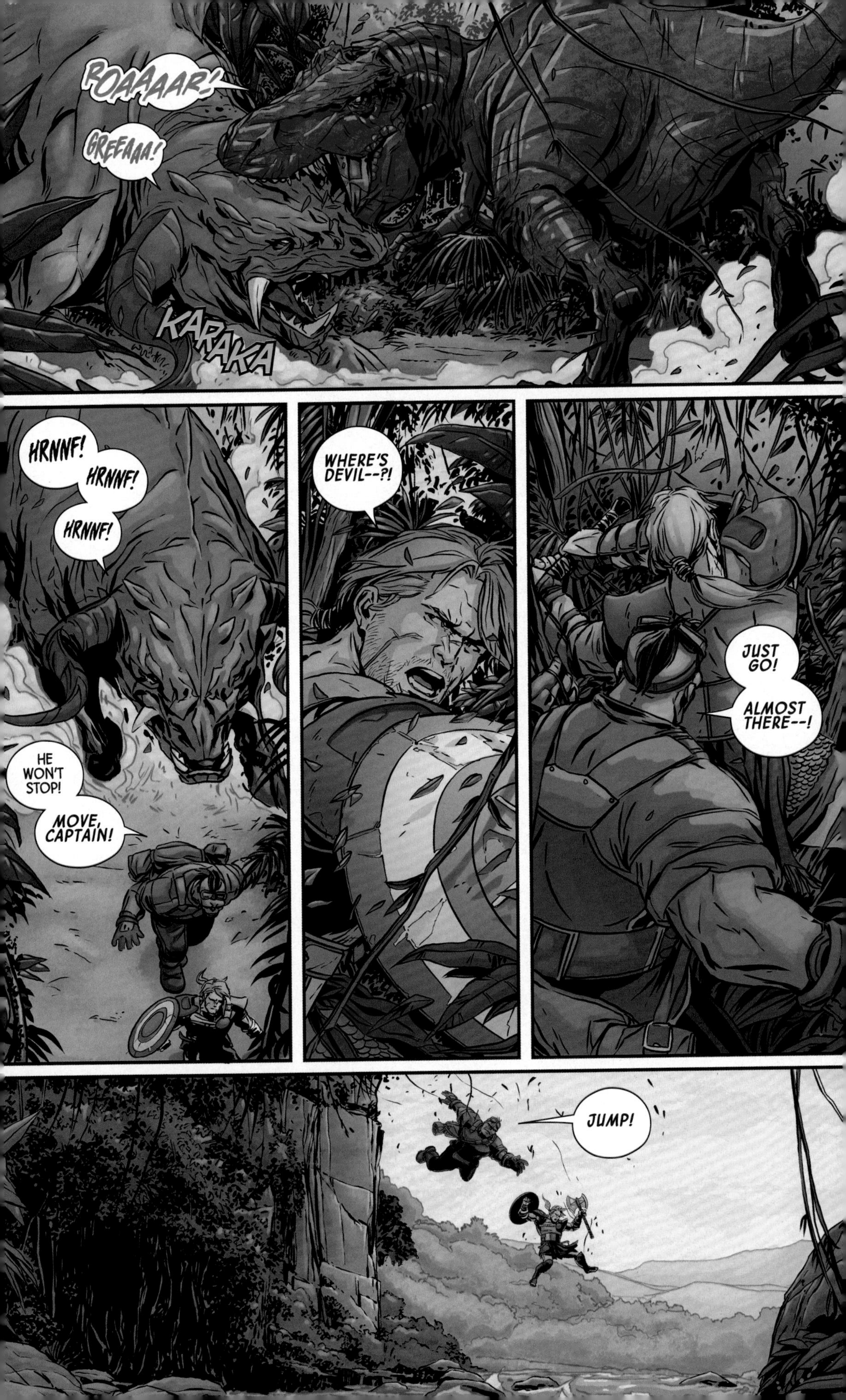
ROAAAAR!
GREEAAA!
KARAKA
HRNNF!
HRNNF!
HRNNF!
HE WON'T STOP!
MOVE, CAPTAIN!
WHERE'S DEVIL--?!
JUST GO!
ALMOST THERE--!
JUMP!

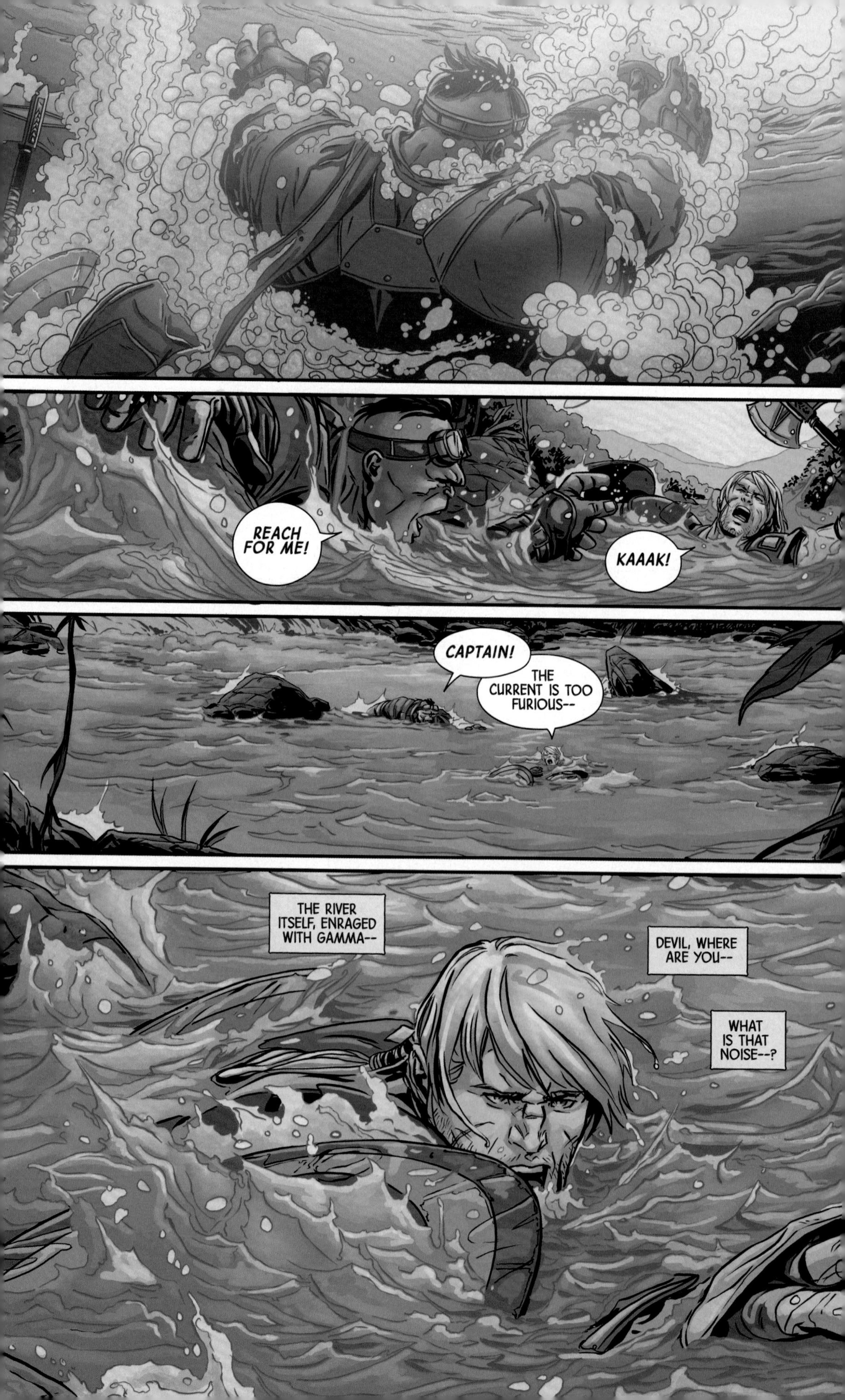
REACH FOR ME!
KAAAK!
CAPTAIN!
THE CURRENT IS TOO FURIOUS--
THE RIVER ITSELF, ENRAGED WITH GAMMA--
DEVIL, WHERE ARE YOU--
WHAT IS THAT NOISE--?

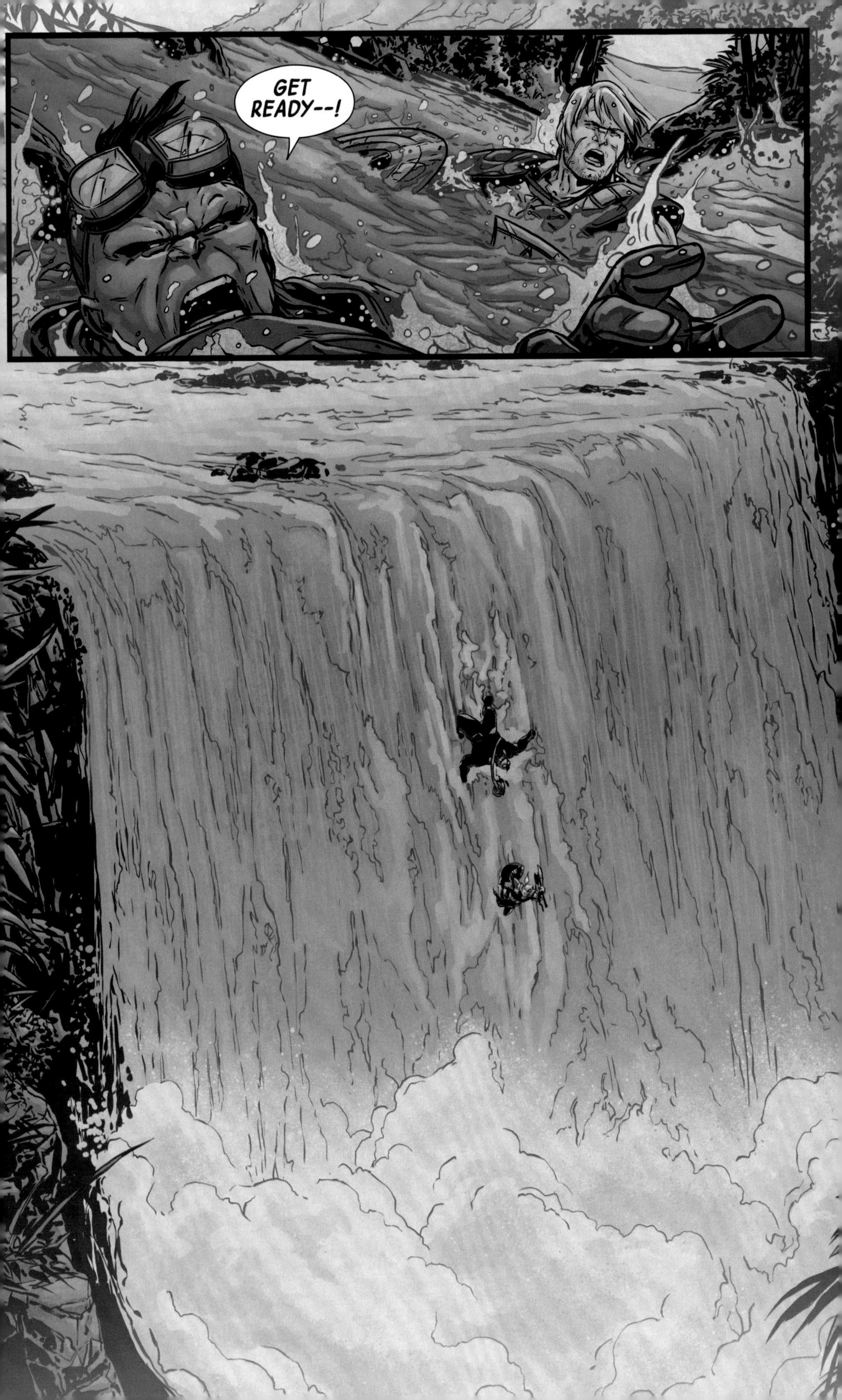

GET READY--!

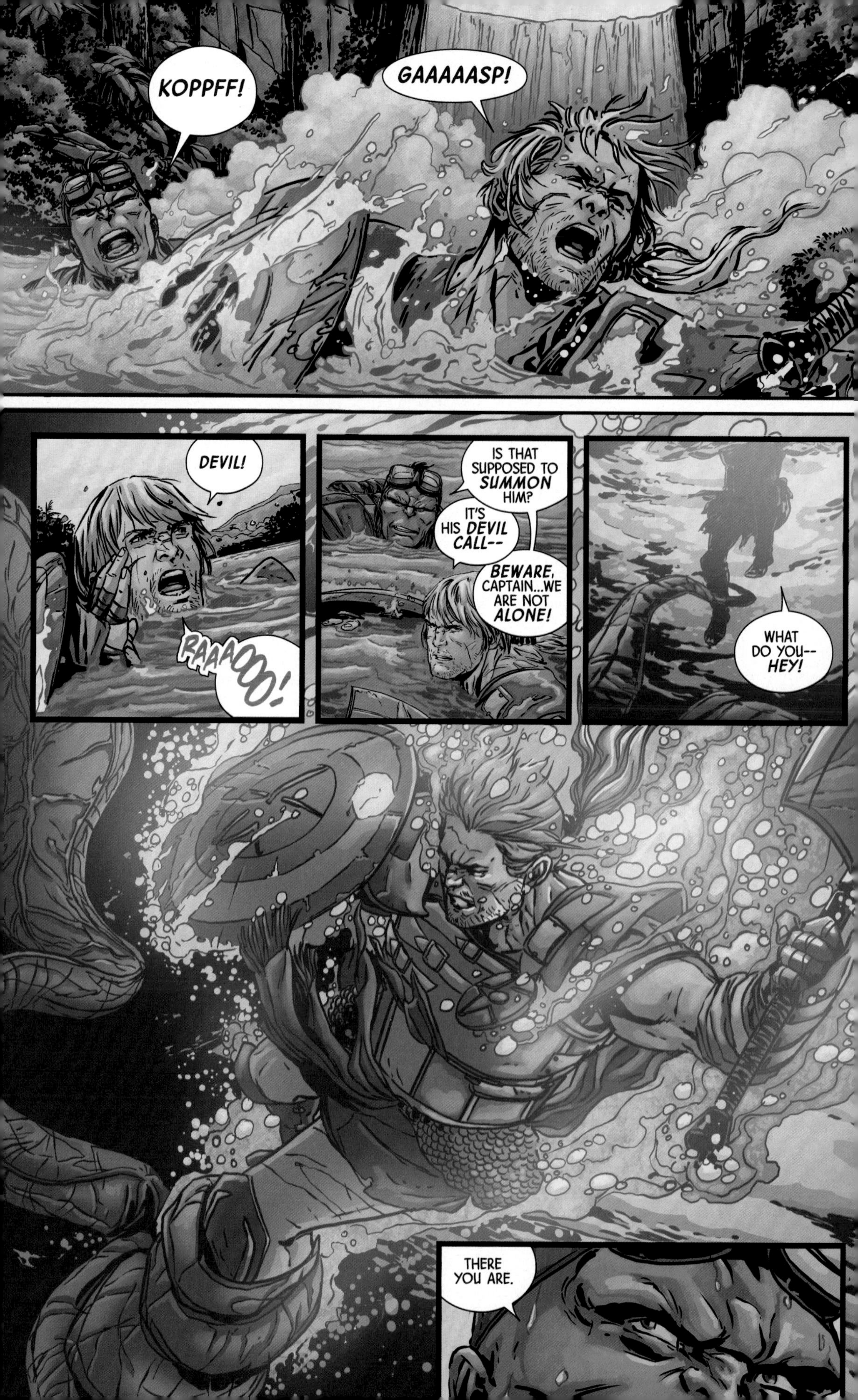
KOPPFF!
GAAAAASP!
DEVIL!
RAAAOOO!
IS THAT SUPPOSED TO SUMMON HIM?
IT'S HIS DEVIL CALL--
BEWARE, CAPTAIN...WE ARE NOT ALONE!
WHAT DO YOU-- HEY!
THERE YOU ARE.

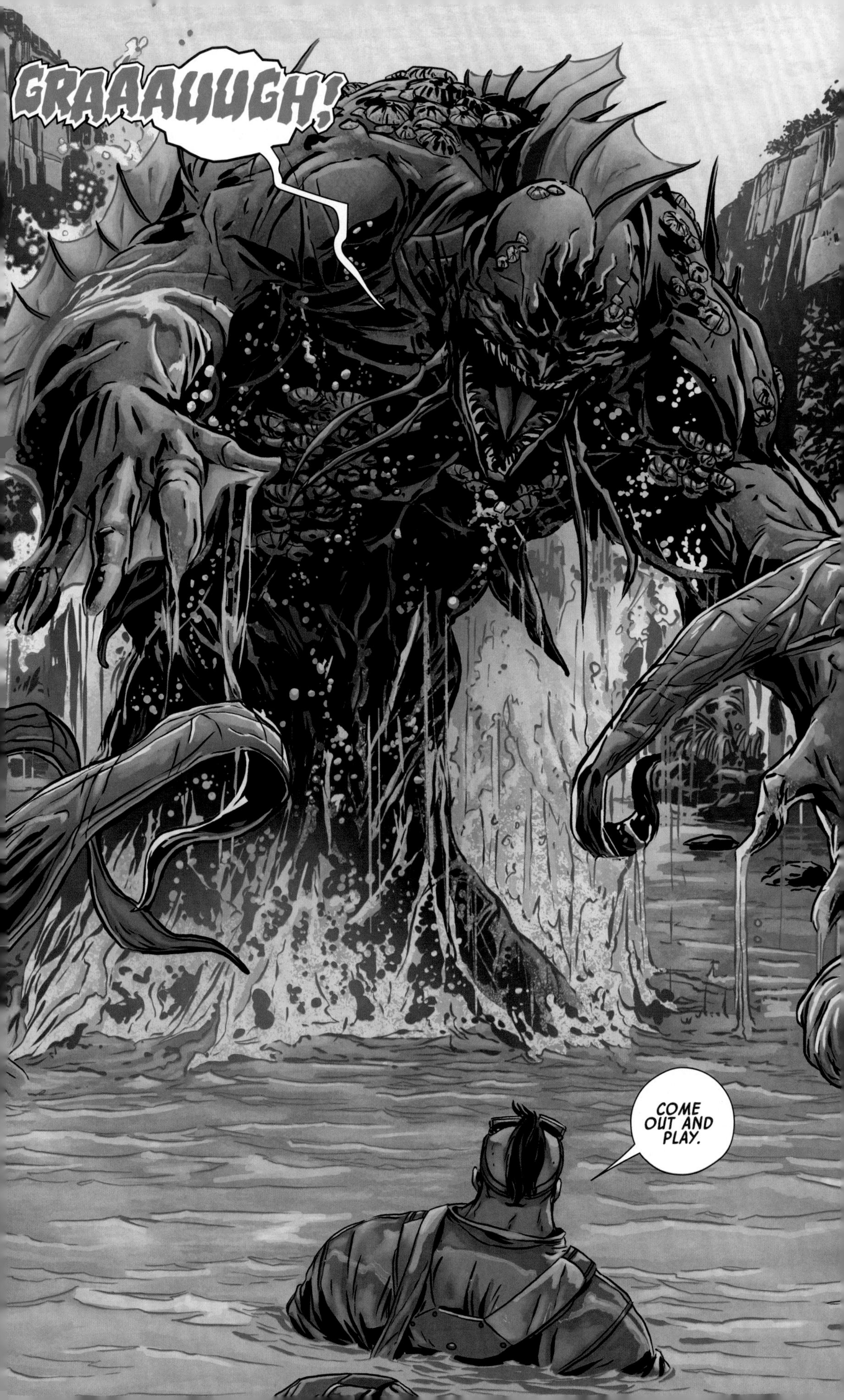
GRAAAUUGH!
COME OUT AND PLAY.

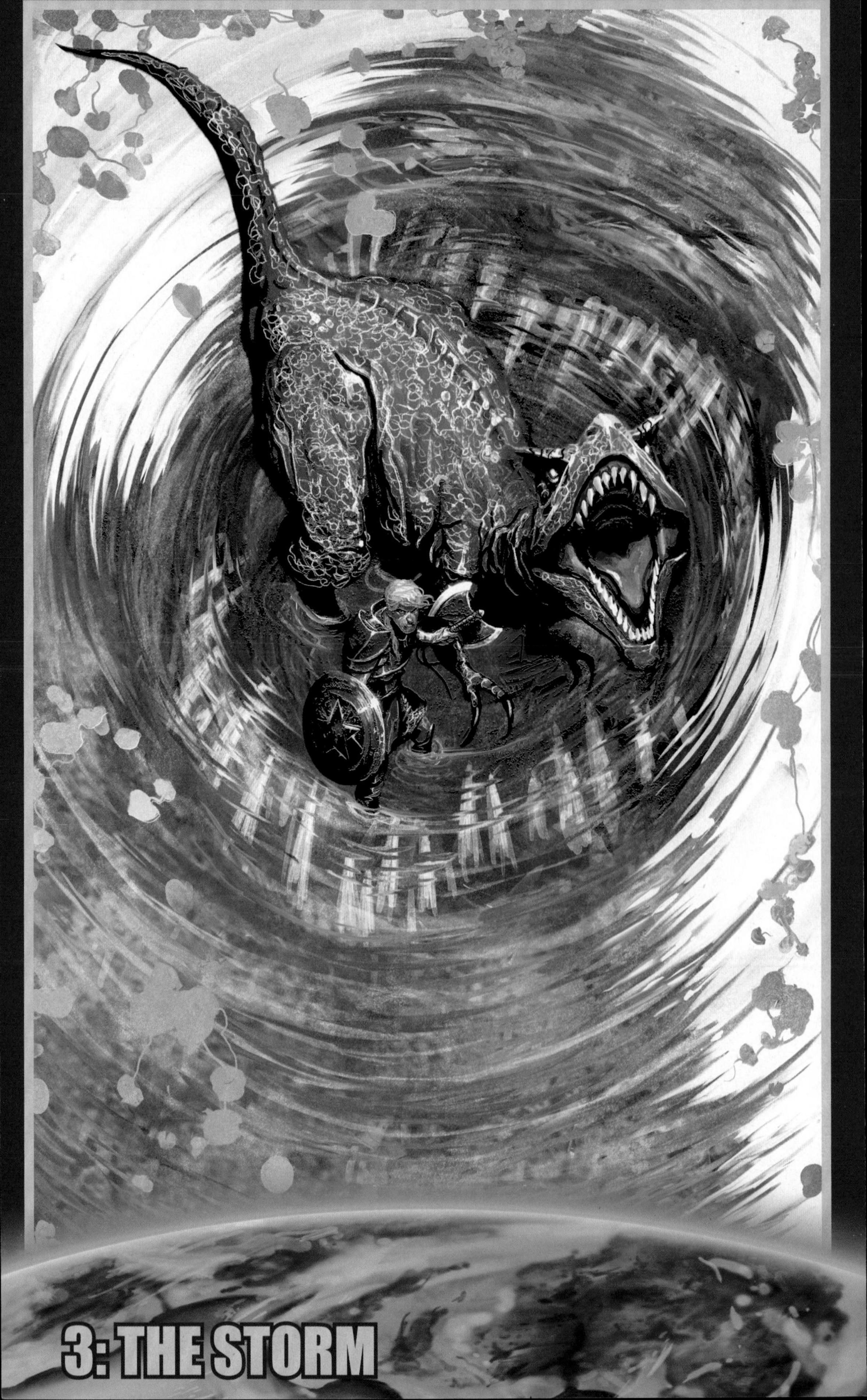
3: THE STORM

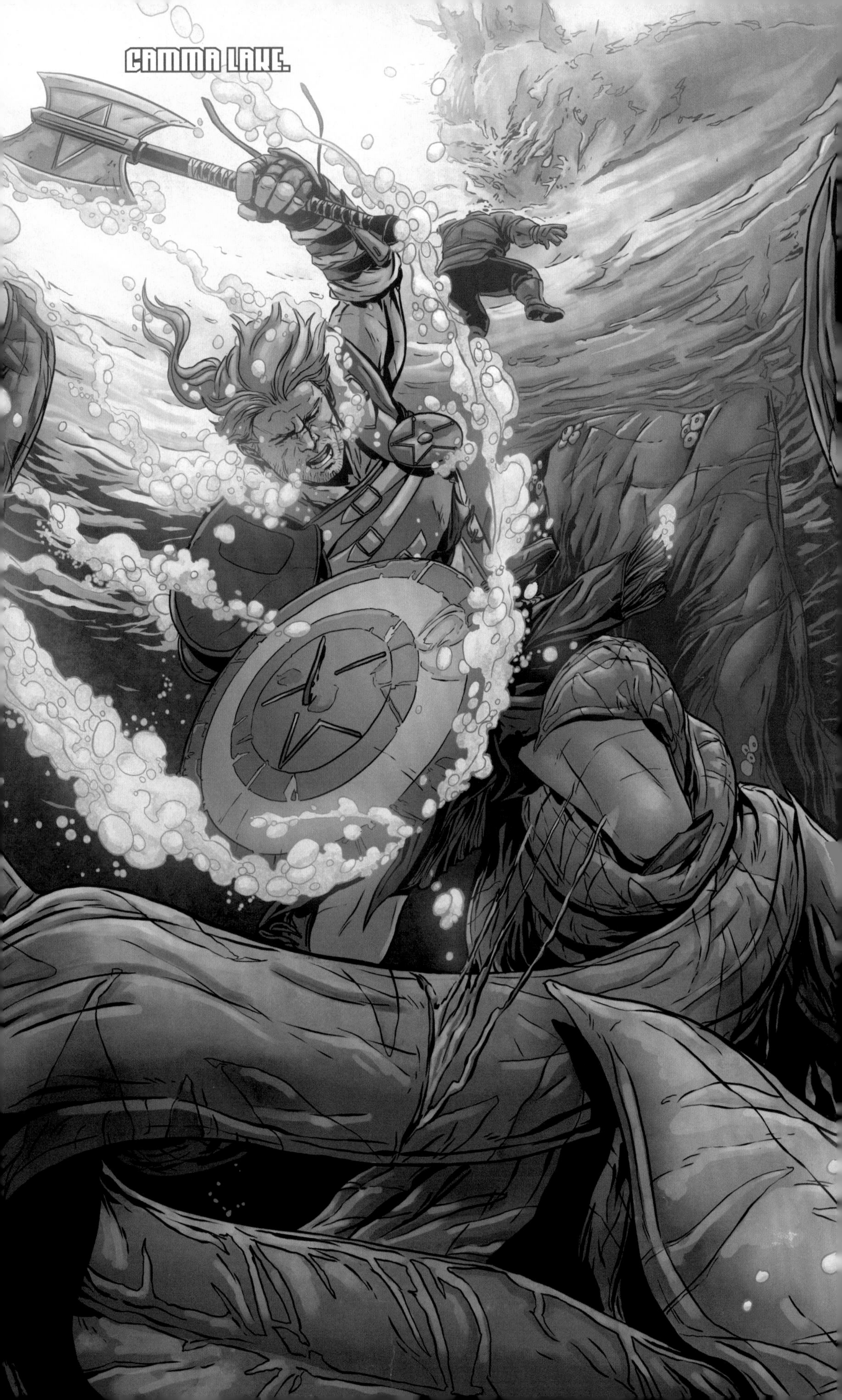
GAMMA LAKE.

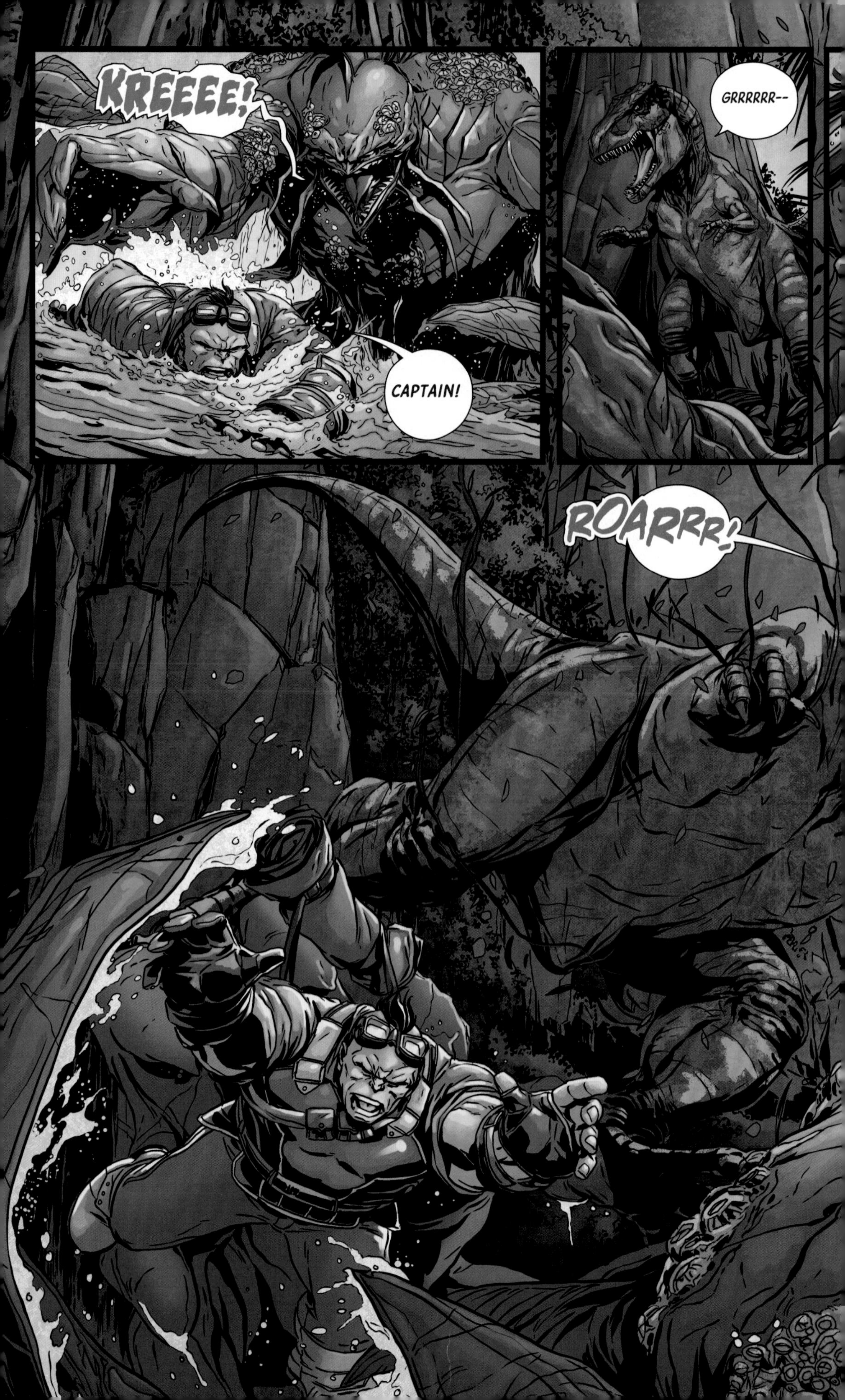
KREEEE!
CAPTAIN!
GRRRRRR--
ROARRR!

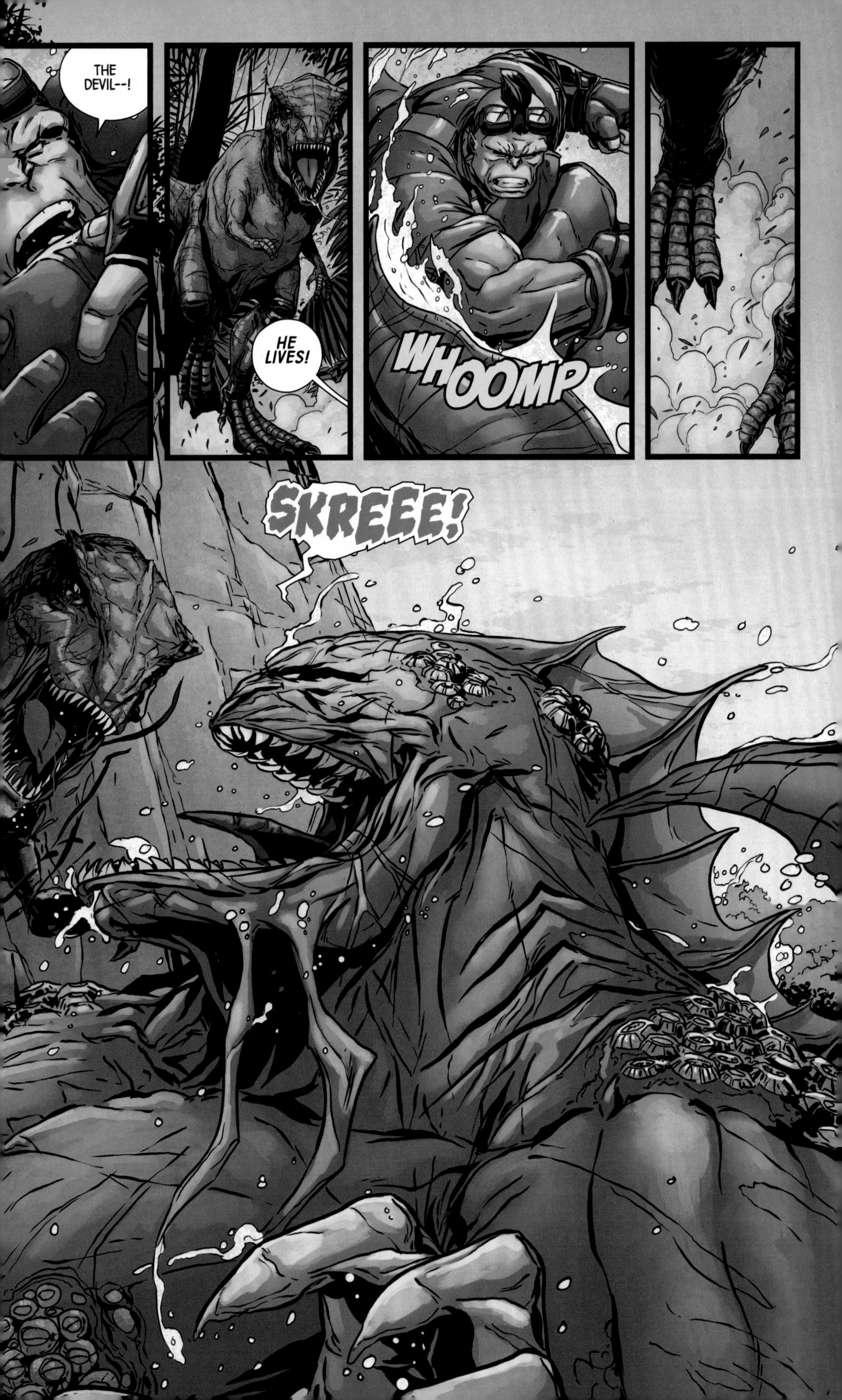
THE DEVIL--!
HE LIVES!
WHOOMP
SKREEE!

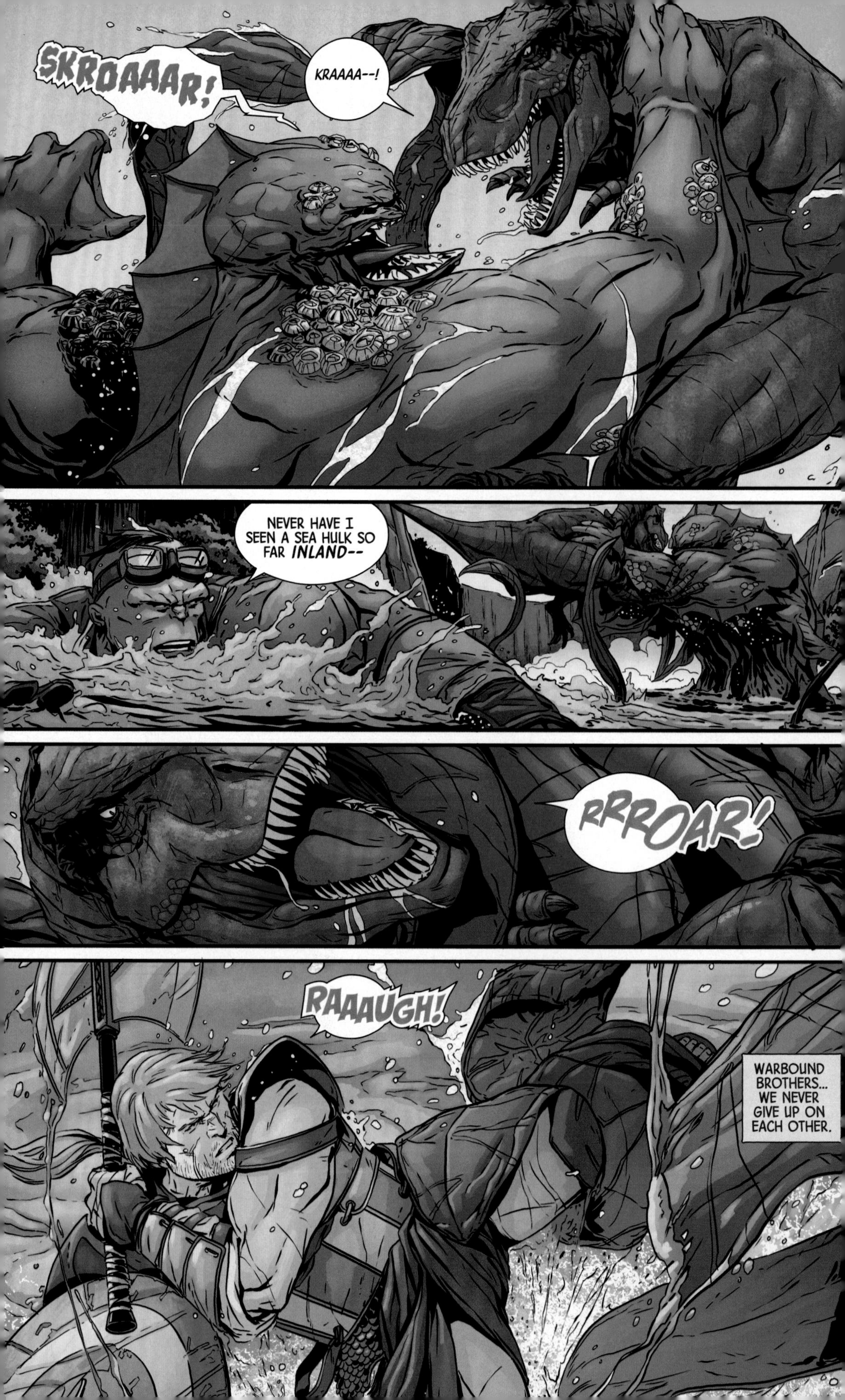
SKROAAAR!
KRAAAA--!
NEVER HAVE I SEEN A SEA HULK SO FAR INLAND--
RRROAR!
RAAAUGH!
WARBOUND BROTHERS... WE NEVER GIVE UP ON EACH OTHER.

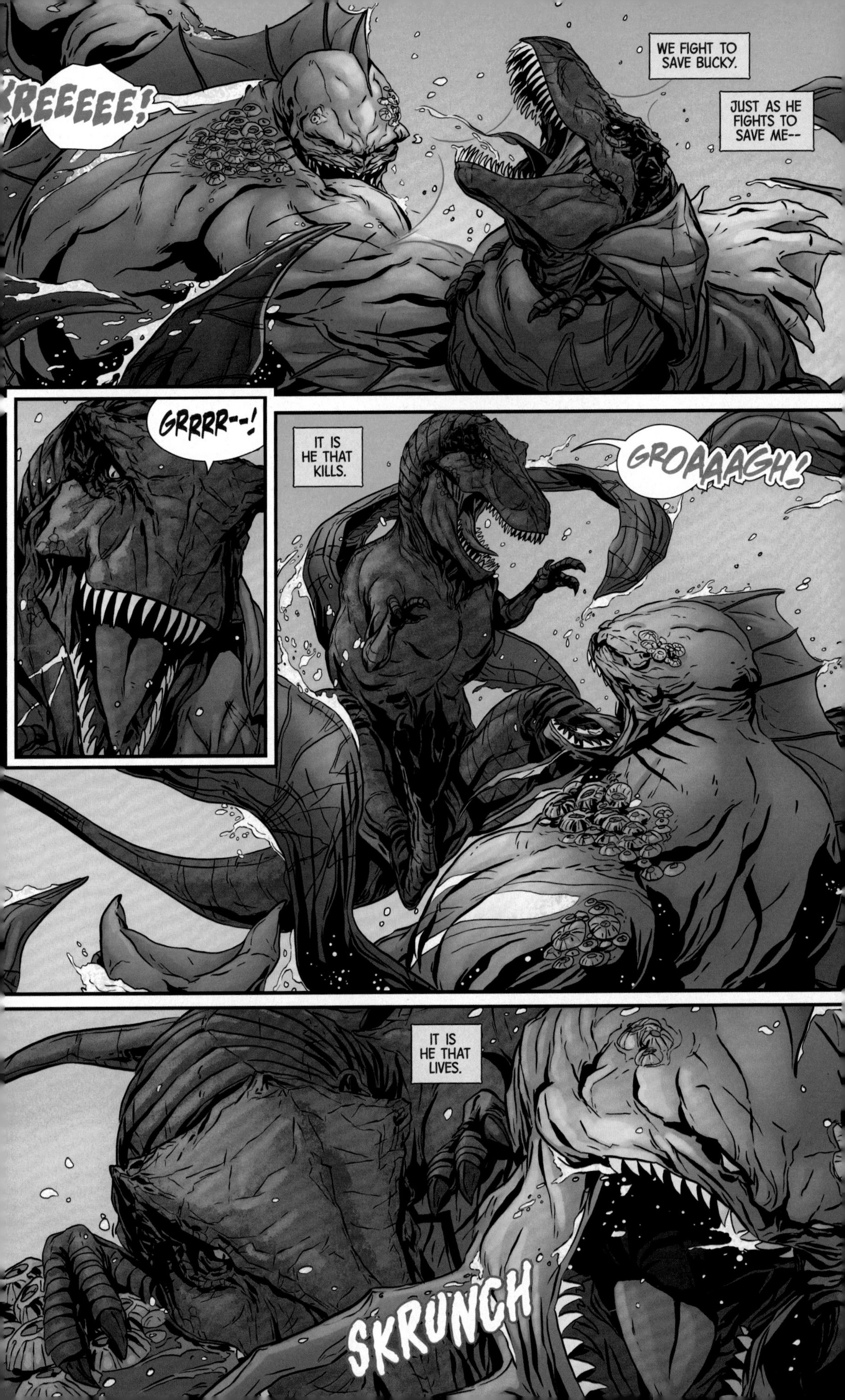
KREEEEE!
WE FIGHT TO SAVE BUCKY.
JUST AS HE FIGHTS TO SAVE ME--
GRRRR--!
IT IS HE THAT KILLS.
GROAAAGH!
IT IS HE THAT LIVES.
SKRUNCH

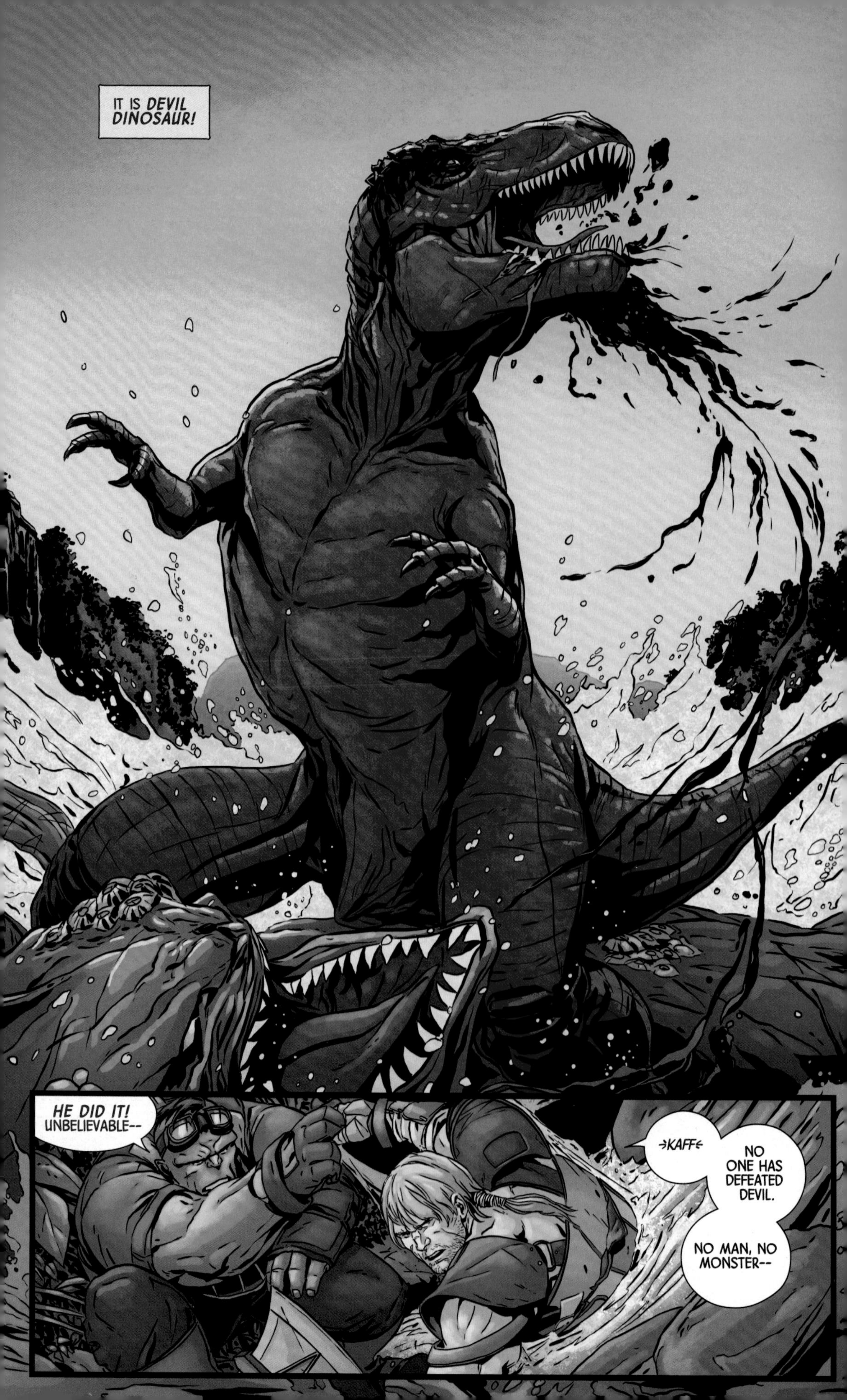
IT IS DEVIL DINOSAUR!
HE DID IT! UNBELIEVABLE--
→KAFF←
NO ONE HAS DEFEATED DEVIL.
NO MAN, NO MONSTER--

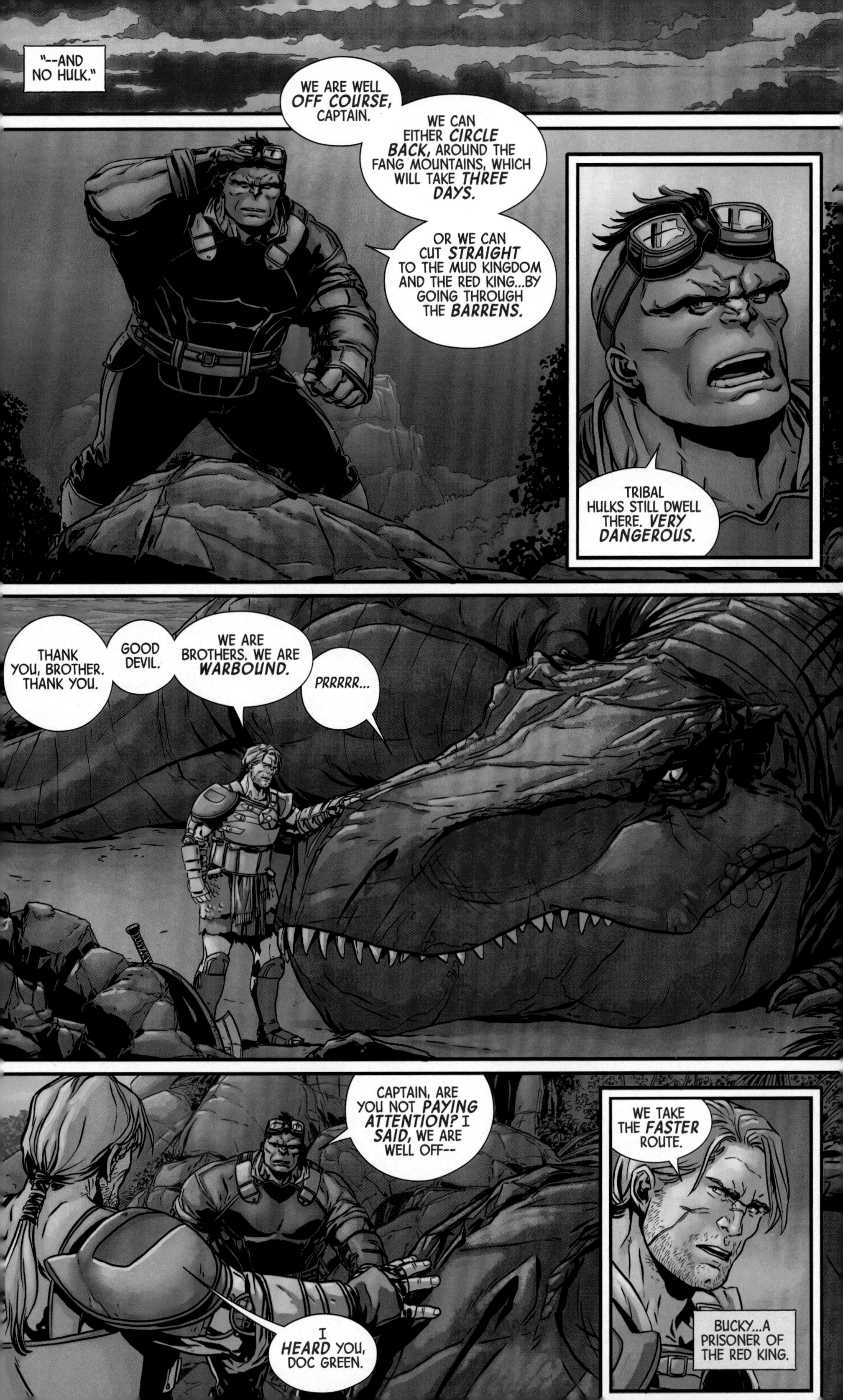
"--AND NO HULK."
WE ARE WELL OFF COURSE, CAPTAIN.
WE CAN EITHER CIRCLE BACK, AROUND THE FANG MOUNTAINS, WHICH WILL TAKE THREE DAYS.
OR WE CAN CUT STRAIGHT TO THE MUD KINGDOM AND THE RED KING...BY GOING THROUGH THE BARRENS.
TRIBAL HULKS STILL DWELL THERE. VERY DANGEROUS.
THANK YOU, BROTHER. THANK YOU.
GOOD DEVIL.
WE ARE BROTHERS. WE ARE WARBOUND.
PRRRRR...
CAPTAIN, ARE YOU NOT PAYING ATTENTION? I SAID, WE ARE WELL OFF--
I HEARD YOU, DOC GREEN.
WE TAKE THE FASTER ROUTE.
BUCKY...A PRISONER OF THE RED KING.

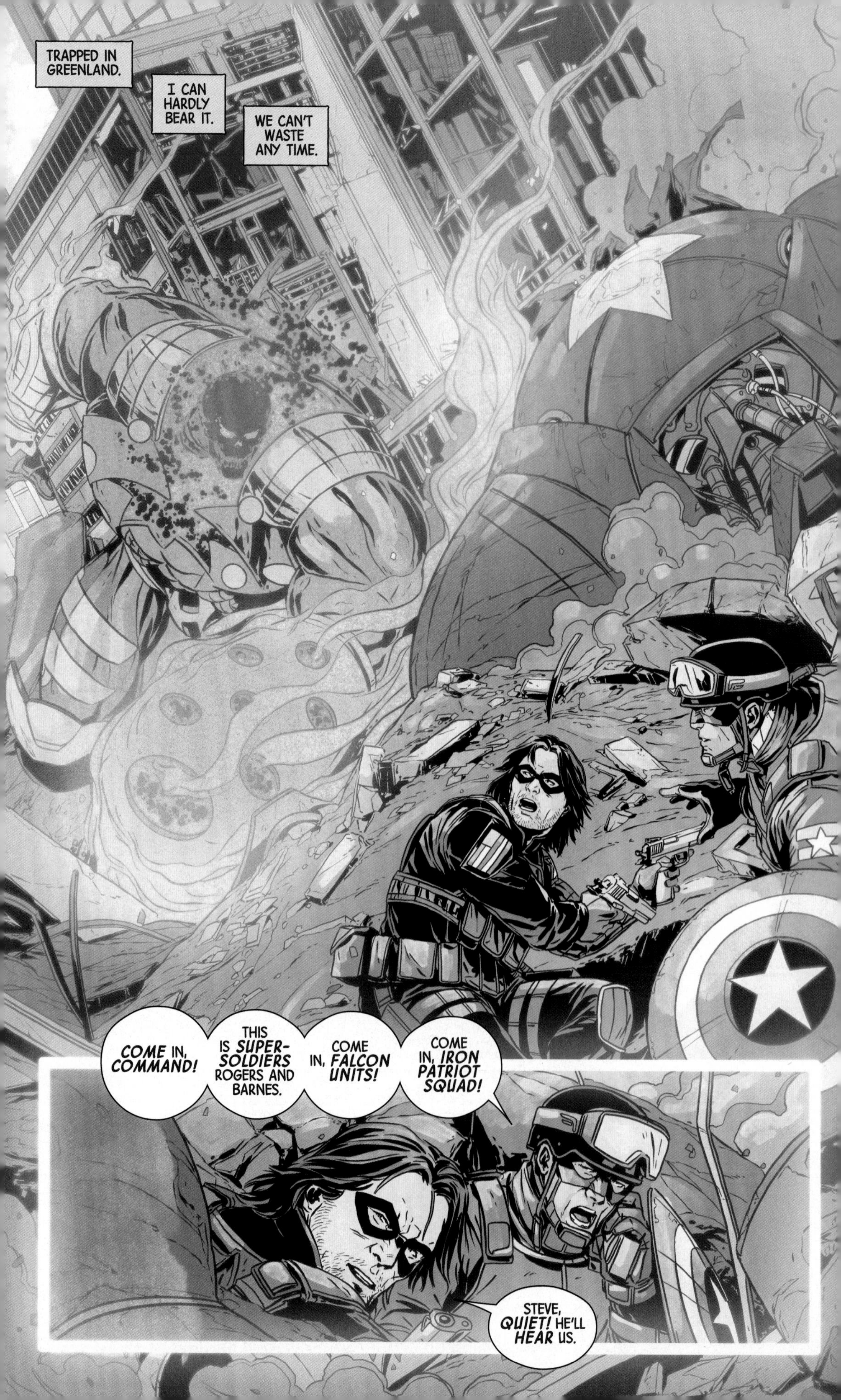
TRAPPED IN GREENLAND.
I CAN HARDLY BEAR IT.
WE CAN'T WASTE ANY TIME.
COME IN, COMMAND!
THIS IS SUPER-SOLDIERS ROGERS AND BARNES.
COME IN, FALCON UNITS!
COME IN, IRON PATRIOT SQUAD!
STEVE, QUIET! HE'LL HEAR US.

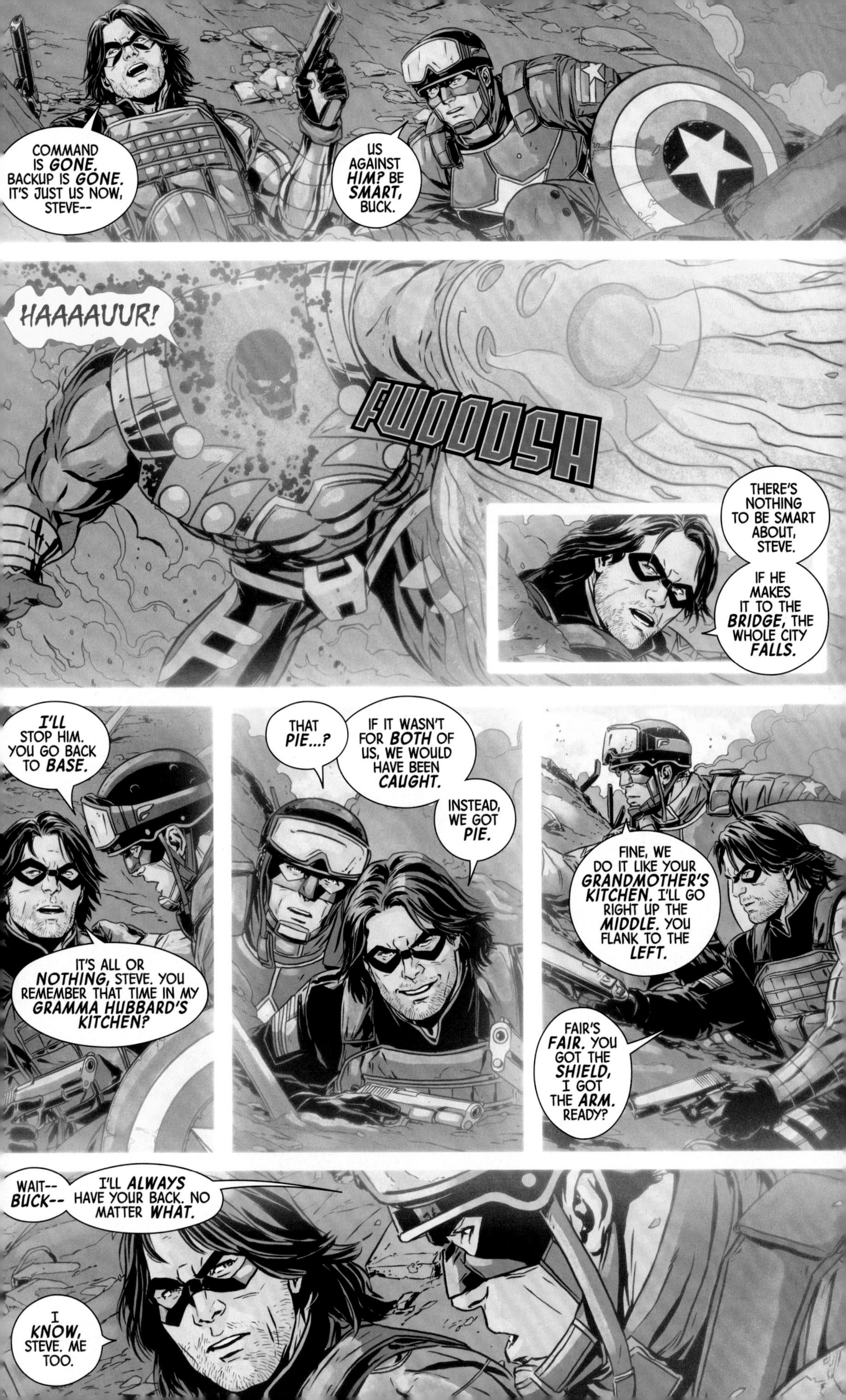
COMMAND IS GONE. BACKUP IS GONE. IT'S JUST US NOW, STEVE--
US AGAINST HIM? BE SMART, BUCK.
HAAAAUUR!
FWOOOSH
THERE'S NOTHING TO BE SMART ABOUT, STEVE.
IF HE MAKES IT TO THE BRIDGE, THE WHOLE CITY FALLS.
I'LL STOP HIM. YOU GO BACK TO BASE.
IT'S ALL OR NOTHING, STEVE. YOU REMEMBER THAT TIME IN MY GRAMMA HUBBARD'S KITCHEN?
THAT PIE...?
IF IT WASN'T FOR BOTH OF US, WE WOULD HAVE BEEN CAUGHT.
INSTEAD, WE GOT PIE.
FINE, WE DO IT LIKE YOUR GRANDMOTHER'S KITCHEN. I'LL GO RIGHT UP THE MIDDLE. YOU FLANK TO THE LEFT.
FAIR'S FAIR. YOU GOT THE SHIELD, I GOT THE ARM. READY?
WAIT-- BUCK--
I'LL ALWAYS HAVE YOUR BACK, NO MATTER WHAT.
I KNOW, STEVE. ME TOO.

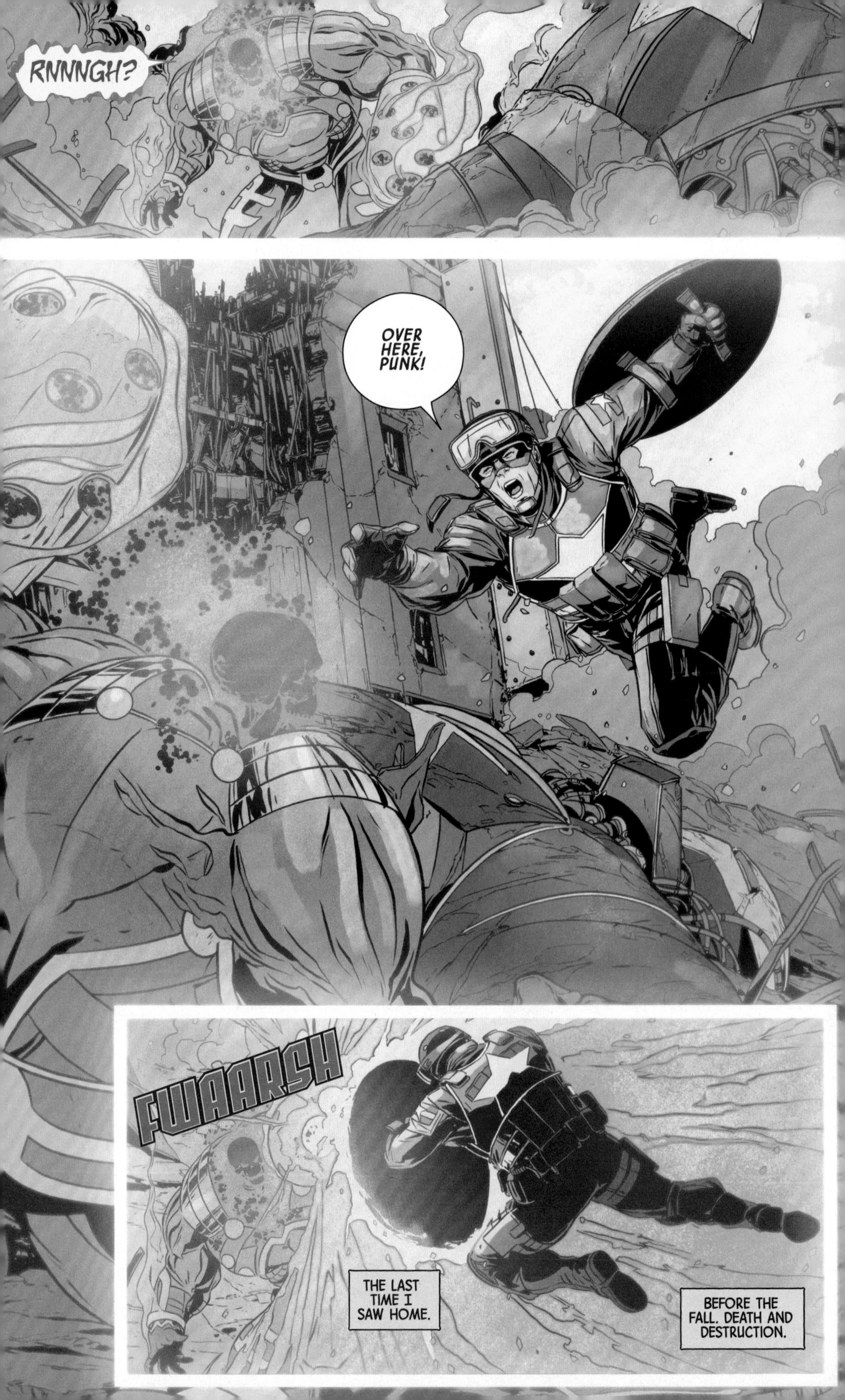
RNNNGH?
OVER HERE, PUNK!
FWAARSH
THE LAST TIME I SAW HOME.
BEFORE THE FALL. DEATH AND DESTRUCTION.

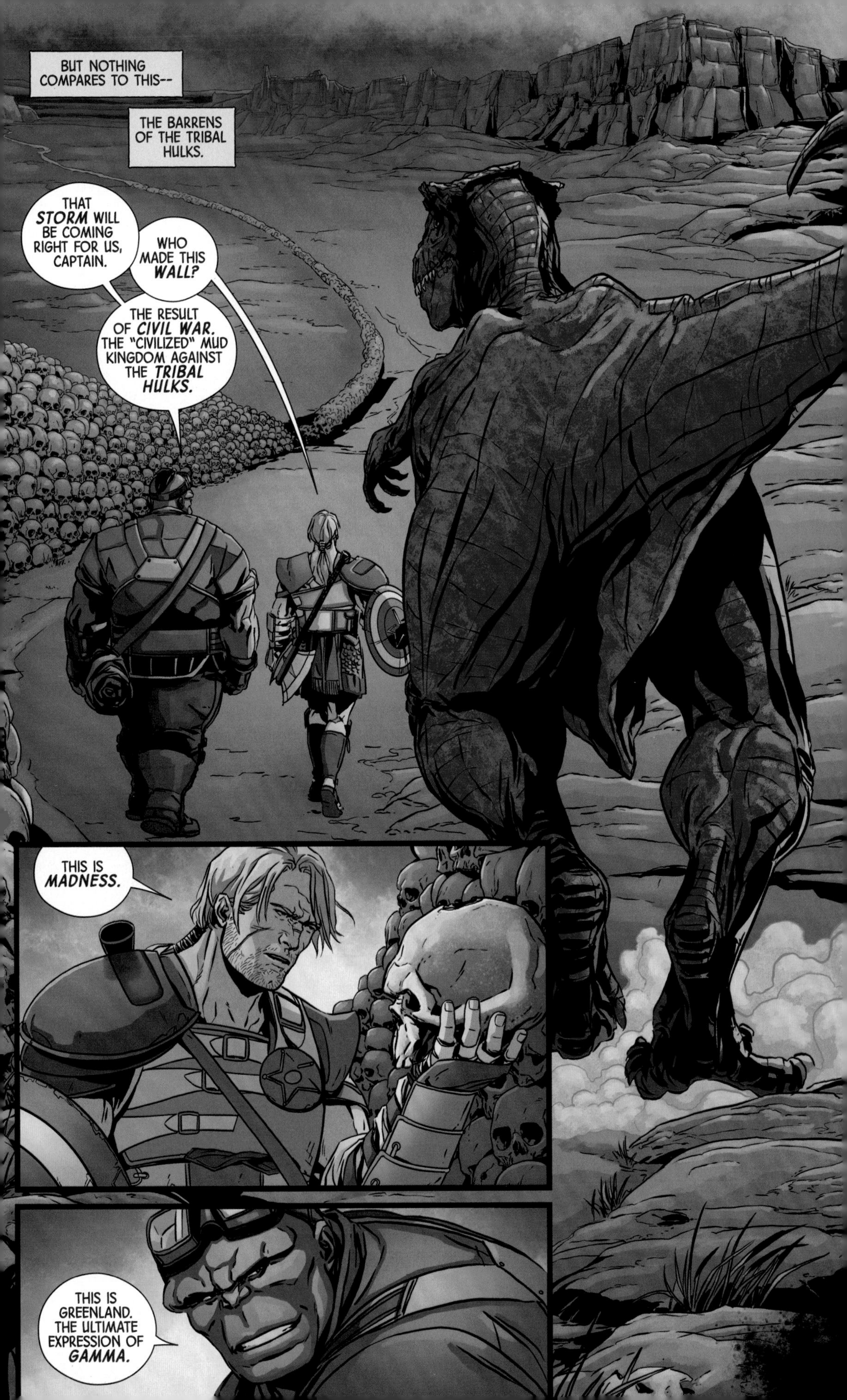
BUT NOTHING COMPARES TO THIS--
THE BARRENS OF THE TRIBAL HULKS.
THAT STORM WILL BE COMING RIGHT FOR US, CAPTAIN.
WHO MADE THIS WALL?
THE RESULT OF CIVIL WAR. THE "CIVILIZED" MUD KINGDOM AGAINST THE TRIBAL HULKS.
THIS IS MADNESS.
THIS IS GREENLAND. THE ULTIMATE EXPRESSION OF GAMMA.

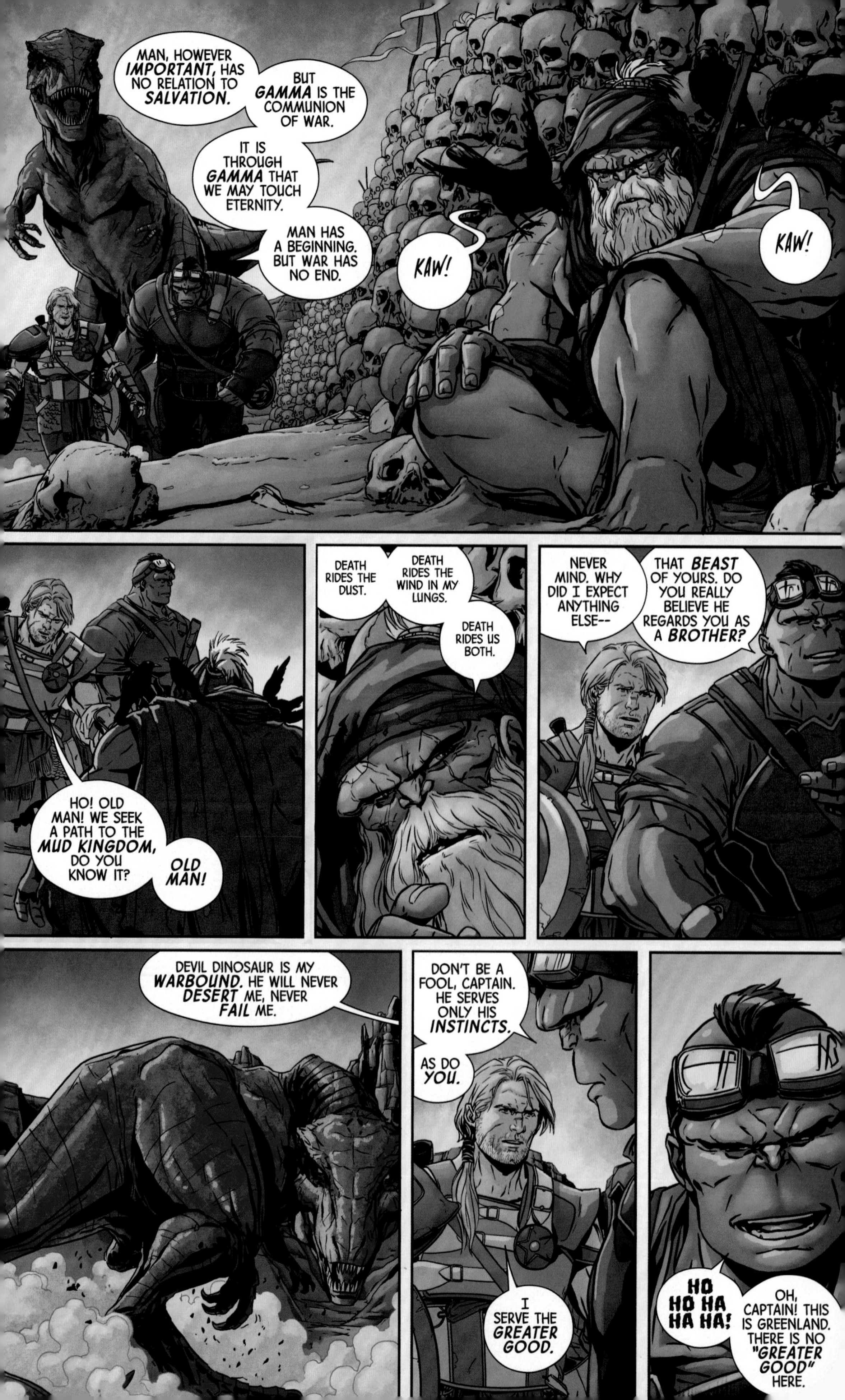
MAN, HOWEVER IMPORTANT, HAS NO RELATION TO SALVATION.
BUT GAMMA IS THE COMMUNION OF WAR.
IT IS THROUGH GAMMA THAT WE MAY TOUCH ETERNITY.
MAN HAS A BEGINNING. BUT WAR HAS NO END.
KAW!
KAW!
HO! OLD MAN! WE SEEK A PATH TO THE MUD KINGDOM, DO YOU KNOW IT?
OLD MAN!
DEATH RIDES THE DUST.
DEATH RIDES THE WIND IN MY LUNGS.
DEATH RIDES US BOTH.
NEVER MIND. WHY DID I EXPECT ANYTHING ELSE--
THAT BEAST OF YOURS. DO YOU REALLY BELIEVE HE REGARDS YOU AS A BROTHER?
DEVIL DINOSAUR IS MY WARBOUND. HE WILL NEVER DESERT ME, NEVER FAIL ME.
DON'T BE A FOOL, CAPTAIN. HE SERVES ONLY HIS INSTINCTS.
AS DO YOU.
I SERVE THE GREATER GOOD.
HO HO HA HA HA!
OH, CAPTAIN! THIS IS GREENLAND. THERE IS NO "GREATER GOOD" HERE.

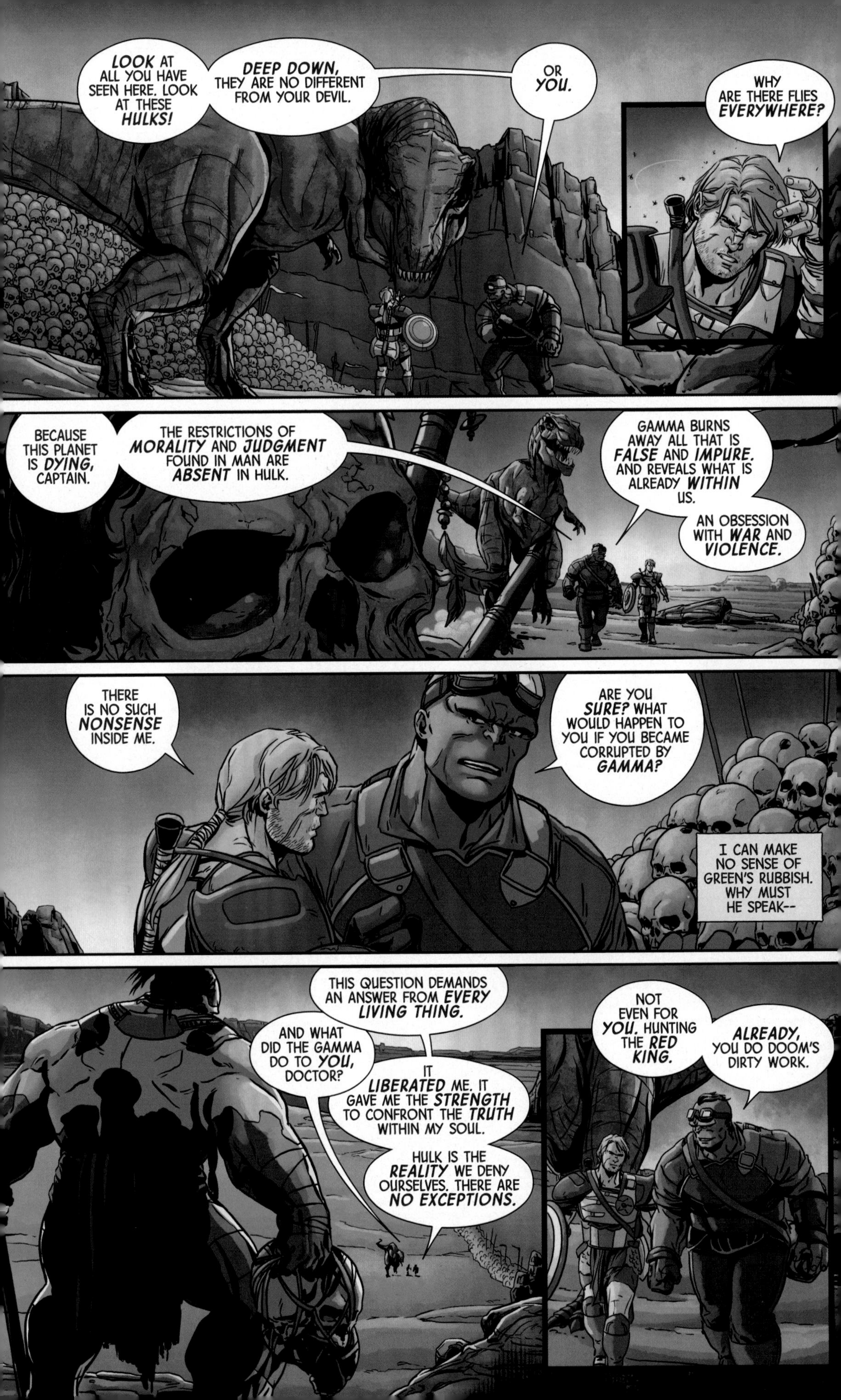

LOOK AT ALL YOU HAVE SEEN HERE. LOOK AT THESE HULKS!
DEEP DOWN, THEY ARE NO DIFFERENT FROM YOUR DEVIL.
OR YOU.
WHY ARE THERE FLIES EVERYWHERE?
BECAUSE THIS PLANET IS DYING, CAPTAIN.
THE RESTRICTIONS OF MORALITY AND JUDGMENT FOUND IN MAN ARE ABSENT IN HULK.
GAMMA BURNS AWAY ALL THAT IS FALSE AND IMPURE. AND REVEALS WHAT IS ALREADY WITHIN US.
AN OBSESSION WITH WAR AND VIOLENCE.
THERE IS NO SUCH NONSENSE INSIDE ME.
ARE YOU SURE? WHAT WOULD HAPPEN TO YOU IF YOU BECAME CORRUPTED BY GAMMA?
I CAN MAKE NO SENSE OF GREEN'S RUBBISH. WHY MUST HE SPEAK--
THIS QUESTION DEMANDS AN ANSWER FROM EVERY LIVING THING.
AND WHAT DID THE GAMMA DO TO YOU, DOCTOR?
IT LIBERATED ME. IT GAVE ME THE STRENGTH TO CONFRONT THE TRUTH WITHIN MY SOUL.
HULK IS THE REALITY WE DENY OURSELVES. THERE ARE NO EXCEPTIONS.
NOT EVEN FOR YOU, HUNTING THE RED KING.
ALREADY, YOU DO DOOM'S DIRTY WORK.

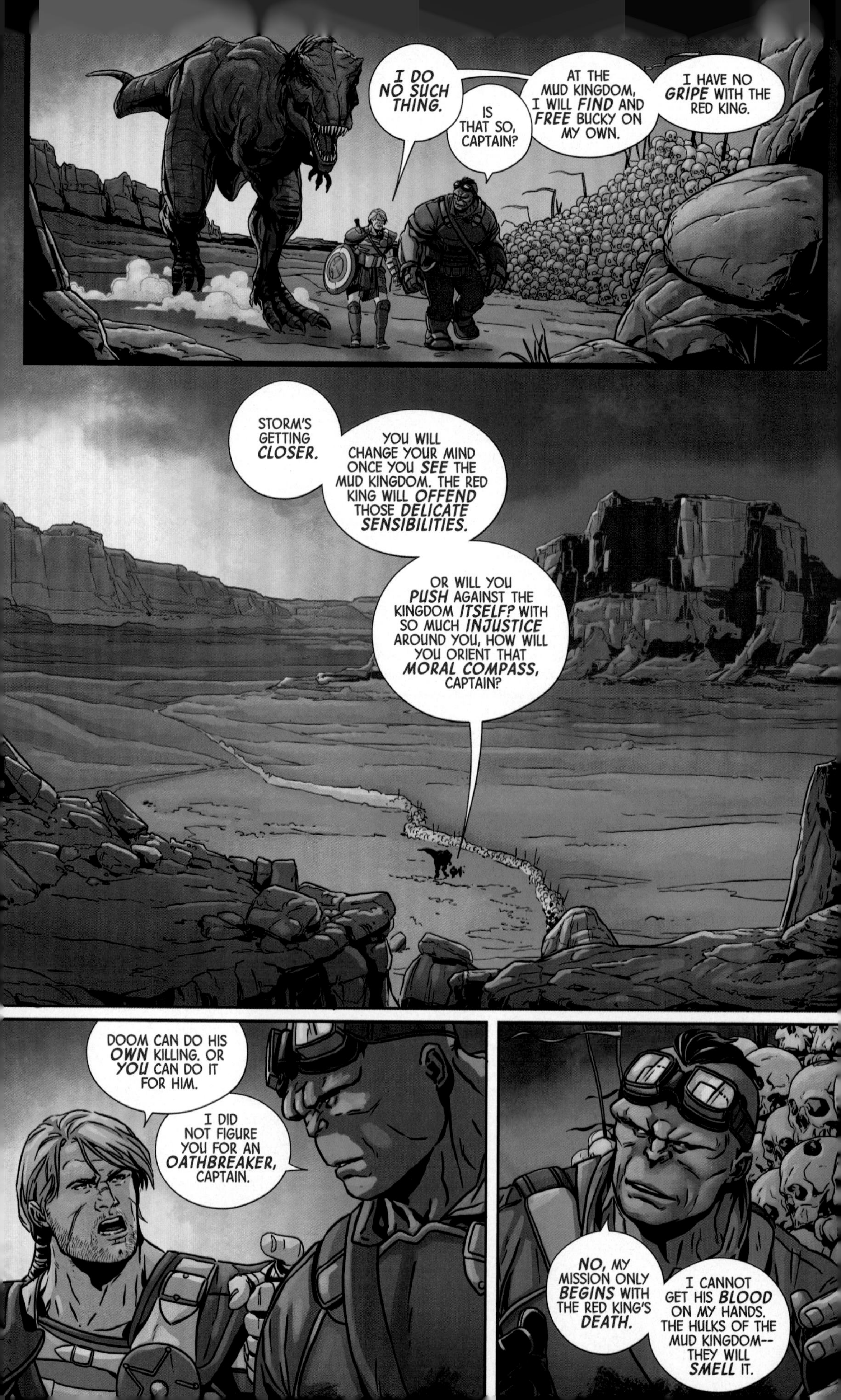

I DO NO SUCH THING.
IS THAT SO, CAPTAIN?
AT THE MUD KINGDOM, I WILL FIND AND FREE BUCKY ON MY OWN.
I HAVE NO GRIPE WITH THE RED KING.
STORM'S GETTING CLOSER.
YOU WILL CHANGE YOUR MIND ONCE YOU SEE THE MUD KINGDOM. THE RED KING WILL OFFEND THOSE DELICATE SENSIBILITIES.
OR WILL YOU PUSH AGAINST THE KINGDOM ITSELF? WITH SO MUCH INJUSTICE AROUND YOU, HOW WILL YOU ORIENT THAT MORAL COMPASS, CAPTAIN?
DOOM CAN DO HIS OWN KILLING. OR YOU CAN DO IT FOR HIM.
I DID NOT FIGURE YOU FOR AN OATHBREAKER, CAPTAIN.
NO, MY MISSION ONLY BEGINS WITH THE RED KING'S DEATH.
I CANNOT GET HIS BLOOD ON MY HANDS. THE HULKS OF THE MUD KINGDOM-- THEY WILL SMELL IT.

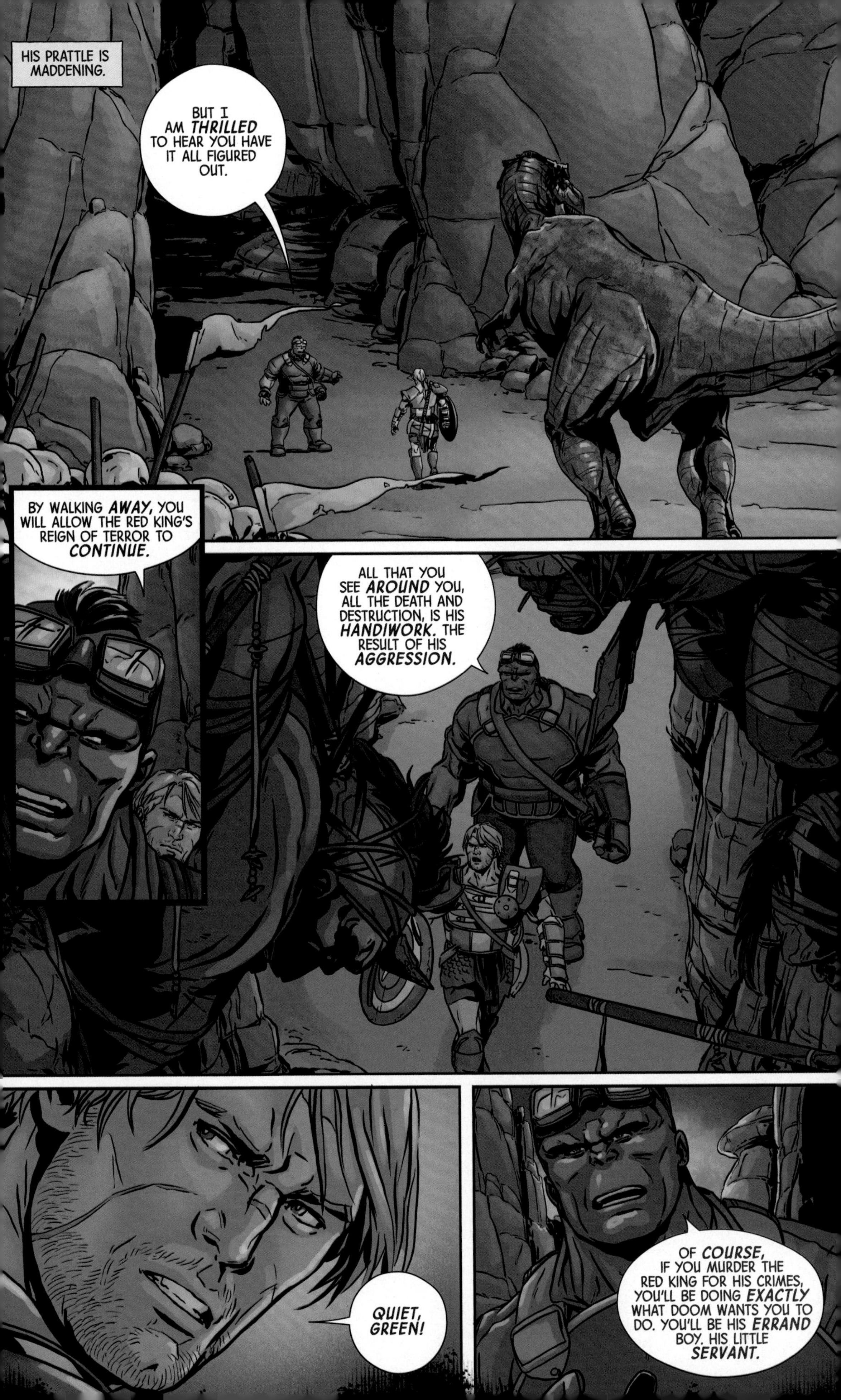
HIS PRATTLE IS MADDENING.
BUT I AM THRILLED TO HEAR YOU HAVE IT ALL FIGURED OUT.
BY WALKING AWAY, YOU WILL ALLOW THE RED KING'S REIGN OF TERROR TO CONTINUE.
ALL THAT YOU SEE AROUND YOU, ALL THE DEATH AND DESTRUCTION, IS HIS HANDIWORK. THE RESULT OF HIS AGGRESSION.
QUIET, GREEN!
OF COURSE, IF YOU MURDER THE RED KING FOR HIS CRIMES, YOU'LL BE DOING EXACTLY WHAT DOOM WANTS YOU TO DO. YOU'LL BE HIS ERRAND BOY. HIS LITTLE SERVANT.

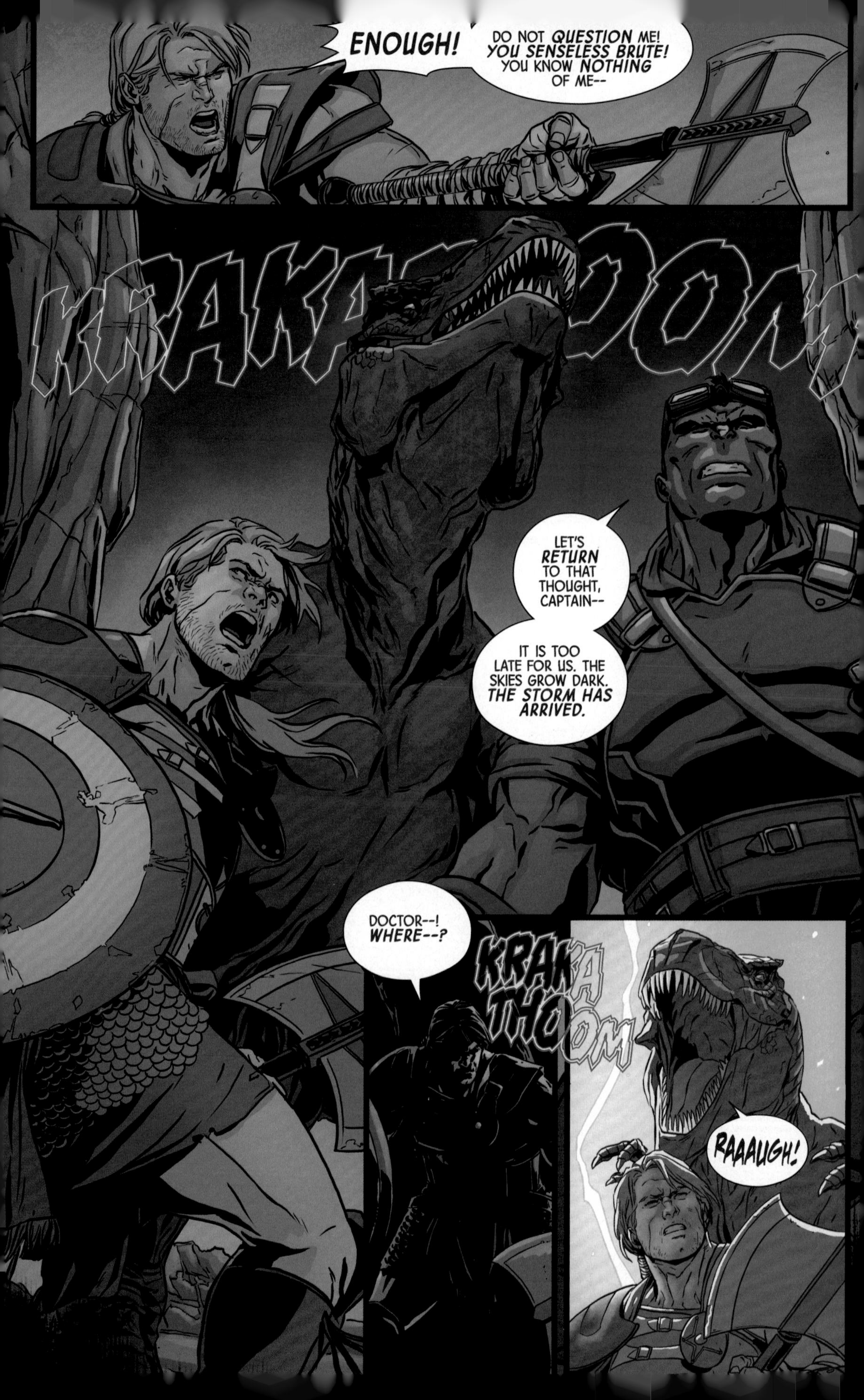
ENOUGH!
DO NOT QUESTION ME! YOU SENSELESS BRUTE! YOU KNOW NOTHING OF ME--
LET'S RETURN TO THAT THOUGHT, CAPTAIN--
IT IS TOO LATE FOR US. THE SKIES GROW DARK. THE STORM HAS ARRIVED.
DOCTOR--! WHERE--?
KRAKATHOOM
RAAAUGH!

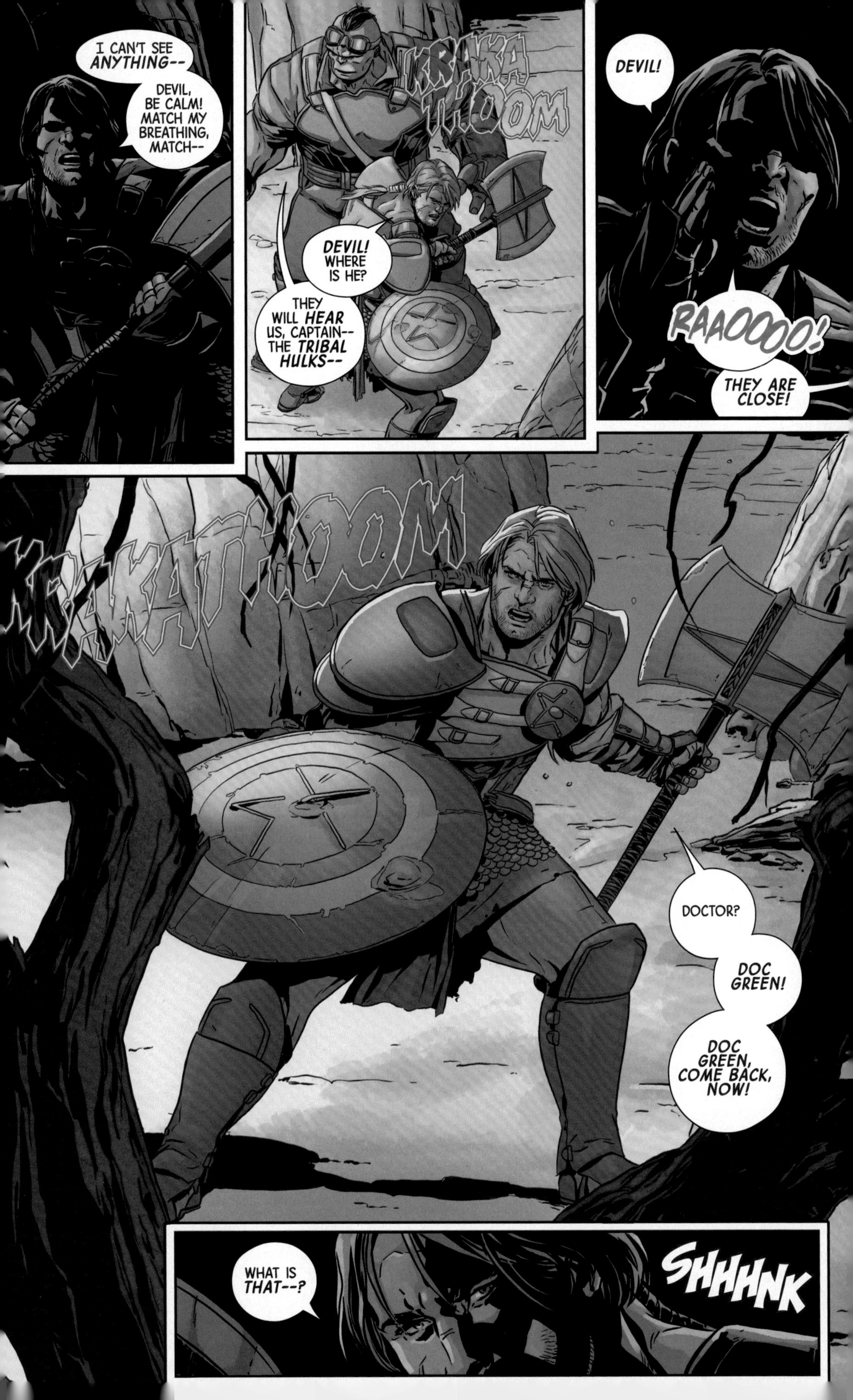
I CAN'T SEE ANYTHING--
DEVIL, BE CALM! MATCH MY BREATHING, MATCH--
KRAKA THOOM
DEVIL! WHERE IS HE?
THEY WILL HEAR US, CAPTAIN-- THE TRIBAL HULKS--
DEVIL!
RAAOOOO!
THEY ARE CLOSE!
KRAKATHOOM
DOCTOR?
DOC GREEN!
DOC GREEN, COME BACK, NOW!
WHAT IS THAT--?
SHHHNK

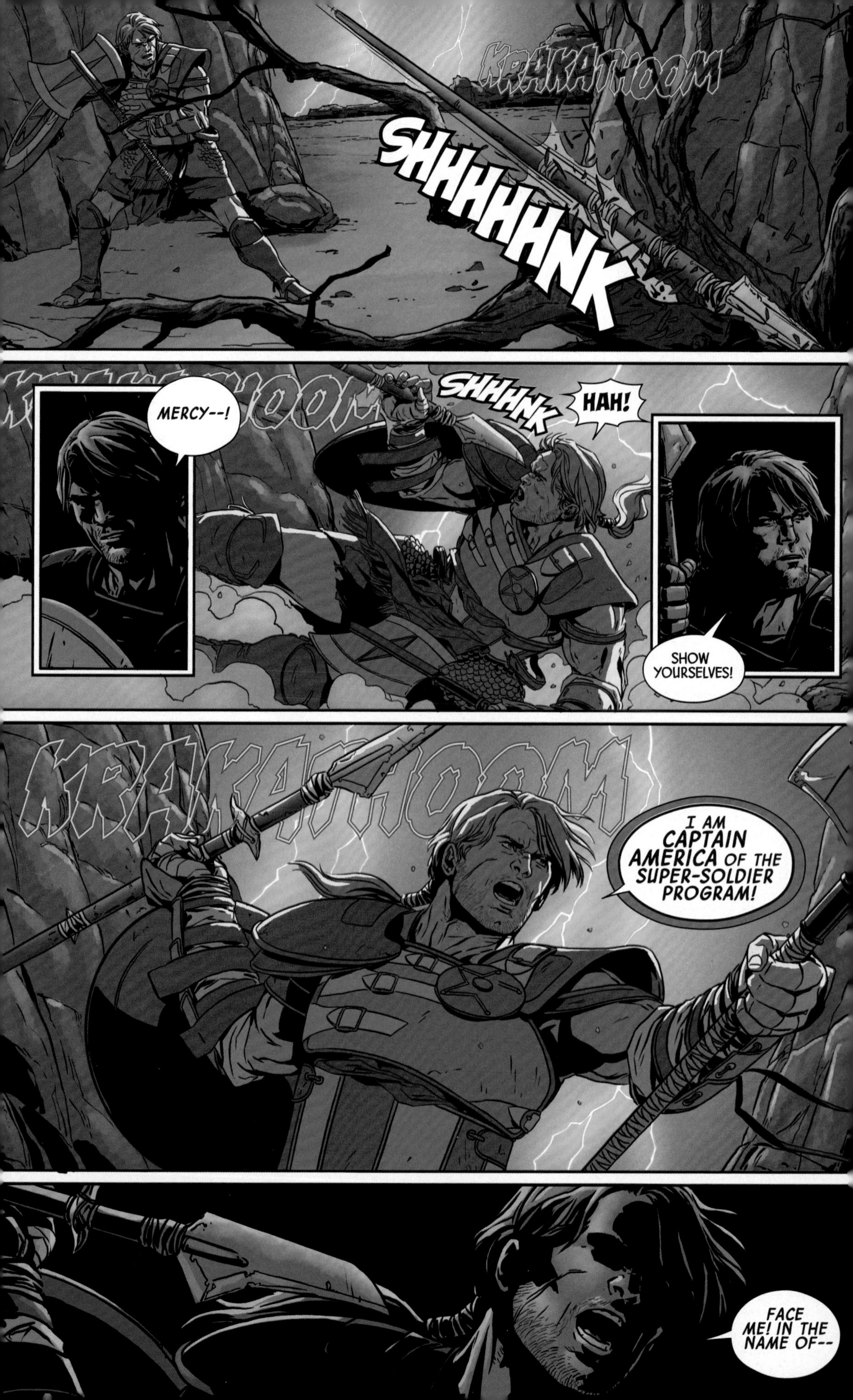
KRAKATHOOM
SHHHHHNK
KRAKATHOOM
MERCY--!
SHHHNK
HAH!
SHOW YOURSELVES!
KRAKATHOOM
I AM CAPTAIN AMERICA OF THE SUPER-SOLDIER PROGRAM!
FACE ME! IN THE NAME OF--

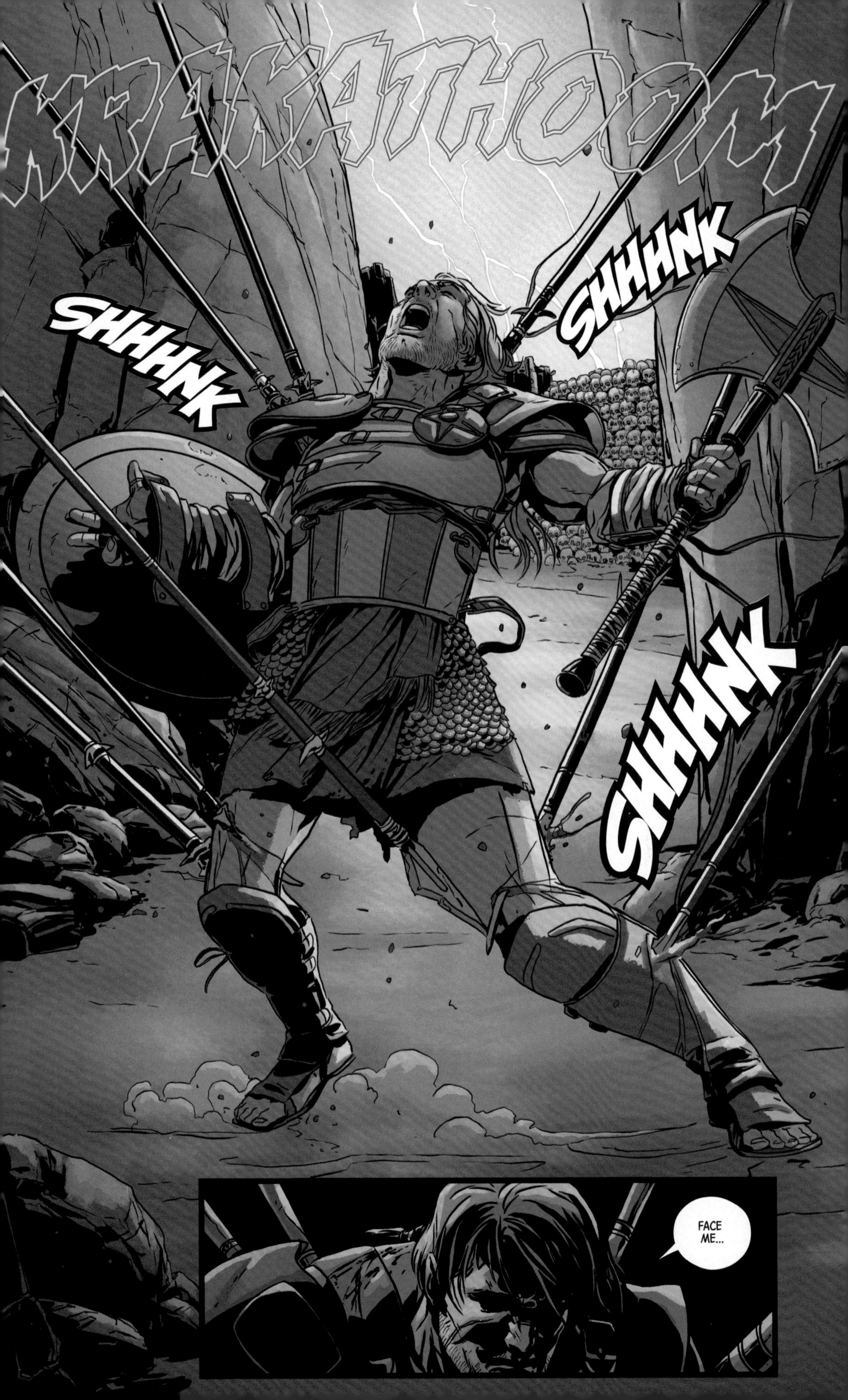
KRAKATHOOM
SHHHNK
SHHHNK
SHHHNK
FACE ME...

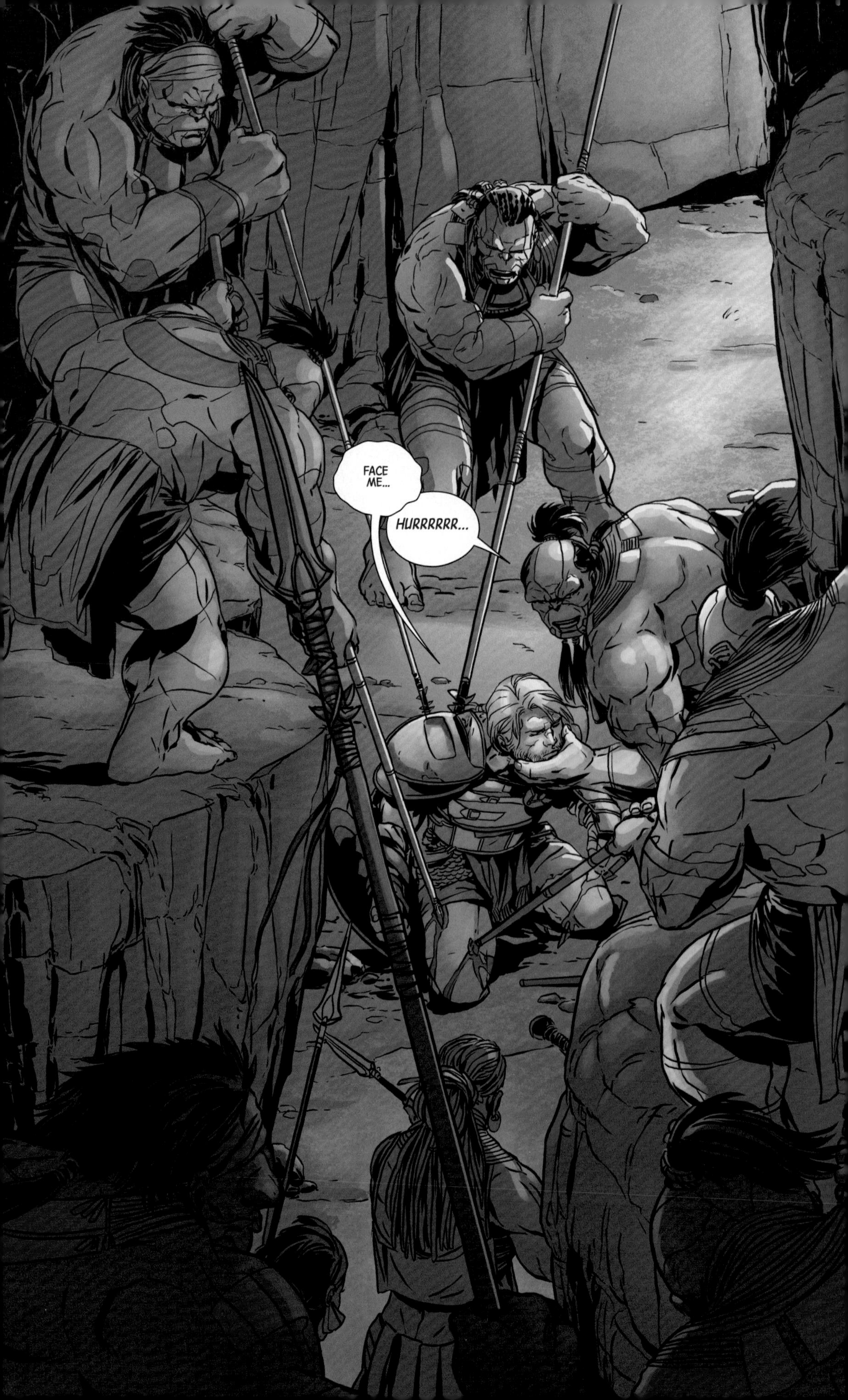
FACE ME...
HURRRRRR...

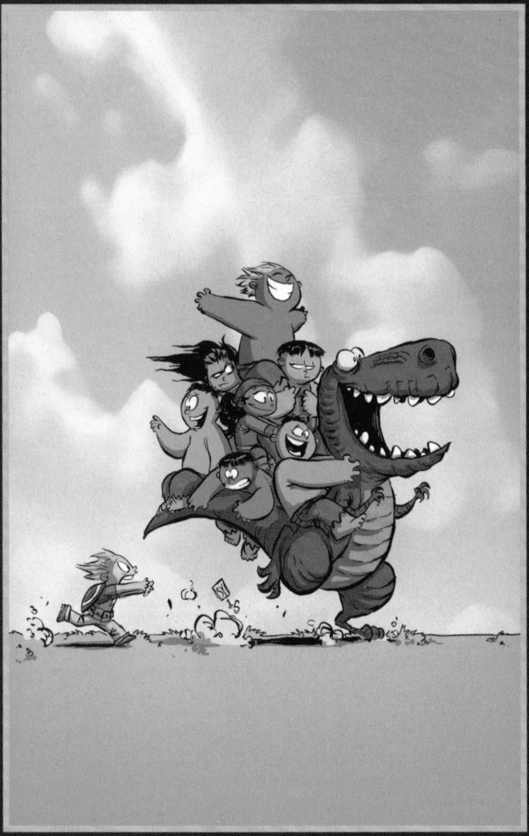

#1 VARIANT BY SKOTTIE YOUNG

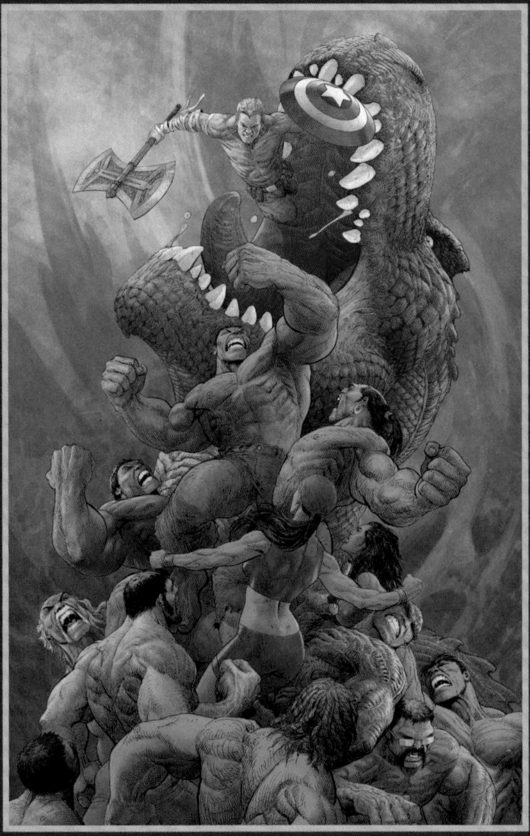

#1 VARIANT BY MUKESH SINGH

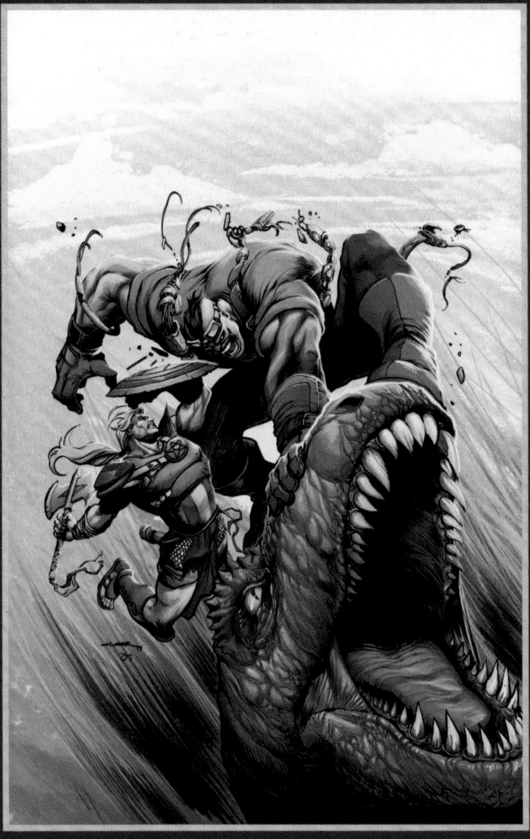

#2 VARIANT BY
YILDIRAY CINAR & FRANK MARTIN

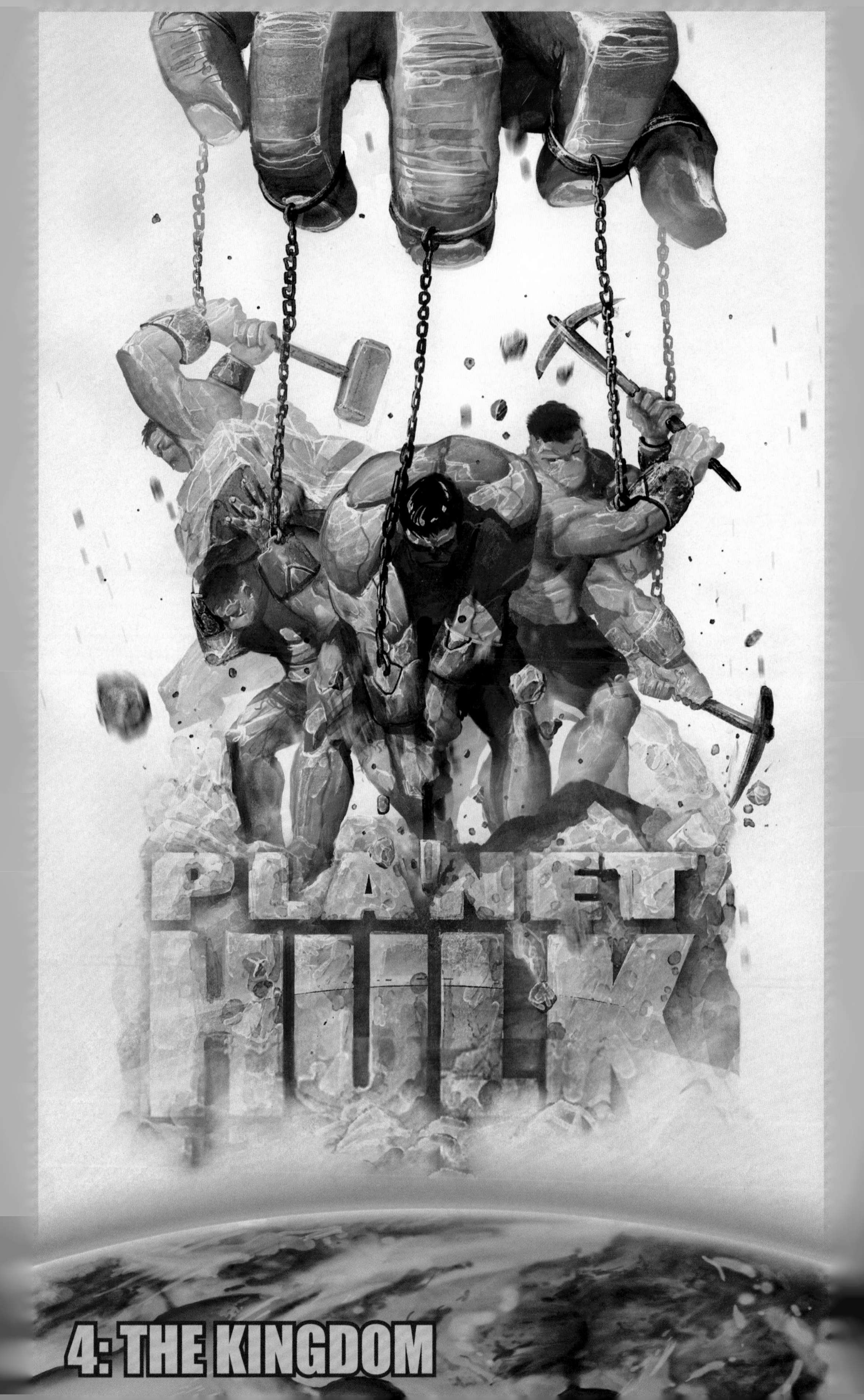
PLANET HULK
4: THE KINGDOM

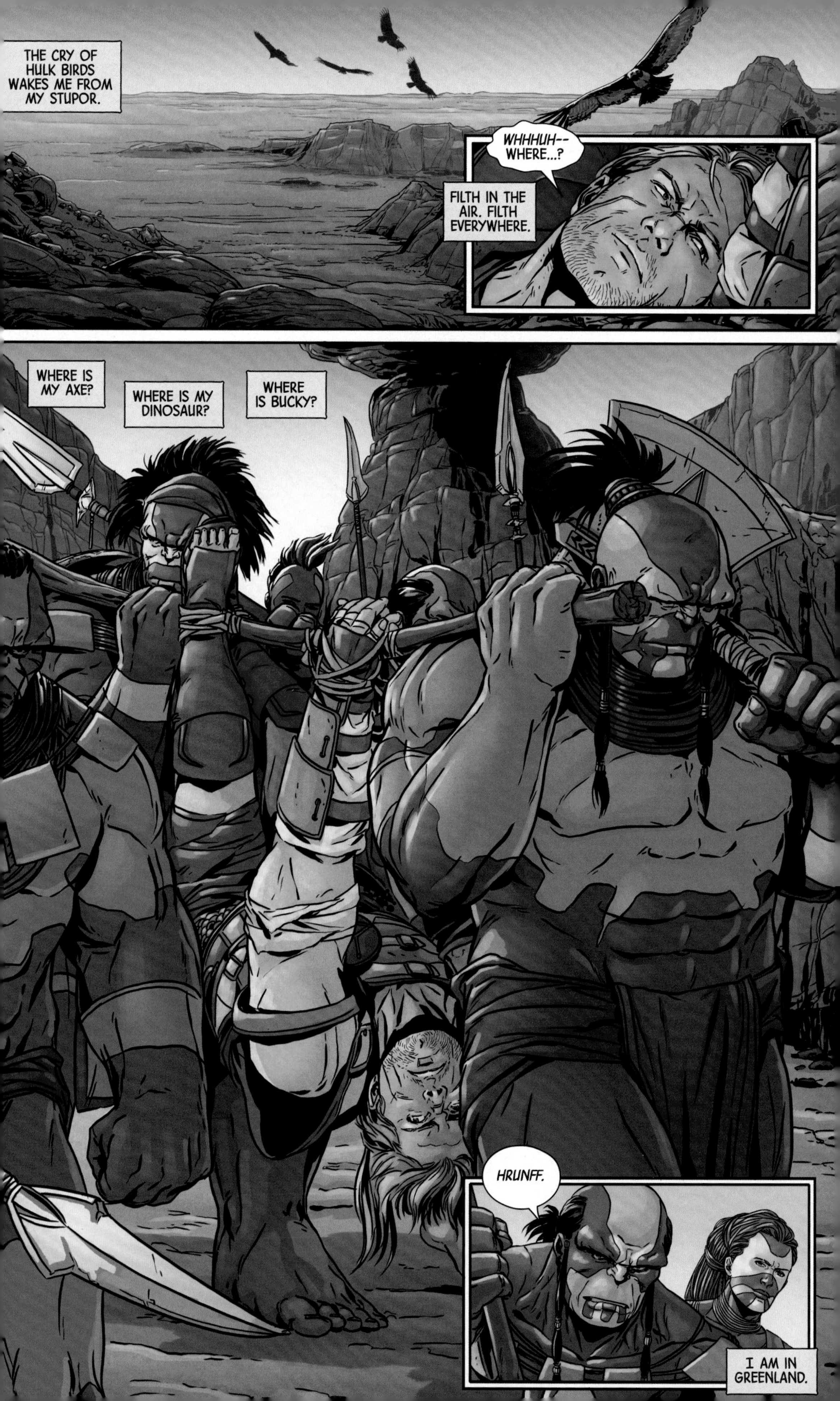

THE CRY OF HULK BIRDS WAKES ME FROM MY STUPOR.
WHHHUH-- WHERE...?
FILTH IN THE AIR. FILTH EVERYWHERE.
WHERE IS MY AXE?
WHERE IS MY DINOSAUR?
WHERE IS BUCKY?
HRUNFF.
I AM IN GREENLAND.

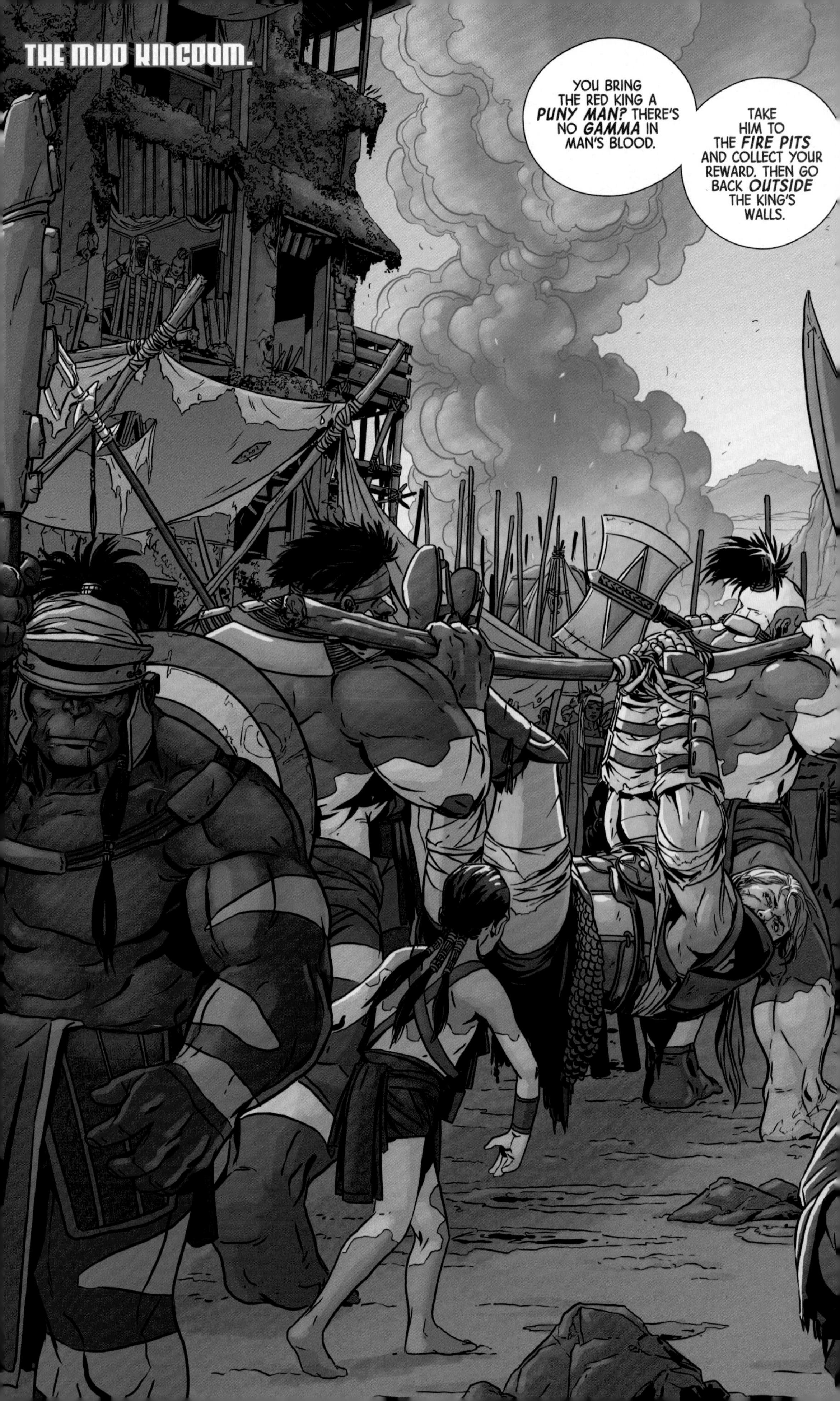
THE MUD KINGDOM.
YOU BRING THE RED KING A PUNY MAN? THERE'S NO GAMMA IN MAN'S BLOOD.
TAKE HIM TO THE FIRE PITS AND COLLECT YOUR REWARD. THEN GO BACK OUTSIDE THE KING'S WALLS.

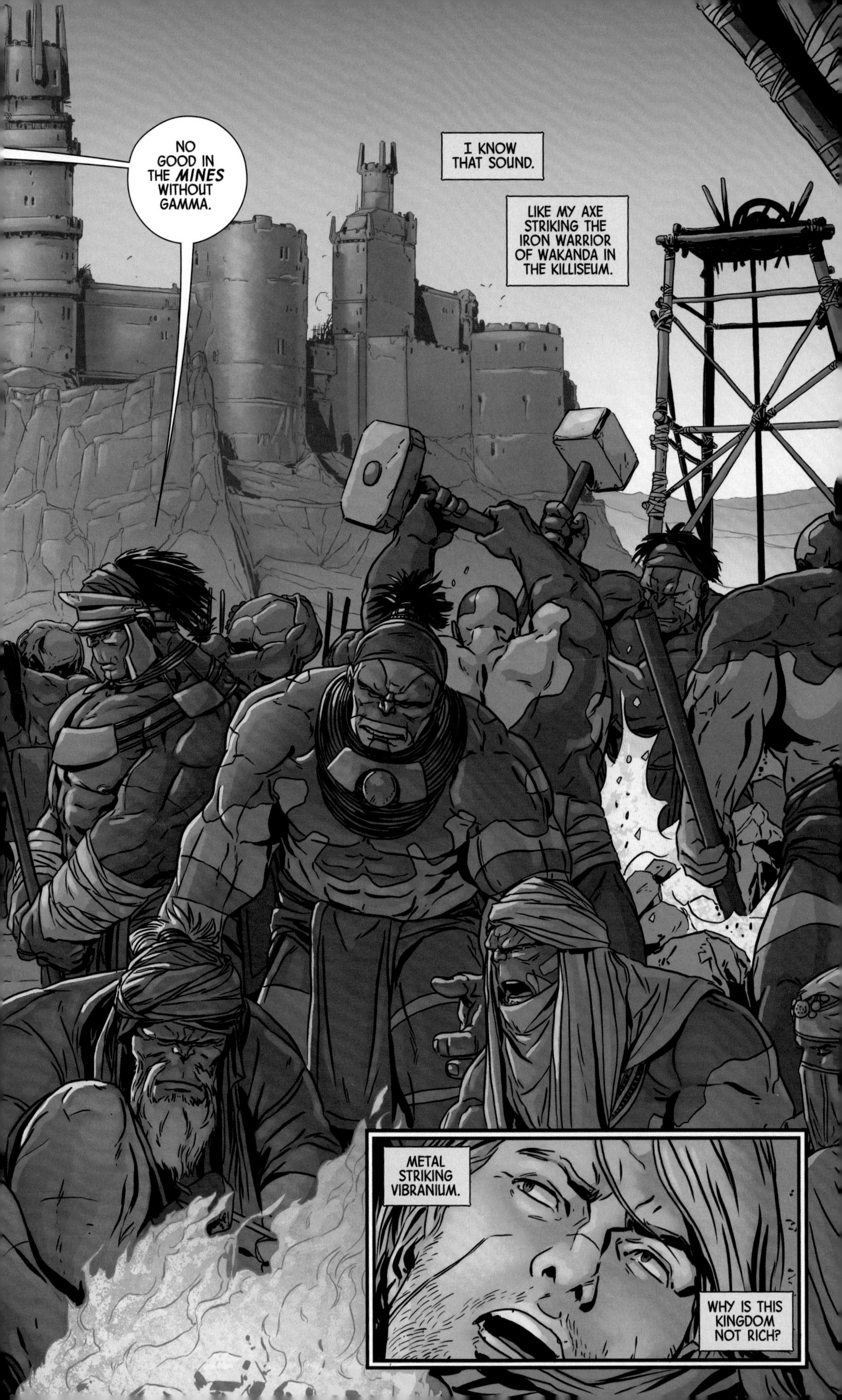
NO GOOD IN THE *MINES* WITHOUT GAMMA.
I KNOW THAT SOUND.
LIKE MY AXE STRIKING THE IRON WARRIOR OF WAKANDA IN THE KILLISEUM.
METAL STRIKING VIBRANIUM.
WHY IS THIS KINGDOM NOT RICH?

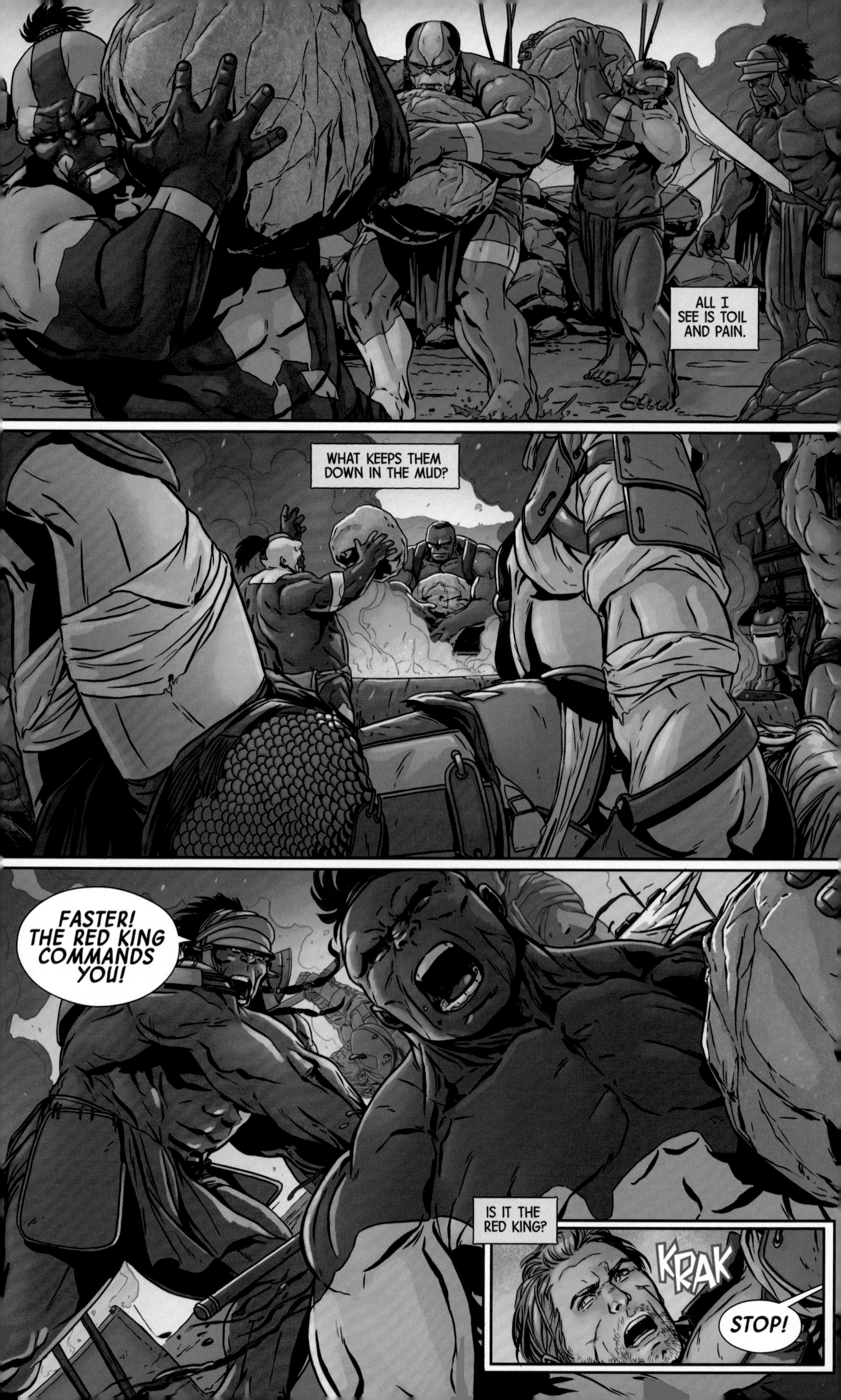
ALL I SEE IS TOIL AND PAIN.
WHAT KEEPS THEM DOWN IN THE MUD?
FASTER! THE RED KING COMMANDS YOU!
IS IT THE RED KING?
KRAK
STOP!

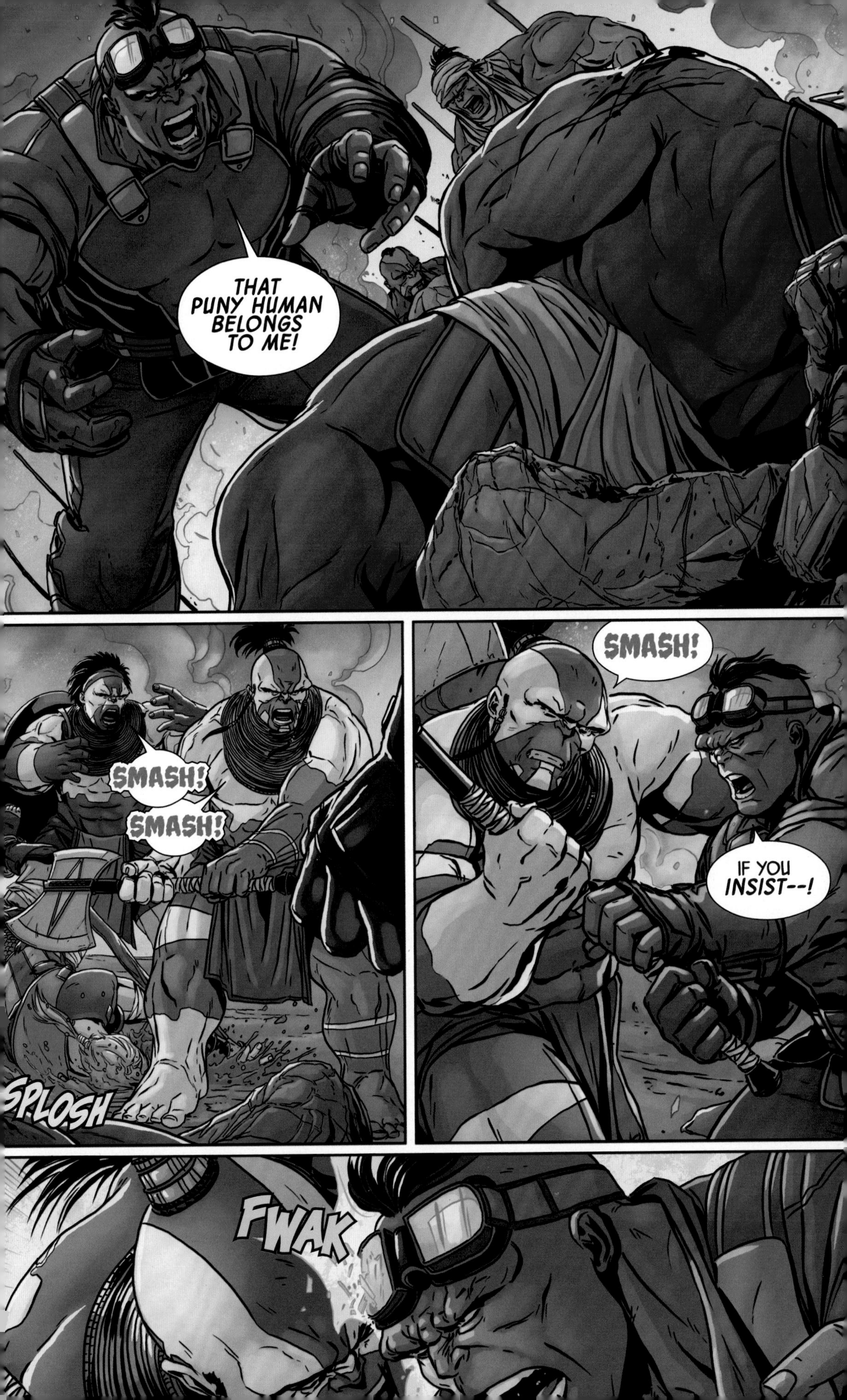
THAT PUNY HUMAN BELONGS TO ME!
SMASH!
SMASH!
SPLOSH
SMASH!
IF YOU INSIST--!
FWAK

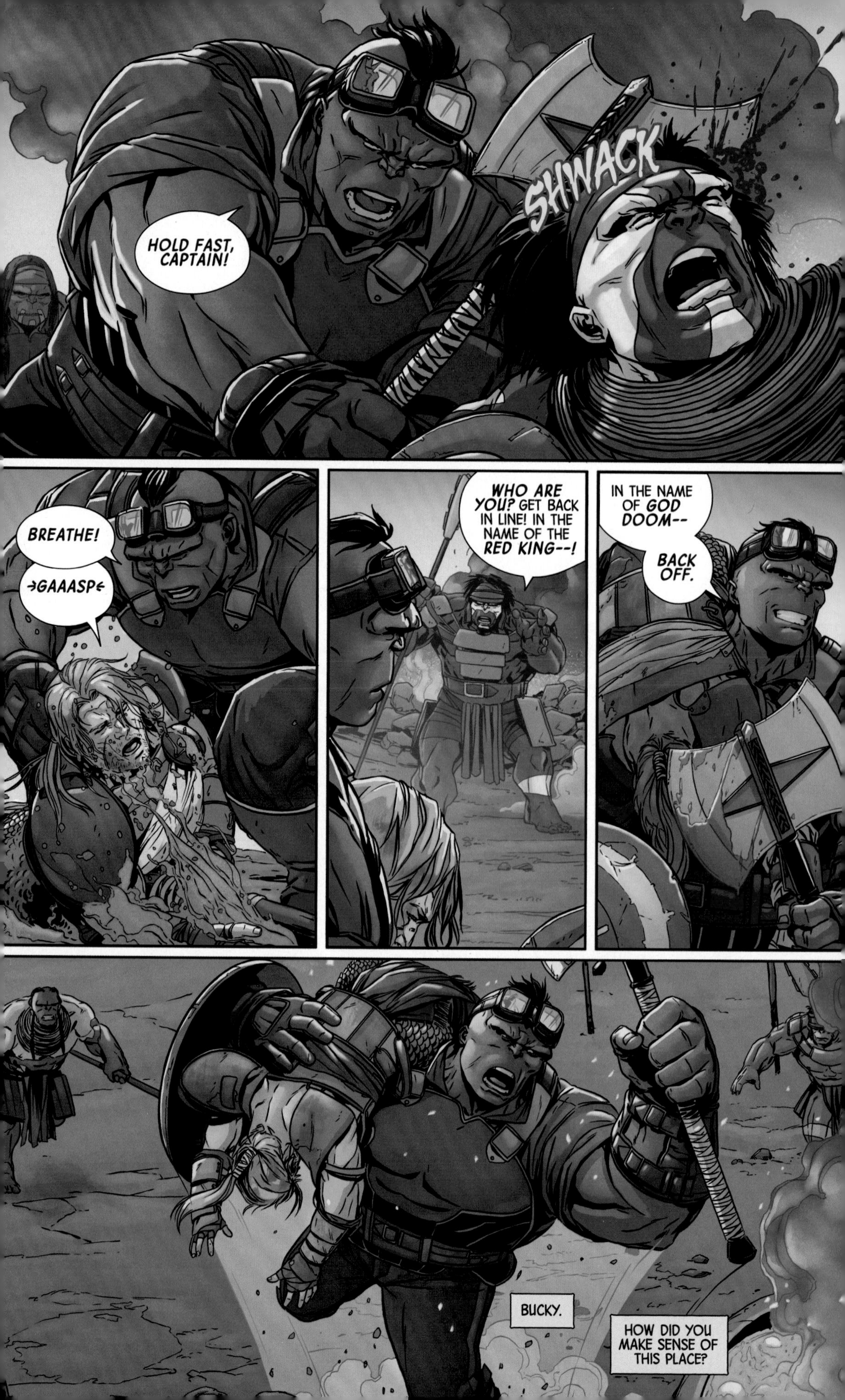
HOLD FAST, CAPTAIN!
SHWACK
BREATHE!
GAAASP
WHO ARE YOU? GET BACK IN LINE! IN THE NAME OF THE RED KING--!
IN THE NAME OF GOD DOOM--
BACK OFF.
BUCKY.
HOW DID YOU MAKE SENSE OF THIS PLACE?

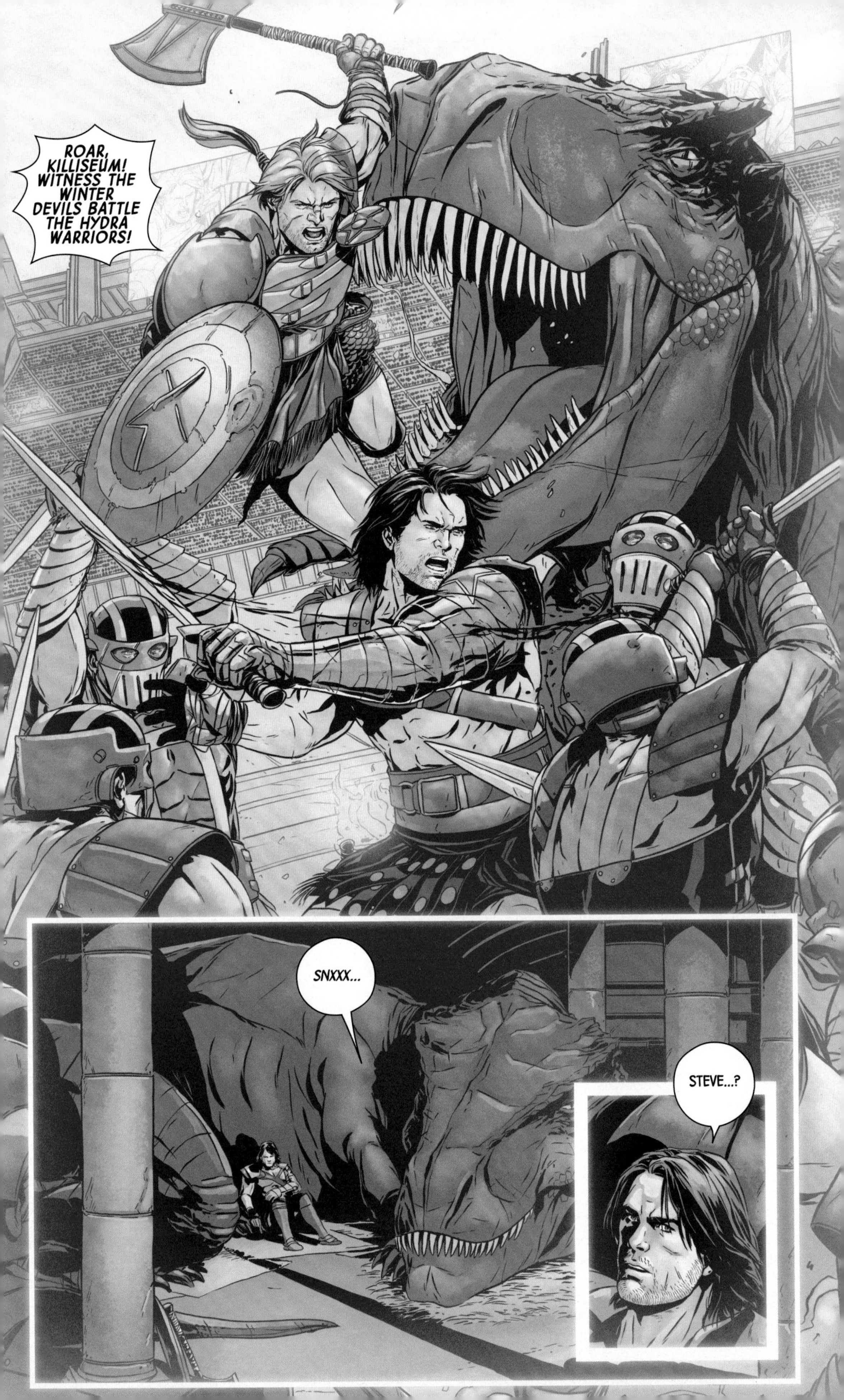
ROAR, KILLISEUM! WITNESS THE WINTER DEVILS BATTLE THE HYDRA WARRIORS!
SNXXX...
STEVE...?

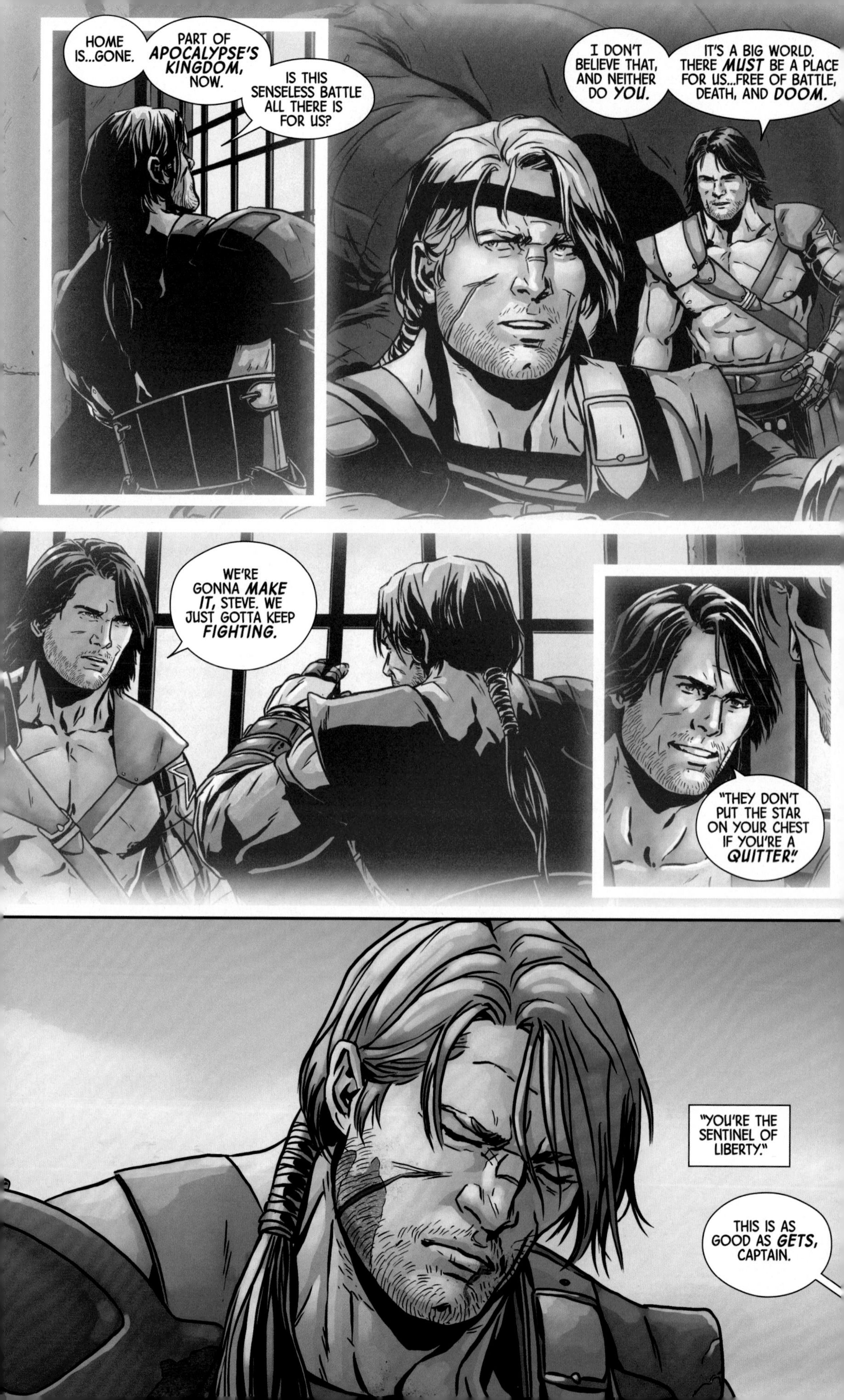
HOME IS...GONE.
PART OF APOCALYPSE'S KINGDOM, NOW.
IS THIS SENSELESS BATTLE ALL THERE IS FOR US?
I DON'T BELIEVE THAT, AND NEITHER DO YOU.
IT'S A BIG WORLD. THERE MUST BE A PLACE FOR US...FREE OF BATTLE, DEATH, AND DOOM.
WE'RE GONNA MAKE IT, STEVE. WE JUST GOTTA KEEP FIGHTING.
"THEY DON'T PUT THE STAR ON YOUR CHEST IF YOU'RE A QUITTER!"
"YOU'RE THE SENTINEL OF LIBERTY."
THIS IS AS GOOD AS GETS, CAPTAIN.

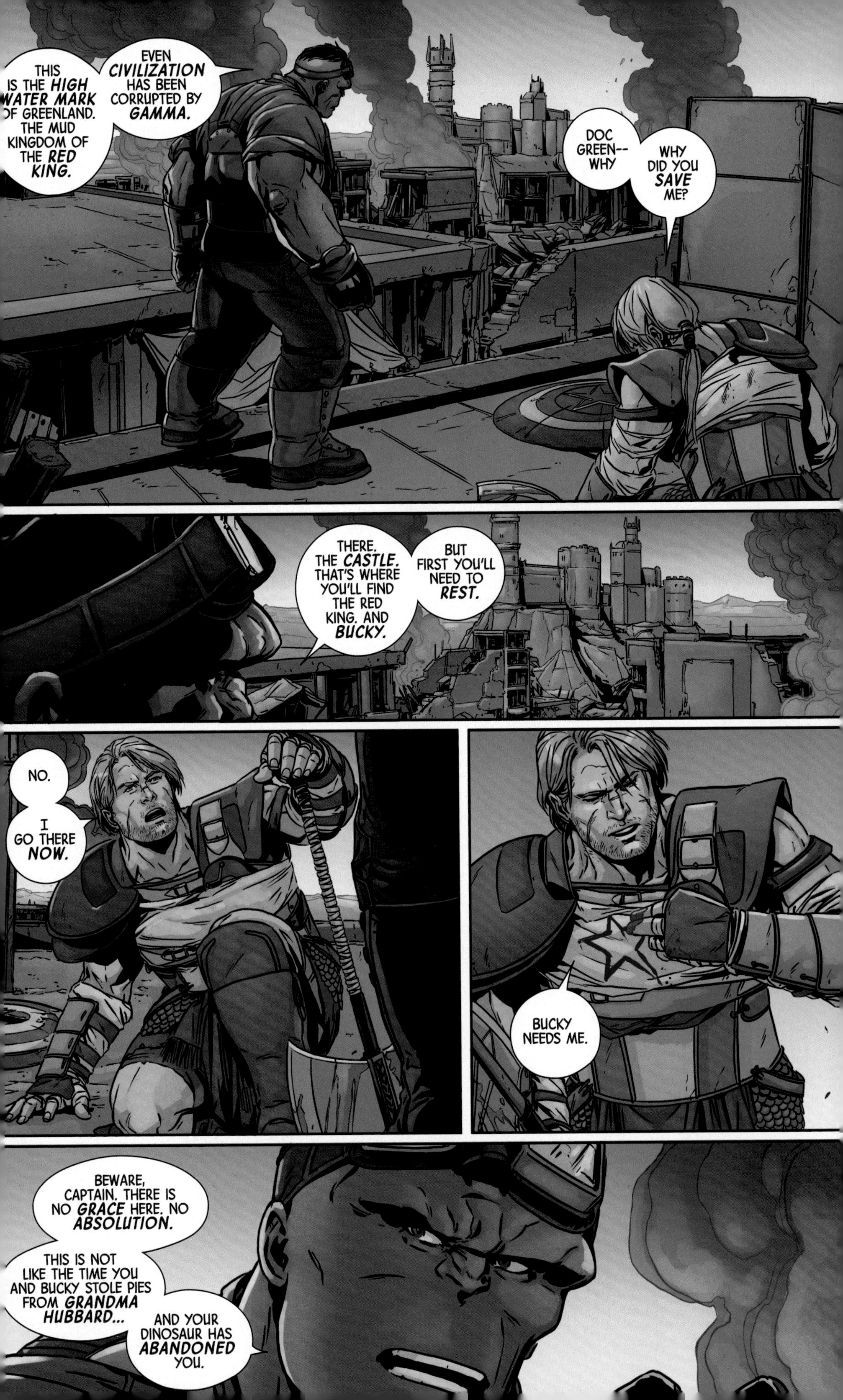
THIS IS THE HIGH WATER MARK OF GREENLAND. THE MUD KINGDOM OF THE RED KING.
EVEN CIVILIZATION HAS BEEN CORRUPTED BY GAMMA.
DOC GREEN-- WHY
WHY DID YOU SAVE ME?
THERE. THE CASTLE. THAT'S WHERE YOU'LL FIND THE RED KING. AND BUCKY.
BUT FIRST YOU'LL NEED TO REST.
NO.
I GO THERE NOW.
BUCKY NEEDS ME.
BEWARE, CAPTAIN. THERE IS NO GRACE HERE. NO ABSOLUTION.
THIS IS NOT LIKE THE TIME YOU AND BUCKY STOLE PIES FROM GRANDMA HUBBARD...
AND YOUR DINOSAUR HAS ABANDONED YOU.

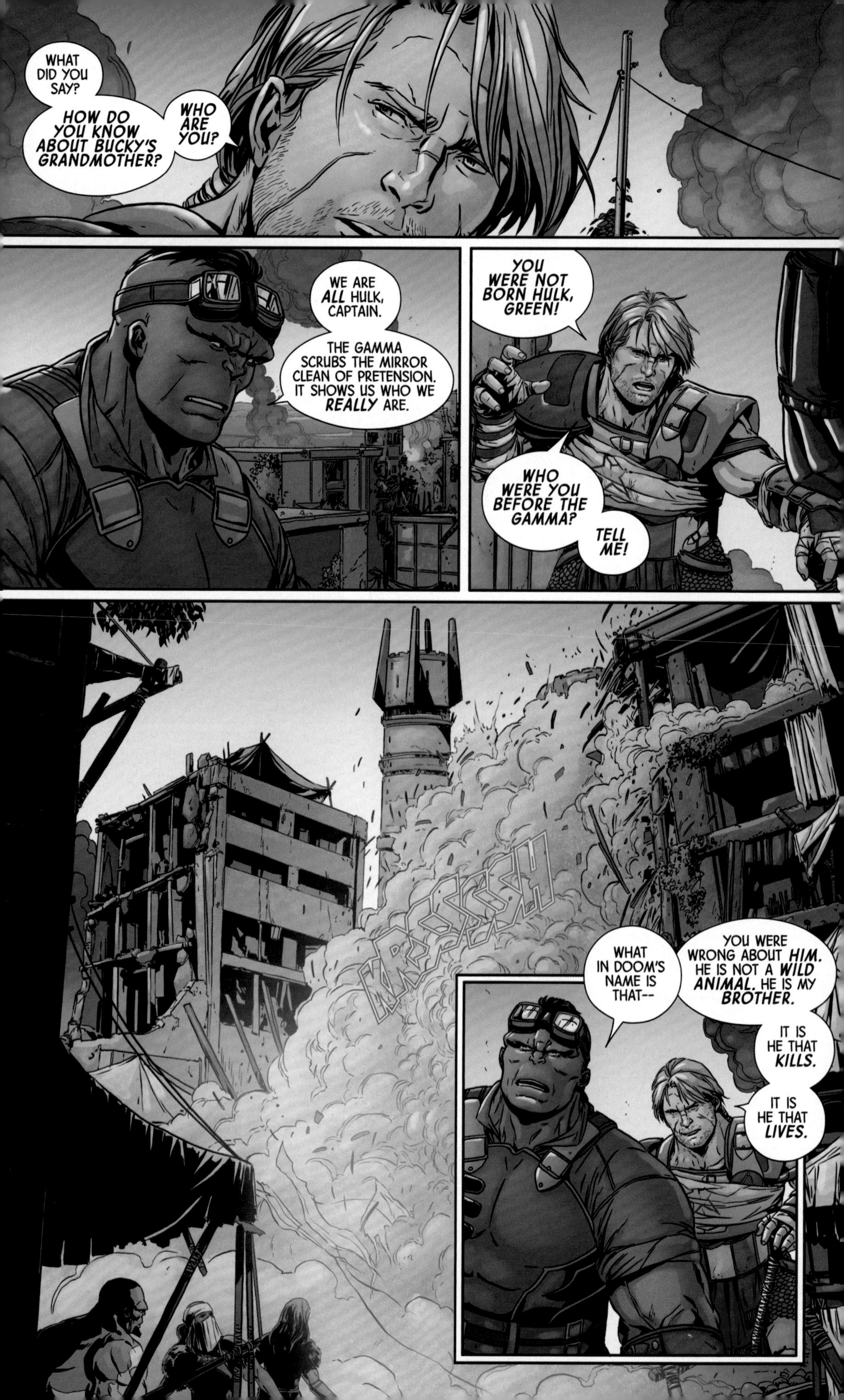

WHAT DID YOU SAY?
HOW DO YOU KNOW ABOUT BUCKY'S GRANDMOTHER?
WHO ARE YOU?
WE ARE ALL HULK, CAPTAIN.
THE GAMMA SCRUBS THE MIRROR CLEAN OF PRETENSION. IT SHOWS US WHO WE REALLY ARE.
YOU WERE NOT BORN HULK, GREEN!
WHO WERE YOU BEFORE THE GAMMA?
TELL ME!
KROOSSSH
WHAT IN DOOM'S NAME IS THAT--
YOU WERE WRONG ABOUT HIM. HE IS NOT A WILD ANIMAL. HE IS MY BROTHER.
IT IS HE THAT KILLS.
IT IS HE THAT LIVES.

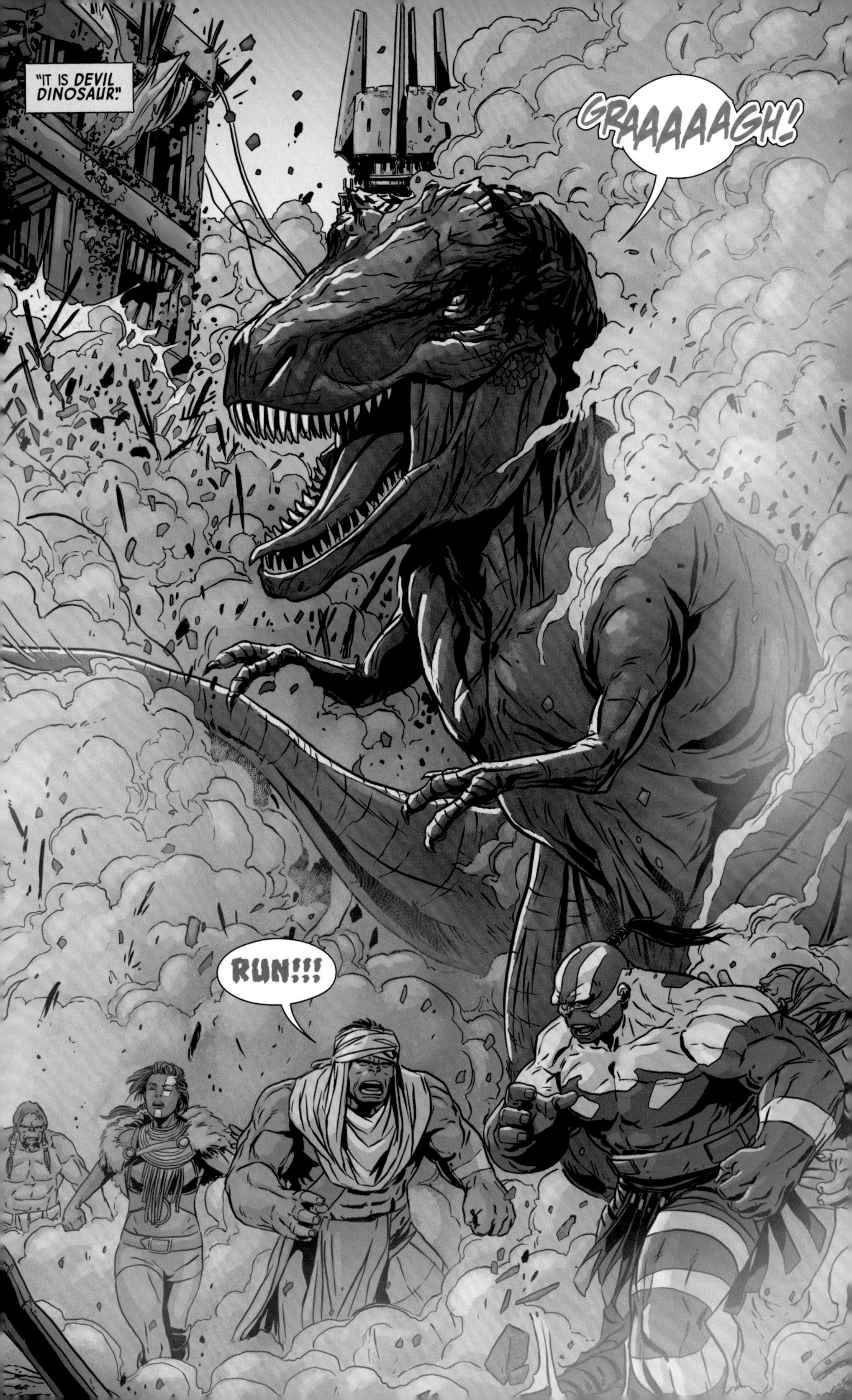
"IT IS DEVIL DINOSAUR."
GRAAAAAAGH!
RUN!!!

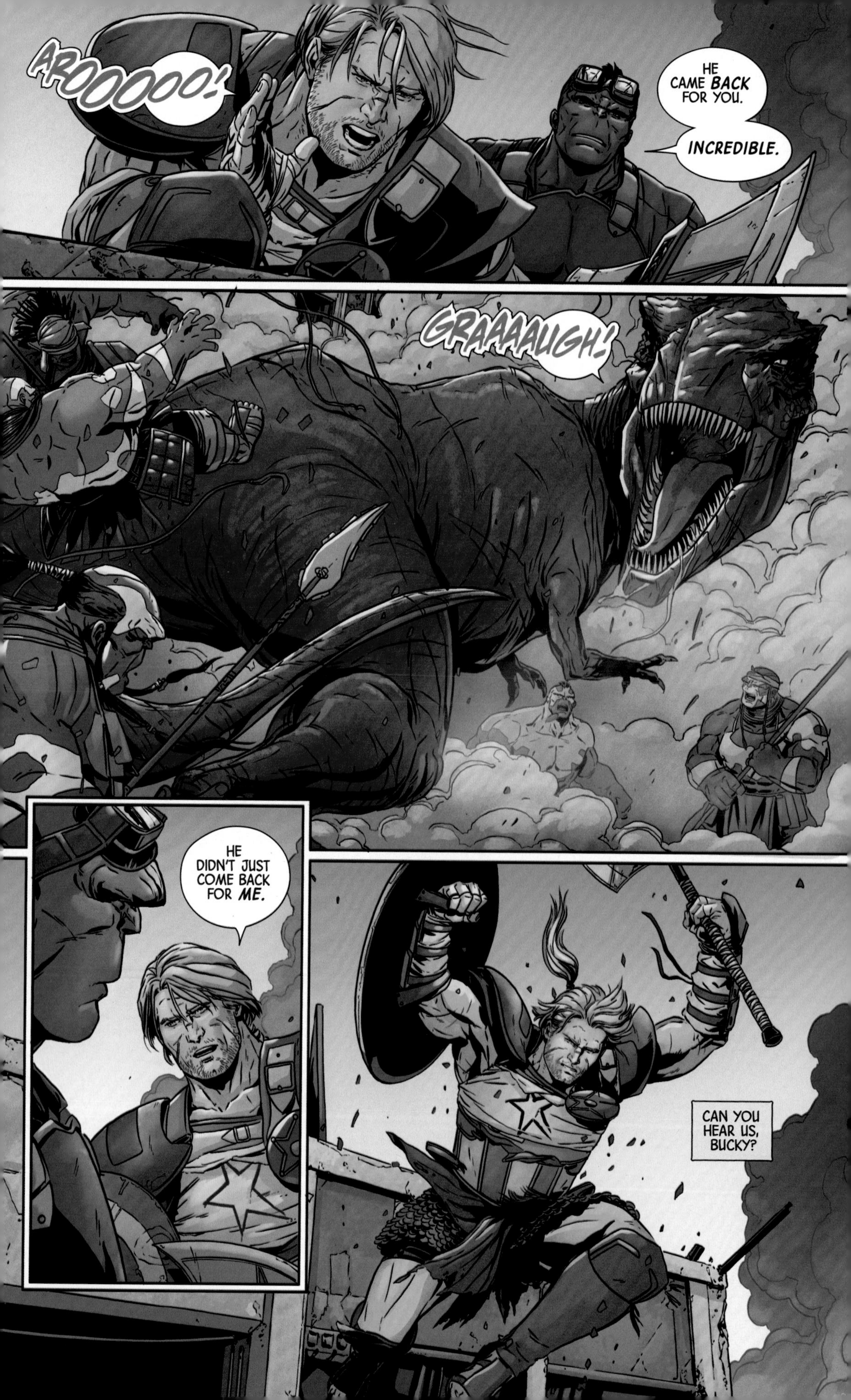
AROOOOO!
HE CAME BACK FOR YOU.
INCREDIBLE.
GRAAAAUGH!
HE DIDN'T JUST COME BACK FOR ME.
CAN YOU HEAR US, BUCKY?

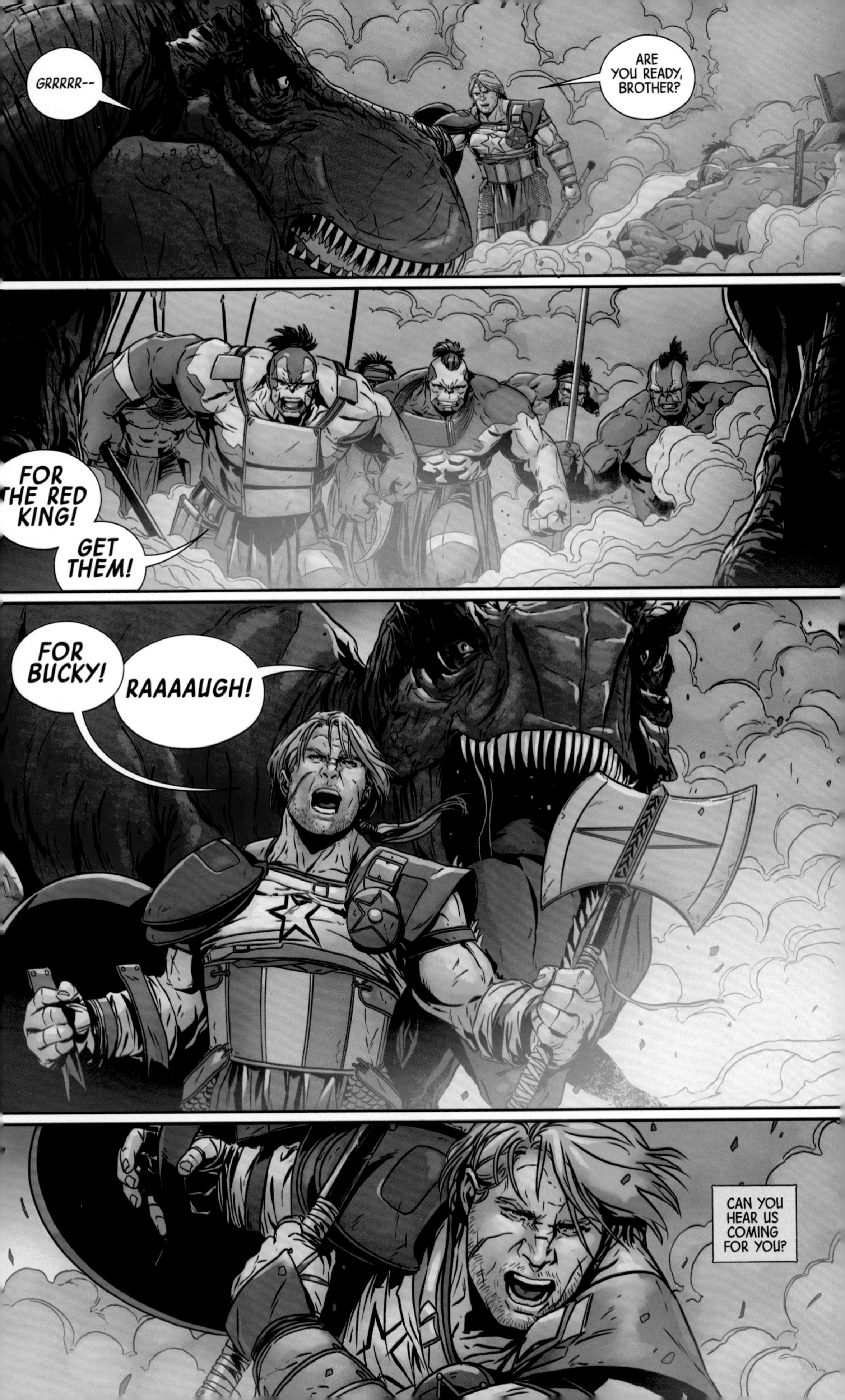
GRRRRR--
ARE YOU READY, BROTHER?
FOR THE RED KING!
GET THEM!
FOR BUCKY!
RAAAAUGH!
CAN YOU HEAR US COMING FOR YOU?

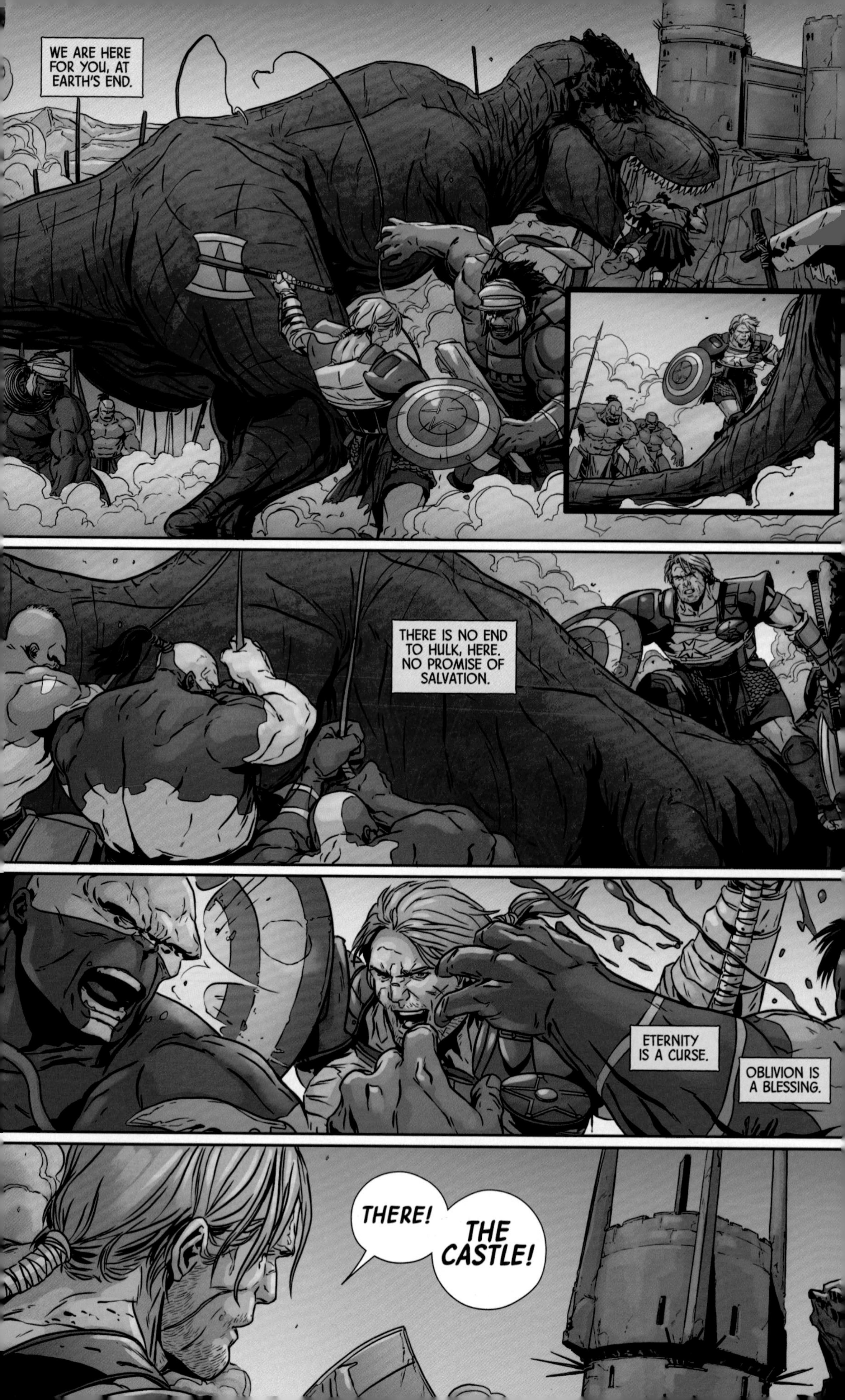
WE ARE HERE FOR YOU, AT EARTH'S END.
THERE IS NO END TO HULK, HERE. NO PROMISE OF SALVATION.
ETERNITY IS A CURSE.
OBLIVION IS A BLESSING.
THERE!
THE CASTLE!

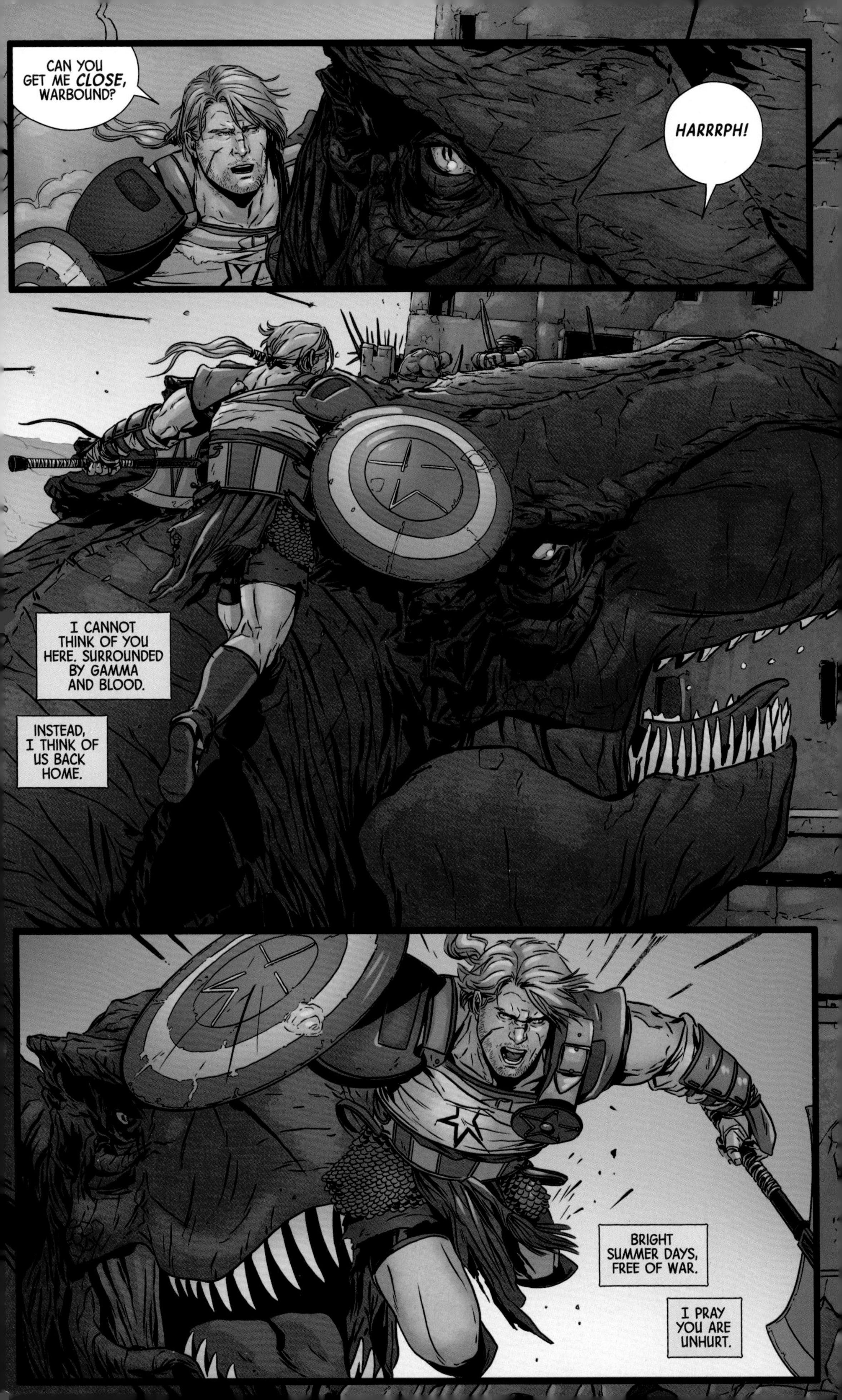
CAN YOU GET ME CLOSE, WARBOUND?
HARRRPH!
I CANNOT THINK OF YOU HERE, SURROUNDED BY GAMMA AND BLOOD.
INSTEAD, I THINK OF US BACK HOME.
BRIGHT SUMMER DAYS, FREE OF WAR.
I PRAY YOU ARE UNHURT.

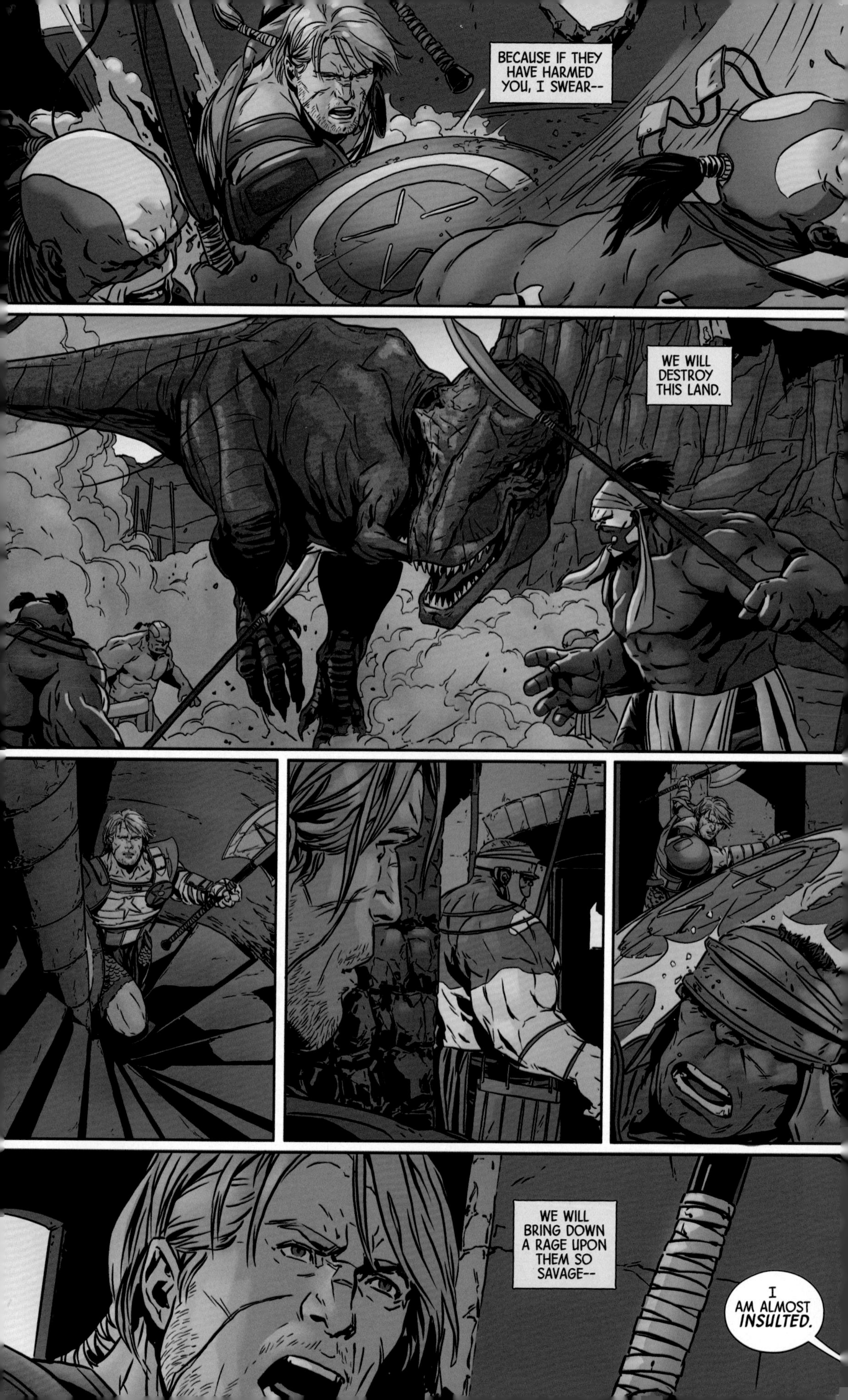
BECAUSE IF THEY HAVE HARMED YOU, I SWEAR--
WE WILL DESTROY THIS LAND.
WE WILL BRING DOWN A RAGE UPON THEM SO SAVAGE--
I AM ALMOST INSULTED.

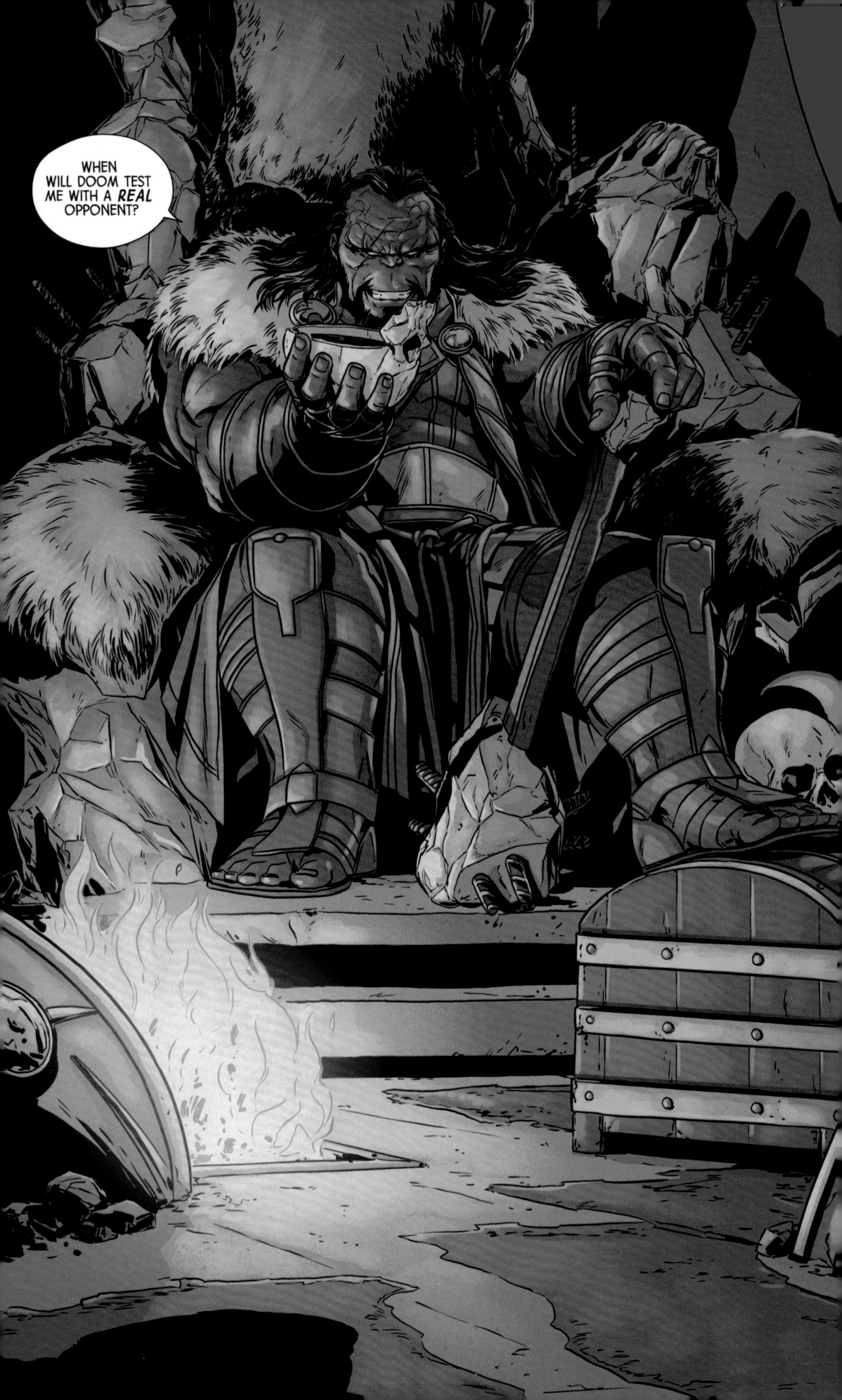
WHEN WILL DOOM TEST ME WITH A REAL OPPONENT?

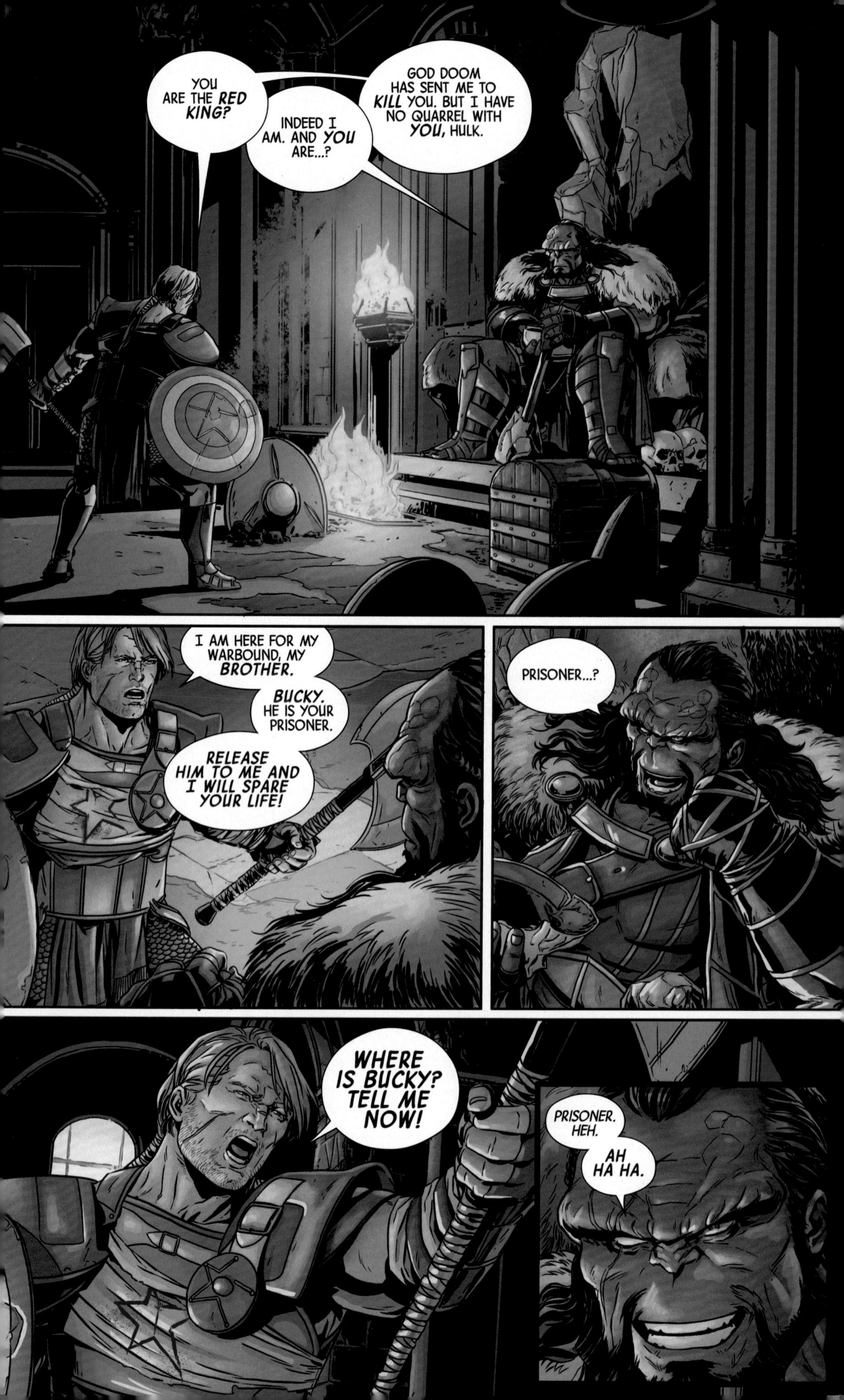
YOU ARE THE RED KING?
INDEED I AM. AND YOU ARE...?
GOD DOOM HAS SENT ME TO KILL YOU. BUT I HAVE NO QUARREL WITH YOU, HULK.
I AM HERE FOR MY WARBOUND, MY BROTHER.
BUCKY. HE IS YOUR PRISONER.
RELEASE HIM TO ME AND I WILL SPARE YOUR LIFE!
PRISONER...?
WHERE IS BUCKY? TELL ME NOW!
PRISONER. HEH.
AH HA HA.

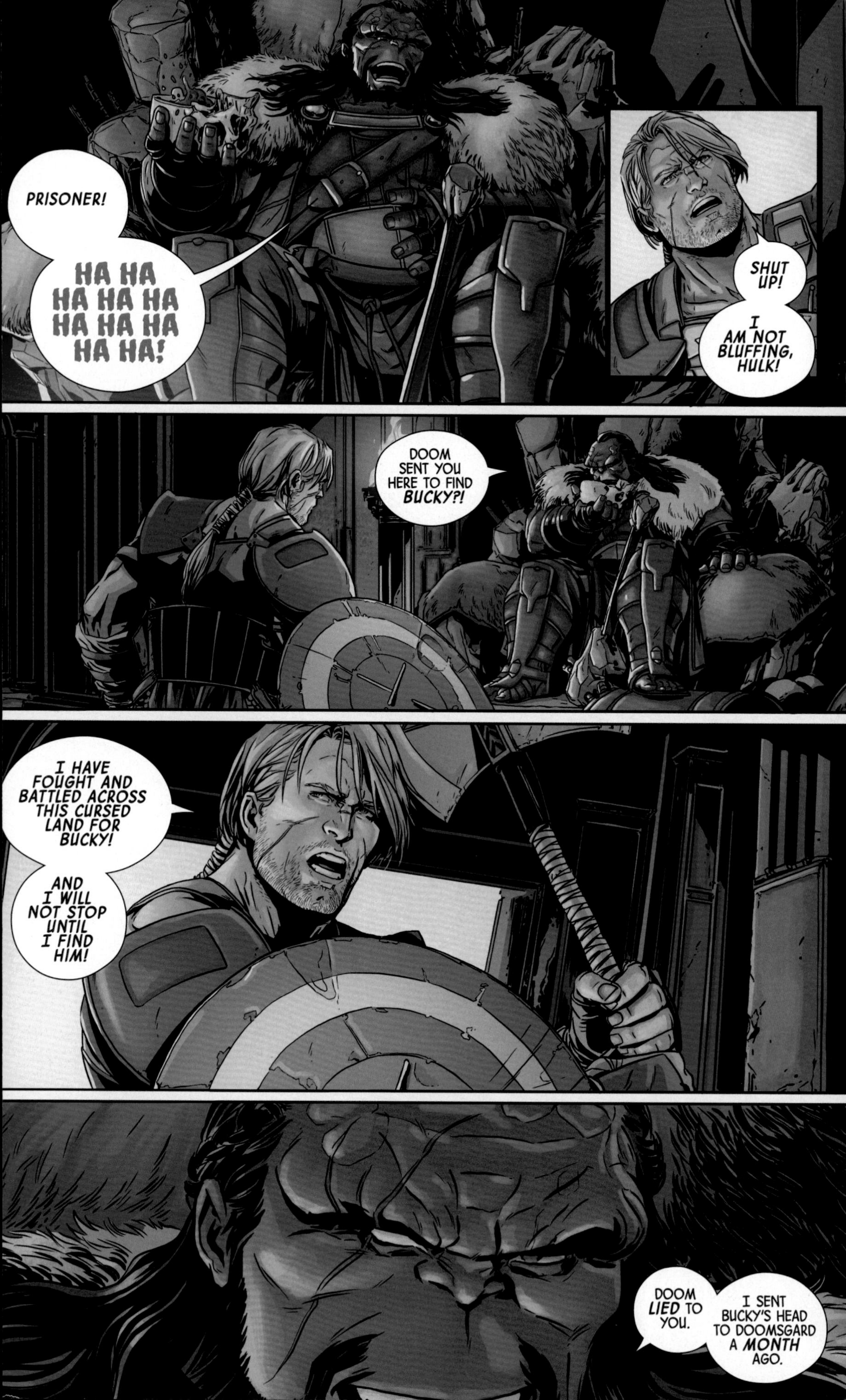
PRISONER!
HA HA HA HA HA HA HA HA HA HA!
SHUT UP!
I AM NOT BLUFFING, HULK!
DOOM SENT YOU HERE TO FIND BUCKY?!
I HAVE FOUGHT AND BATTLED ACROSS THIS CURSED LAND FOR BUCKY!
AND I WILL NOT STOP UNTIL I FIND HIM!
DOOM LIED TO YOU.
I SENT BUCKY'S HEAD TO DOOMSGARD A MONTH AGO.

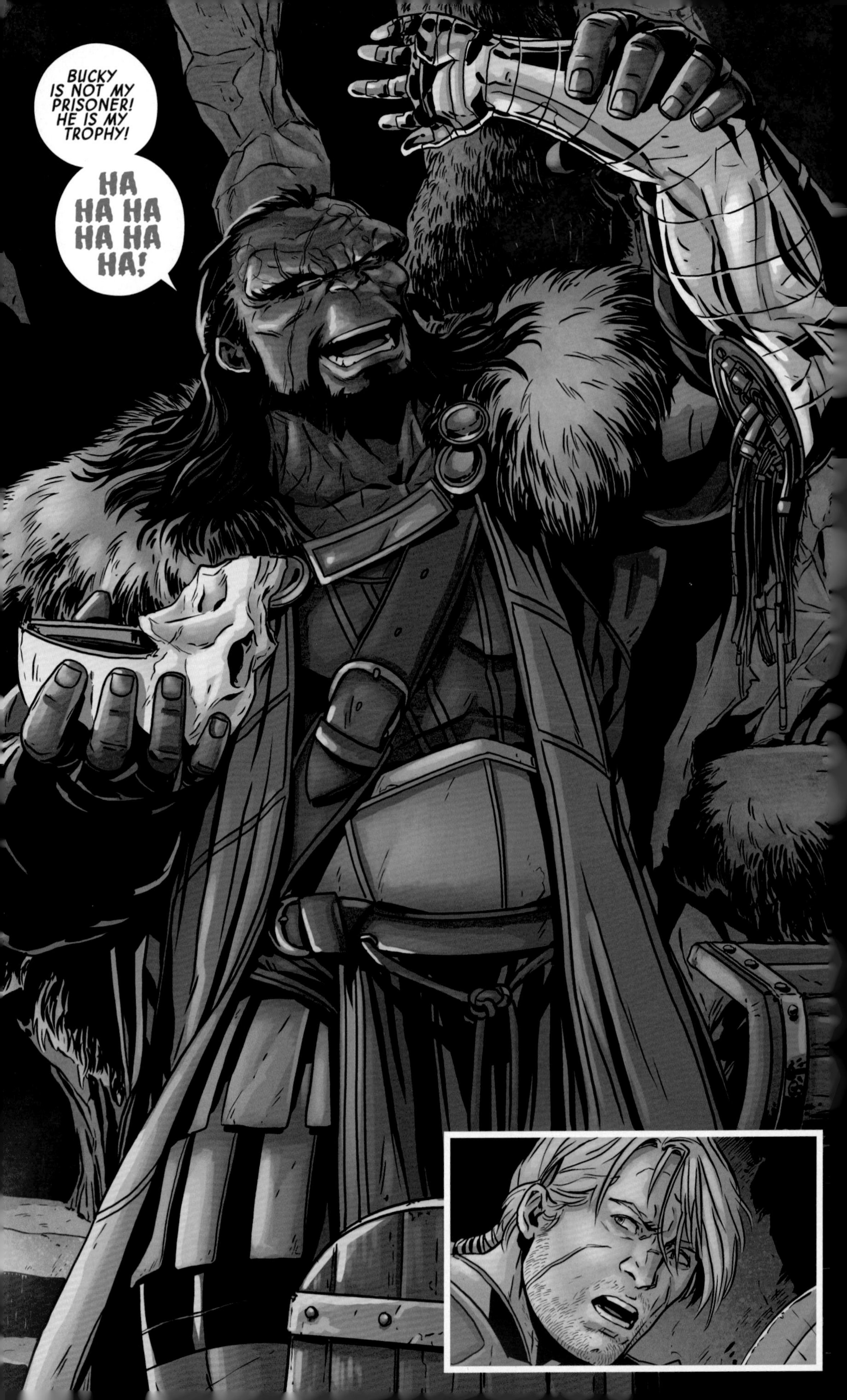
BUCKY IS NOT MY PRISONER! HE IS MY TROPHY!
HA HA HA HA HA HA!

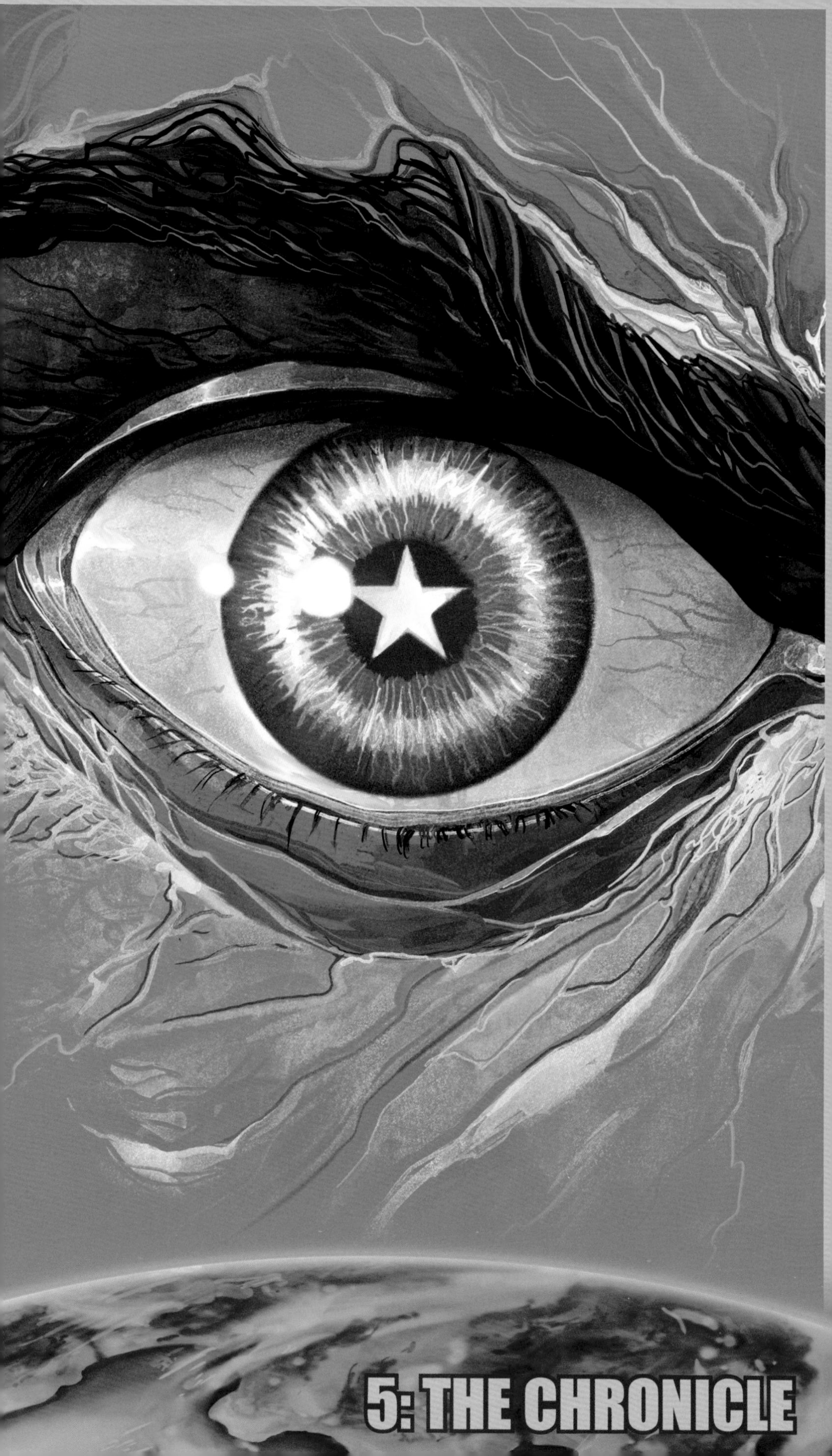

5: THE CHRONICLE

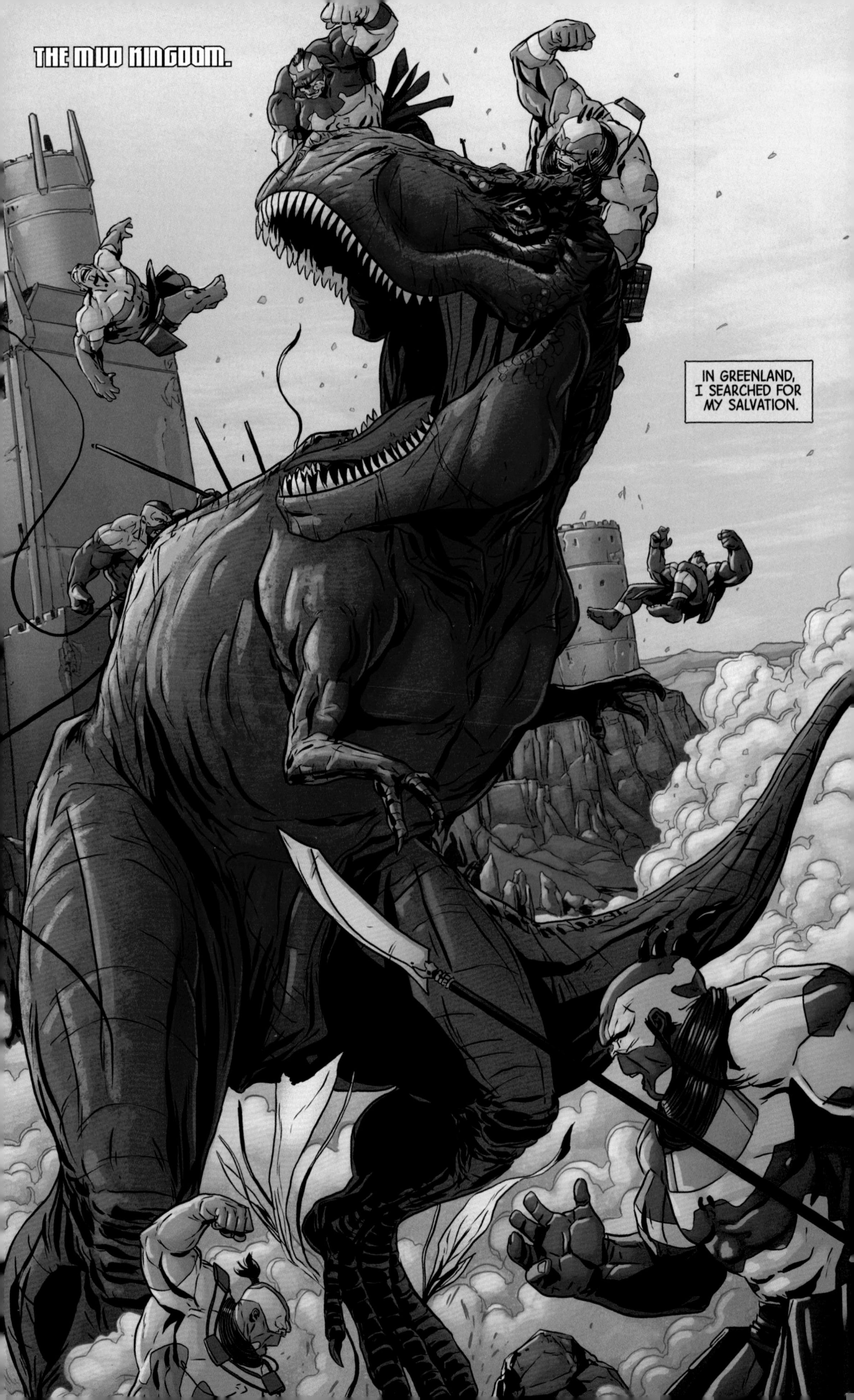
THE MUD KINGDOM.
IN GREENLAND, I SEARCHED FOR MY SALVATION.

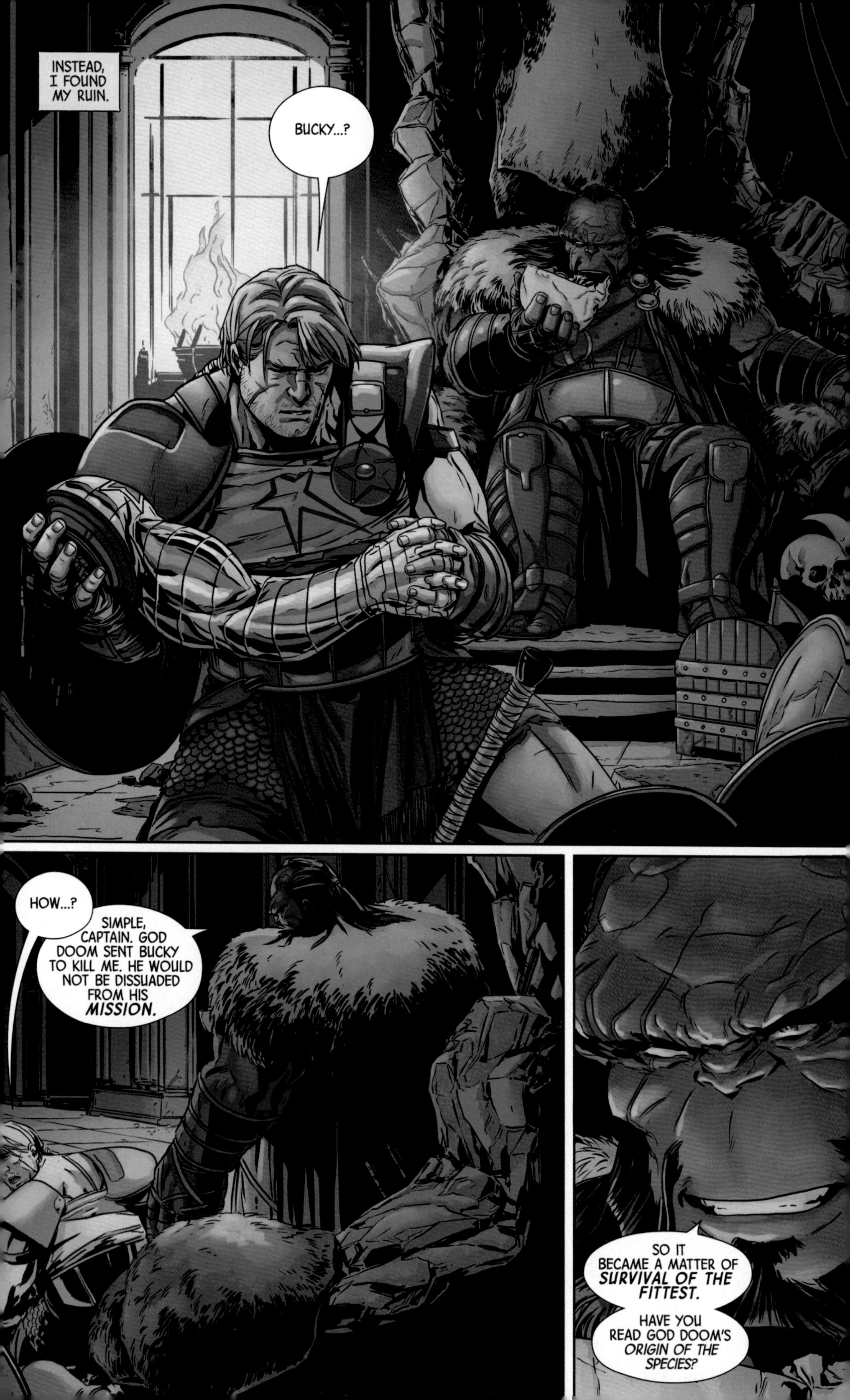
INSTEAD, I FOUND MY RUIN.
BUCKY...?
HOW...?
SIMPLE, CAPTAIN. GOD DOOM SENT BUCKY TO KILL ME. HE WOULD NOT BE DISSUADED FROM HIS *MISSION.*
SO IT BECAME A MATTER OF ***SURVIVAL OF THE FITTEST.***
HAVE YOU READ GOD DOOM'S *ORIGIN OF THE SPECIES?*

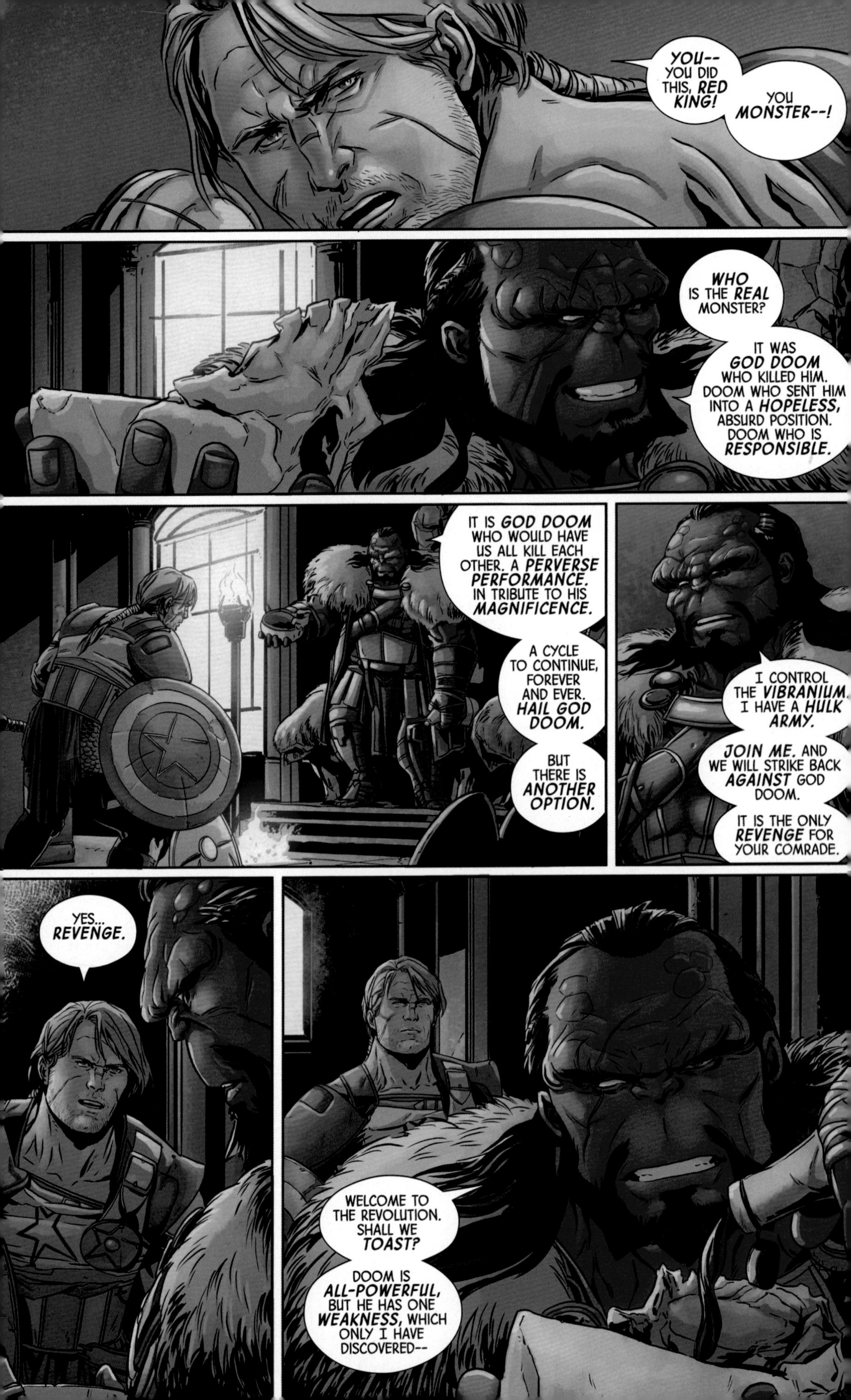

YOU-- YOU DID THIS, RED KING!
YOU MONSTER--!
WHO IS THE REAL MONSTER?
IT WAS GOD DOOM WHO KILLED HIM. DOOM WHO SENT HIM INTO A HOPELESS, ABSURD POSITION. DOOM WHO IS RESPONSIBLE.
IT IS GOD DOOM WHO WOULD HAVE US ALL KILL EACH OTHER. A PERVERSE PERFORMANCE. IN TRIBUTE TO HIS MAGNIFICENCE.
A CYCLE TO CONTINUE, FOREVER AND EVER. HAIL GOD DOOM.
BUT THERE IS ANOTHER OPTION.
I CONTROL THE VIBRANIUM. I HAVE A HULK ARMY.
JOIN ME. AND WE WILL STRIKE BACK AGAINST GOD DOOM.
IT IS THE ONLY REVENGE FOR YOUR COMRADE.
YES... REVENGE.
WELCOME TO THE REVOLUTION. SHALL WE TOAST?
DOOM IS ALL-POWERFUL, BUT HE HAS ONE WEAKNESS, WHICH ONLY I HAVE DISCOVERED--

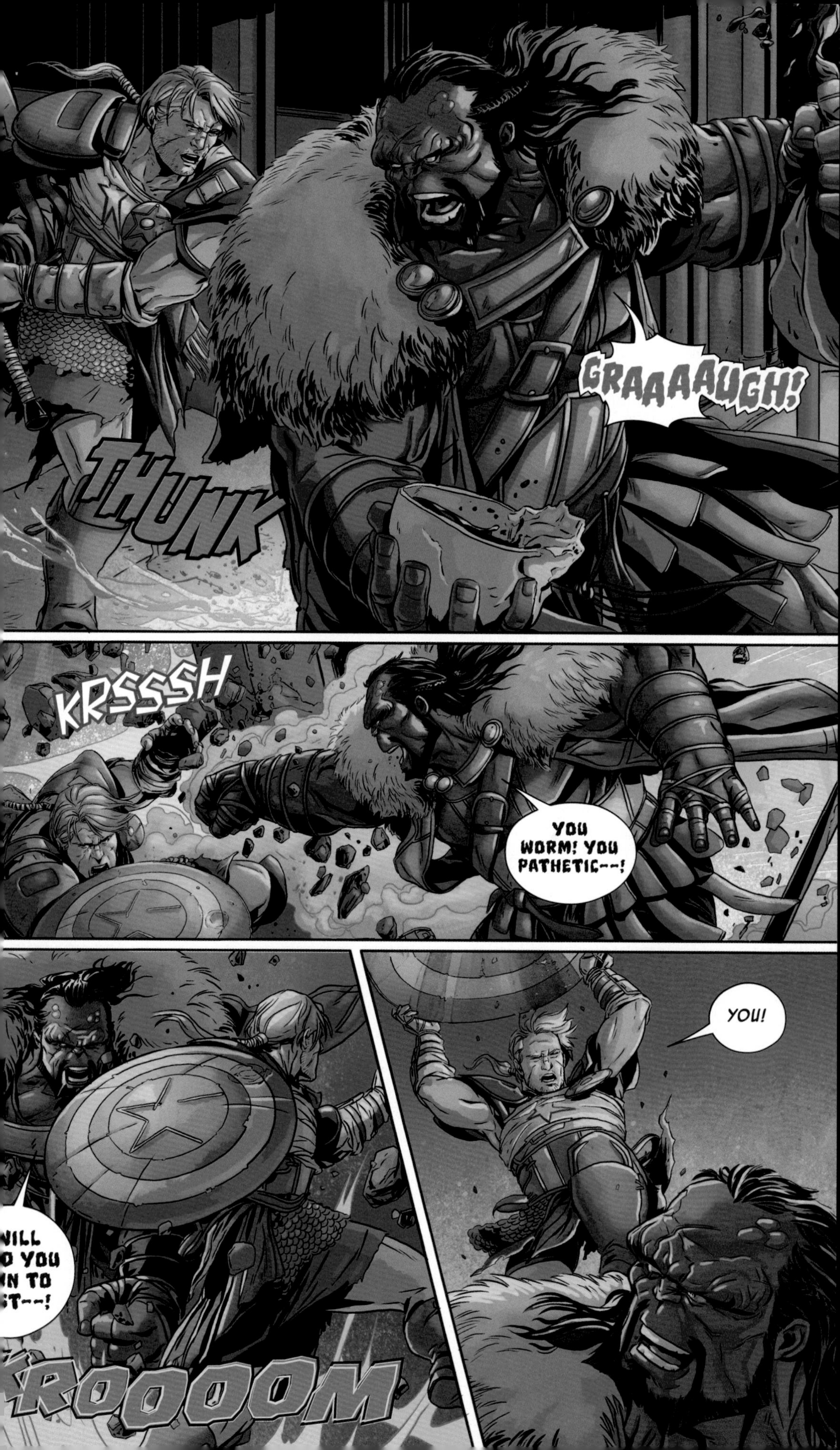
GRAAAAUGH!
THUNK
KRSSSH
YOU WORM! YOU PATHETIC--!
YOU!
ROOOOM

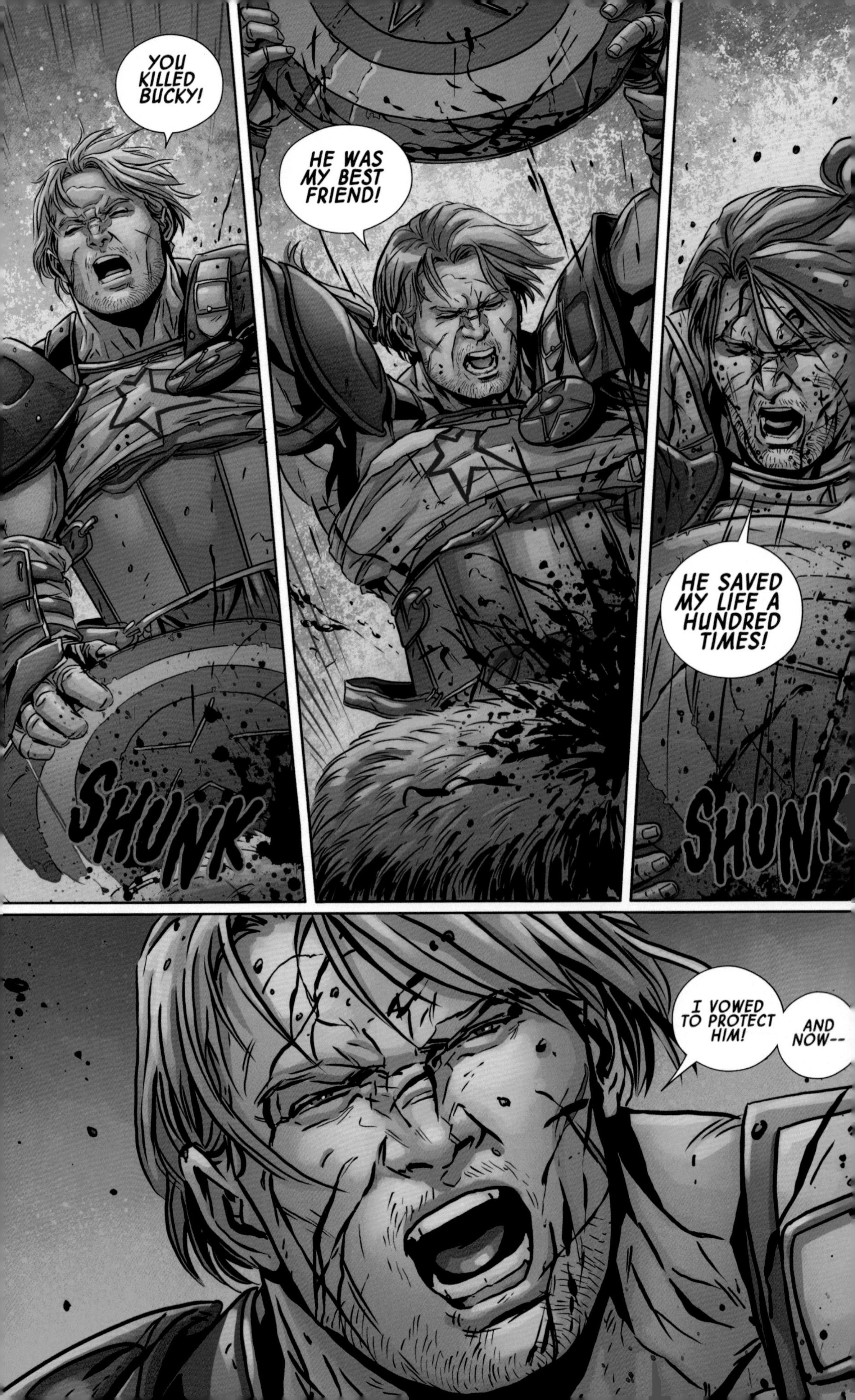
YOU KILLED BUCKY!
SHUNK
HE WAS MY BEST FRIEND!
HE SAVED MY LIFE A HUNDRED TIMES!
SHUNK
I VOWED TO PROTECT HIM!
AND NOW--

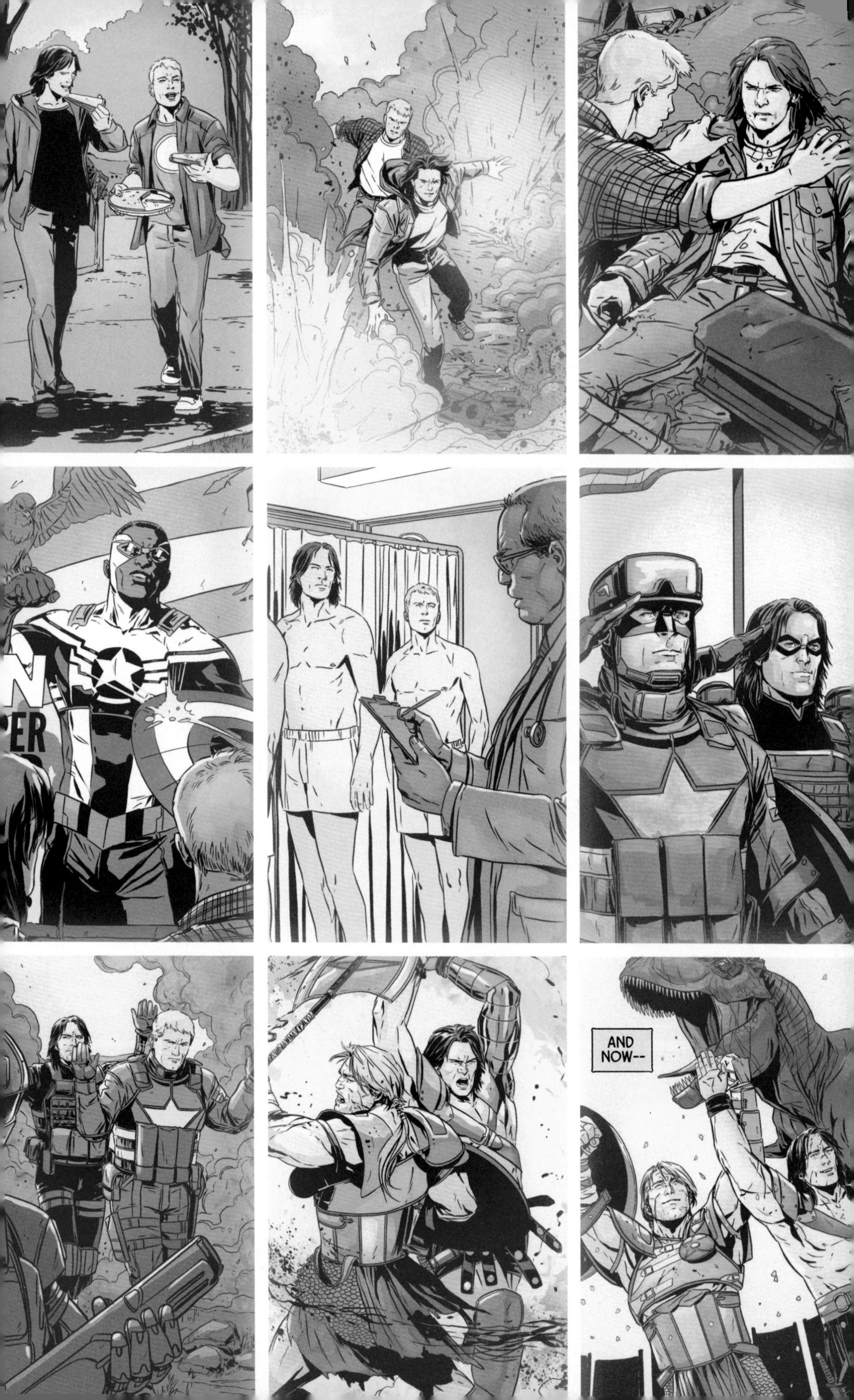
AND
NOW--

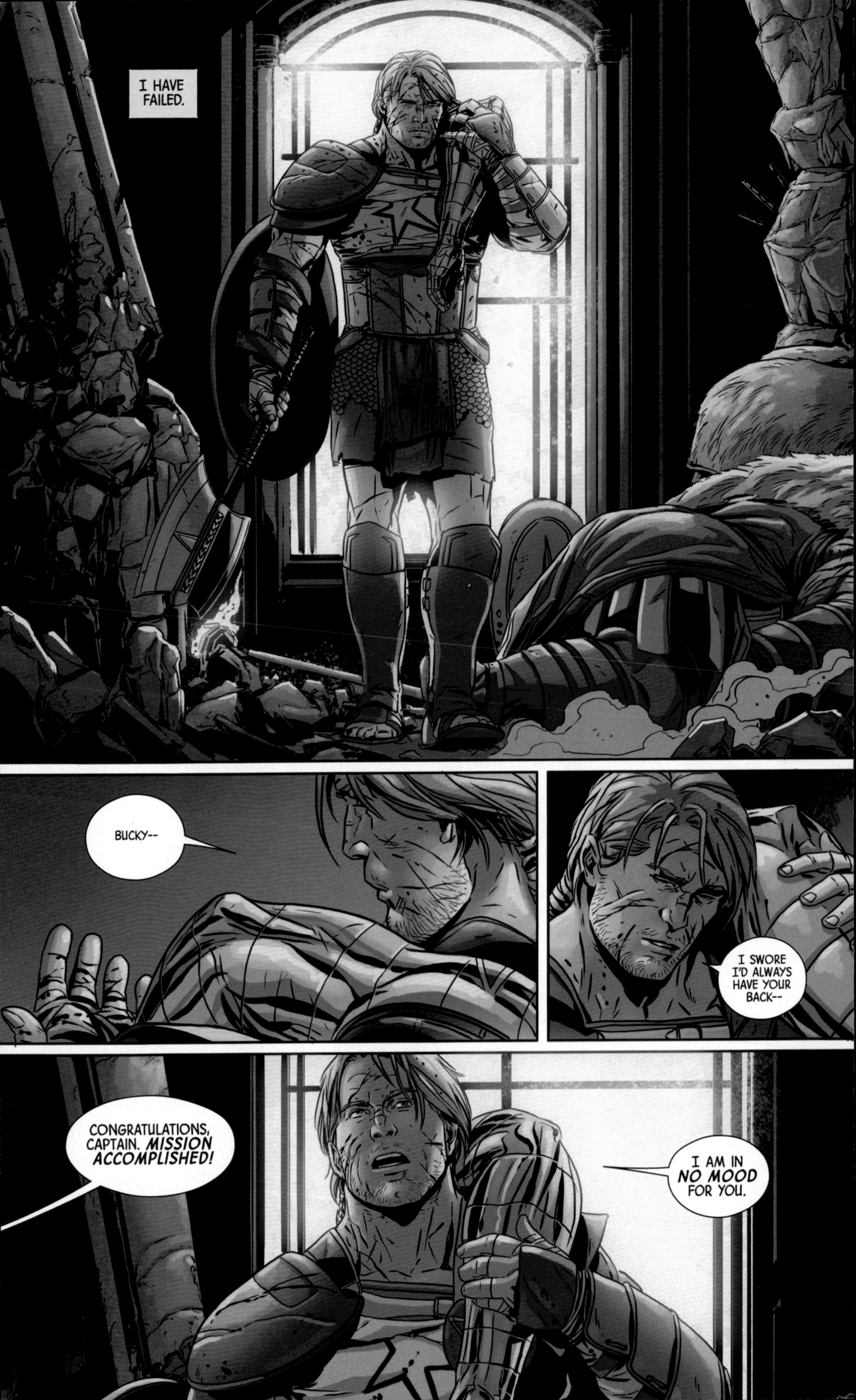
I HAVE FAILED.
BUCKY--
I SWORE I'D ALWAYS HAVE YOUR BACK--
CONGRATULATIONS, CAPTAIN. *MISSION ACCOMPLISHED!*
I AM IN *NO MOOD* FOR YOU.

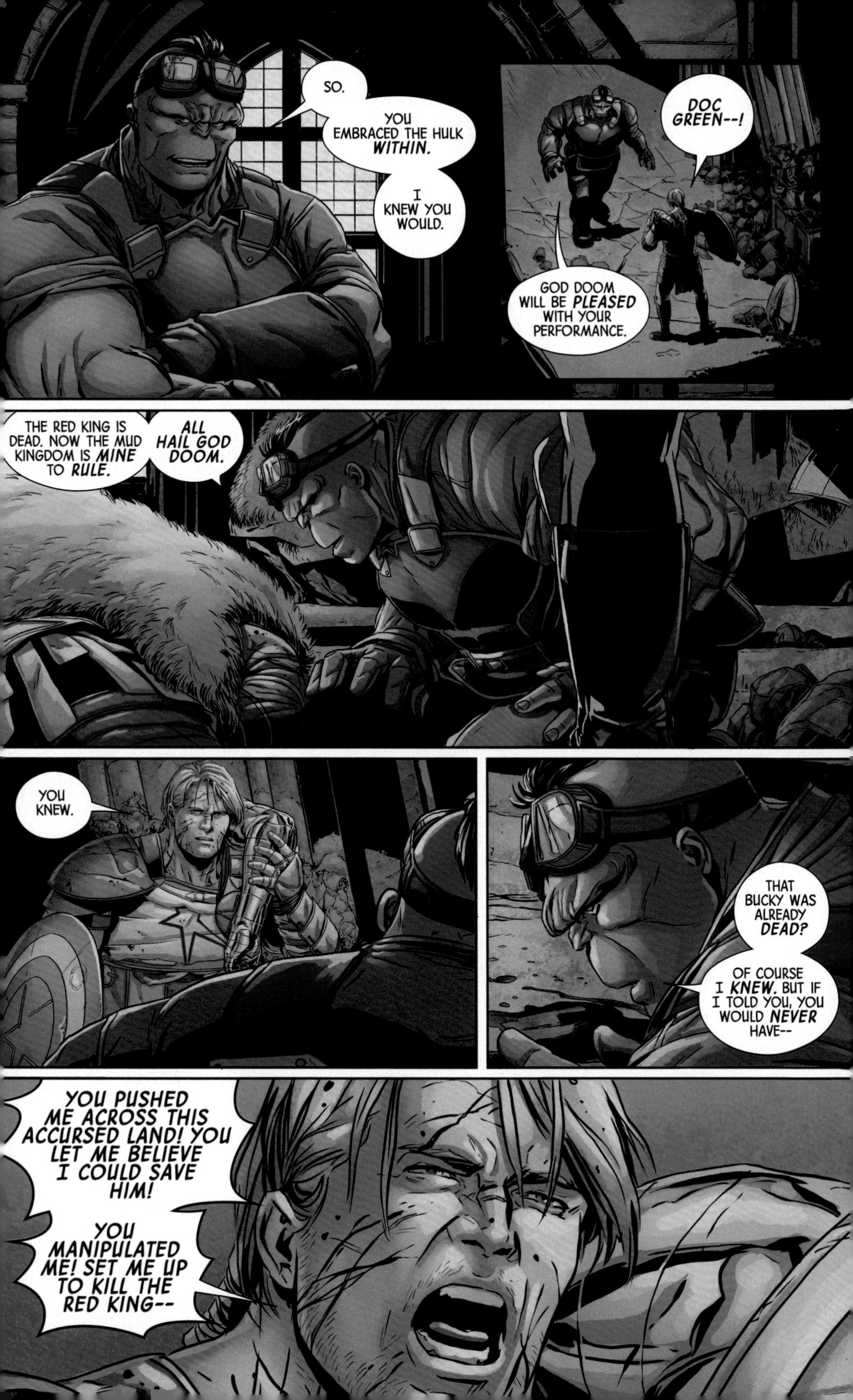
SO.
YOU EMBRACED THE HULK WITHIN.
I KNEW YOU WOULD.
DOC GREEN--!
GOD DOOM WILL BE PLEASED WITH YOUR PERFORMANCE.
THE RED KING IS DEAD. NOW THE MUD KINGDOM IS MINE TO RULE.
ALL HAIL GOD DOOM.
YOU KNEW.
THAT BUCKY WAS ALREADY DEAD?
OF COURSE I KNEW. BUT IF I TOLD YOU, YOU WOULD NEVER HAVE--
YOU PUSHED ME ACROSS THIS ACCURSED LAND! YOU LET ME BELIEVE I COULD SAVE HIM!
YOU MANIPULATED ME! SET ME UP TO KILL THE RED KING--

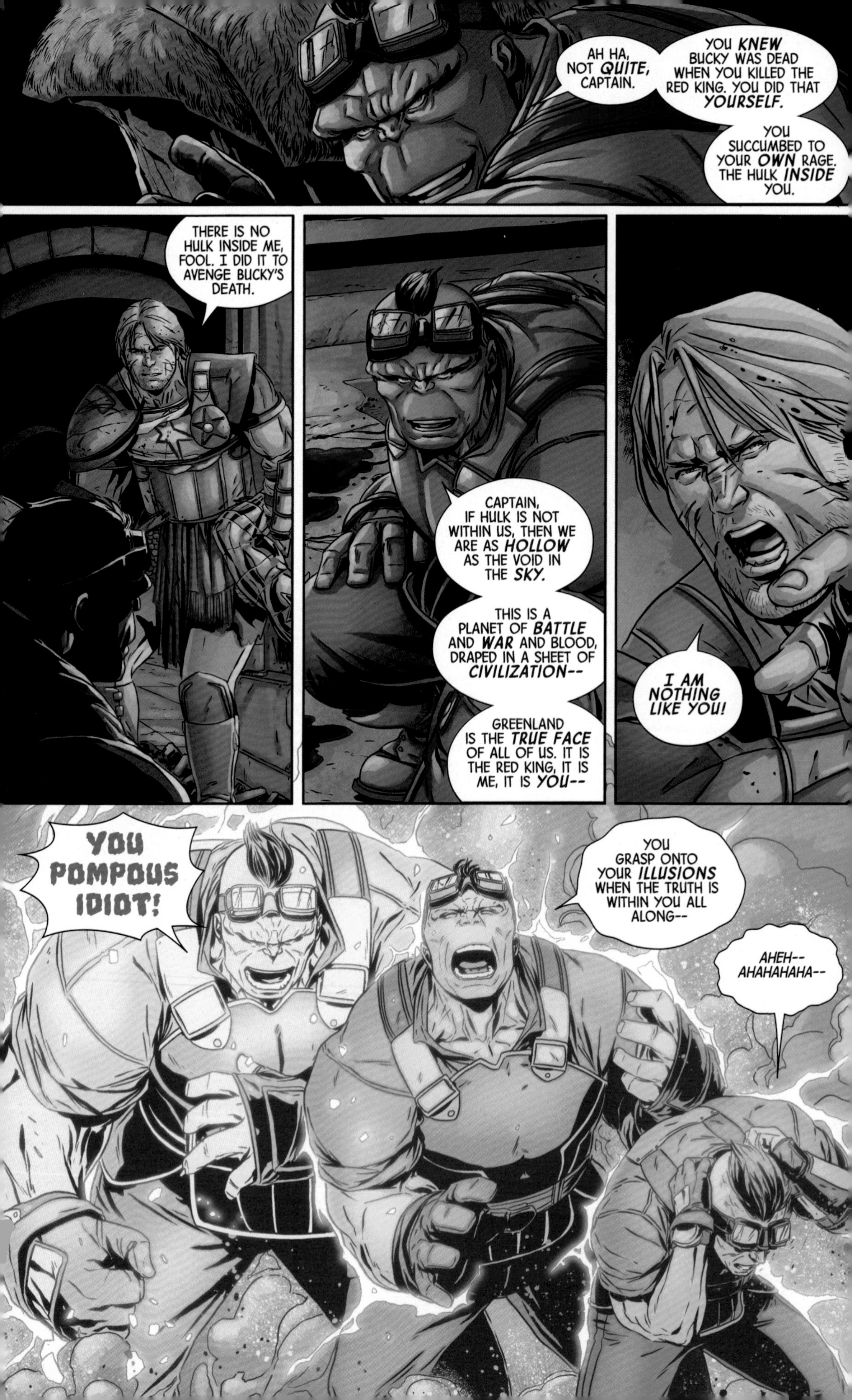
AH HA, NOT QUITE, CAPTAIN.
YOU KNEW BUCKY WAS DEAD WHEN YOU KILLED THE RED KING. YOU DID THAT YOURSELF.
YOU SUCCUMBED TO YOUR OWN RAGE. THE HULK INSIDE YOU.
THERE IS NO HULK INSIDE ME, FOOL. I DID IT TO AVENGE BUCKY'S DEATH.
CAPTAIN, IF HULK IS NOT WITHIN US, THEN WE ARE AS HOLLOW AS THE VOID IN THE SKY.
THIS IS A PLANET OF BATTLE AND WAR AND BLOOD, DRAPED IN A SHEET OF CIVILIZATION--
GREENLAND IS THE TRUE FACE OF ALL OF US. IT IS THE RED KING, IT IS ME, IT IS YOU--
I AM NOTHING LIKE YOU!
YOU POMPOUS IDIOT!
YOU GRASP ONTO YOUR ILLUSIONS WHEN THE TRUTH IS WITHIN YOU ALL ALONG--
AHEH-- AHAHAHAHA--

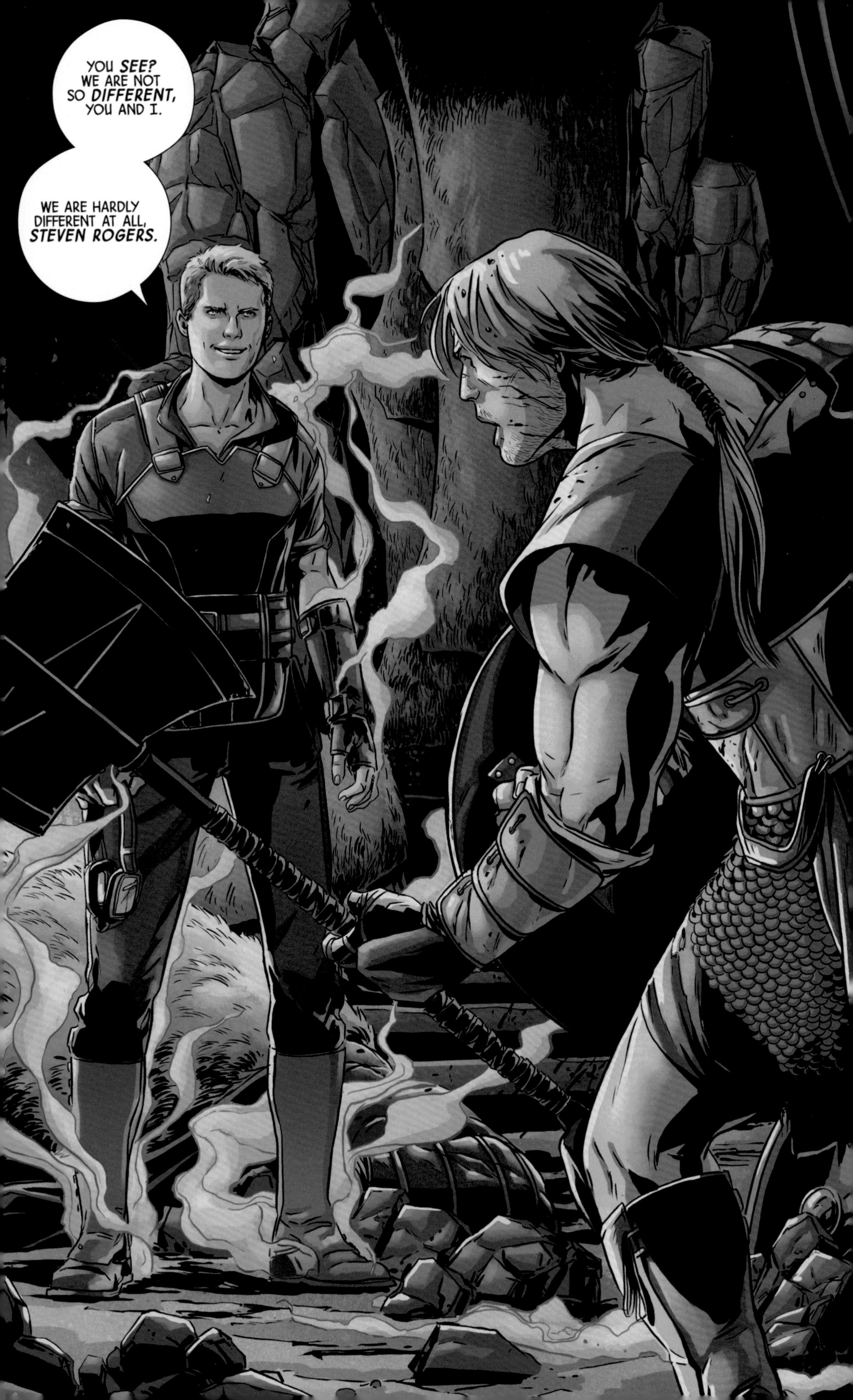
YOU **SEE?** WE ARE NOT SO ***DIFFERENT,*** YOU AND I.
WE ARE HARDLY DIFFERENT AT ALL, ***STEVEN ROGERS.***

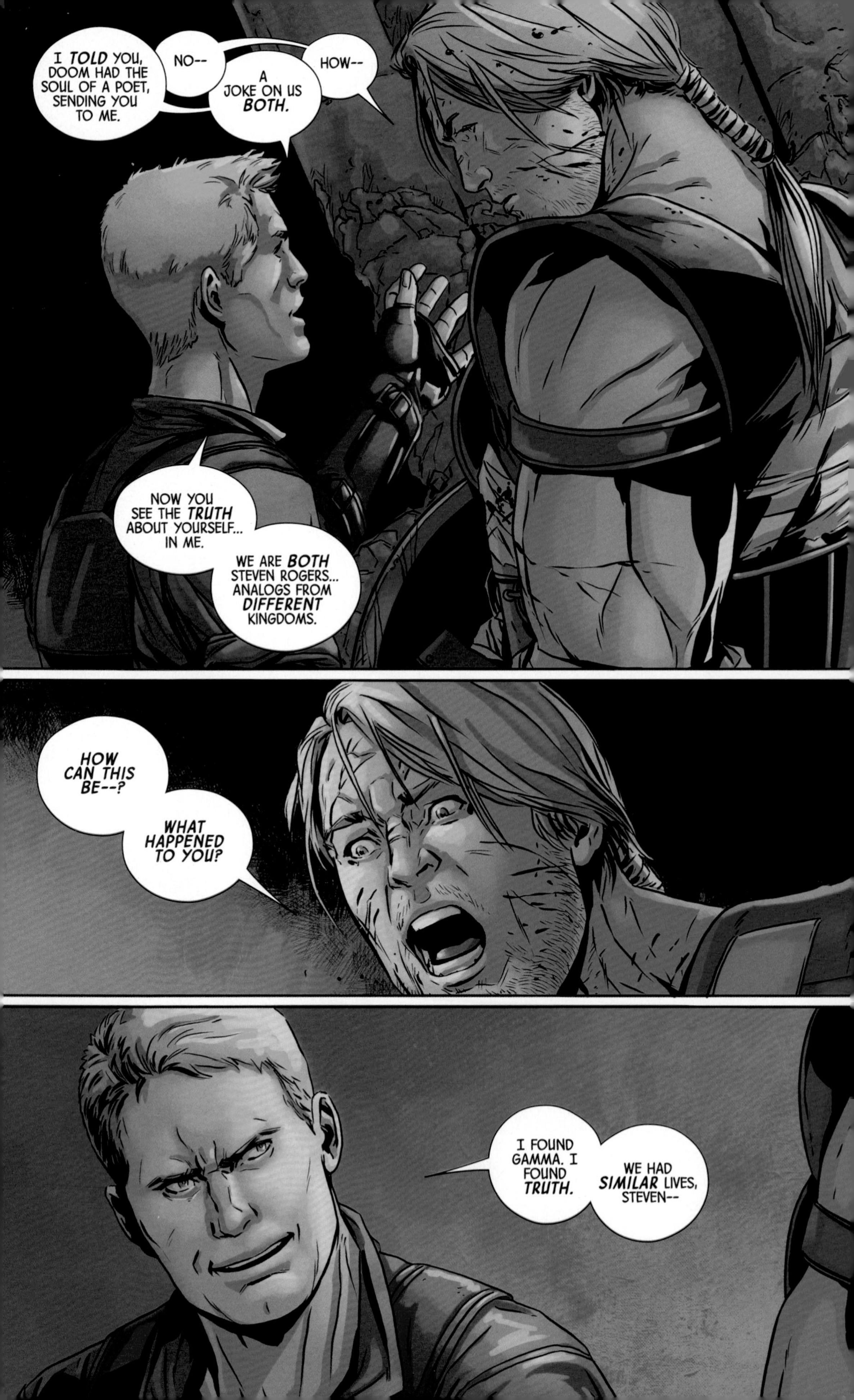
I TOLD YOU, DOOM HAD THE SOUL OF A POET, SENDING YOU TO ME.
NO--
A JOKE ON US BOTH.
HOW--
NOW YOU SEE THE TRUTH ABOUT YOURSELF... IN ME.
WE ARE BOTH STEVEN ROGERS... ANALOGS FROM DIFFERENT KINGDOMS.
HOW CAN THIS BE--?
WHAT HAPPENED TO YOU?
I FOUND GAMMA. I FOUND TRUTH.
WE HAD SIMILAR LIVES, STEVEN--

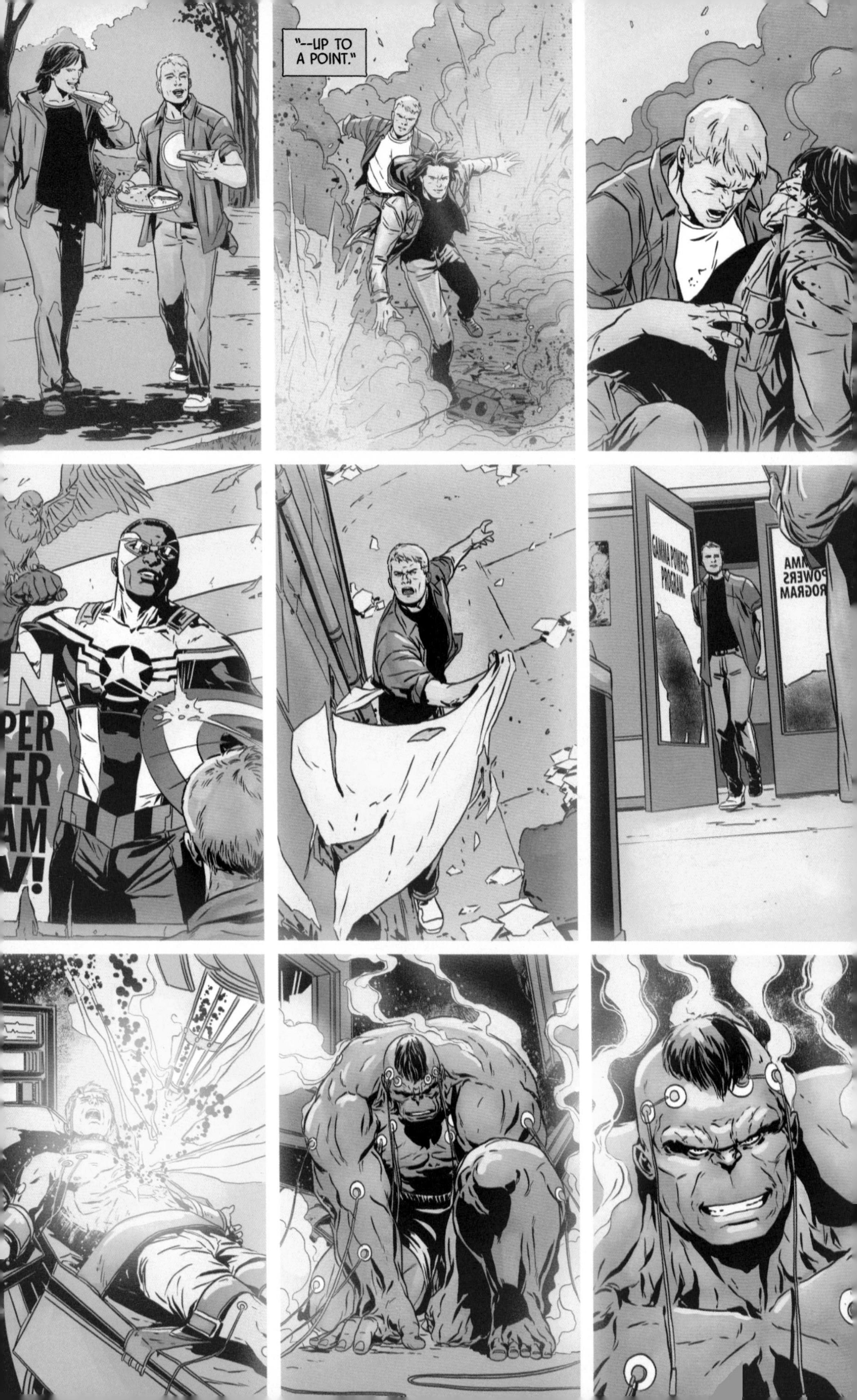
"--UP TO A POINT."
GAMMA POWERS PROGRAM

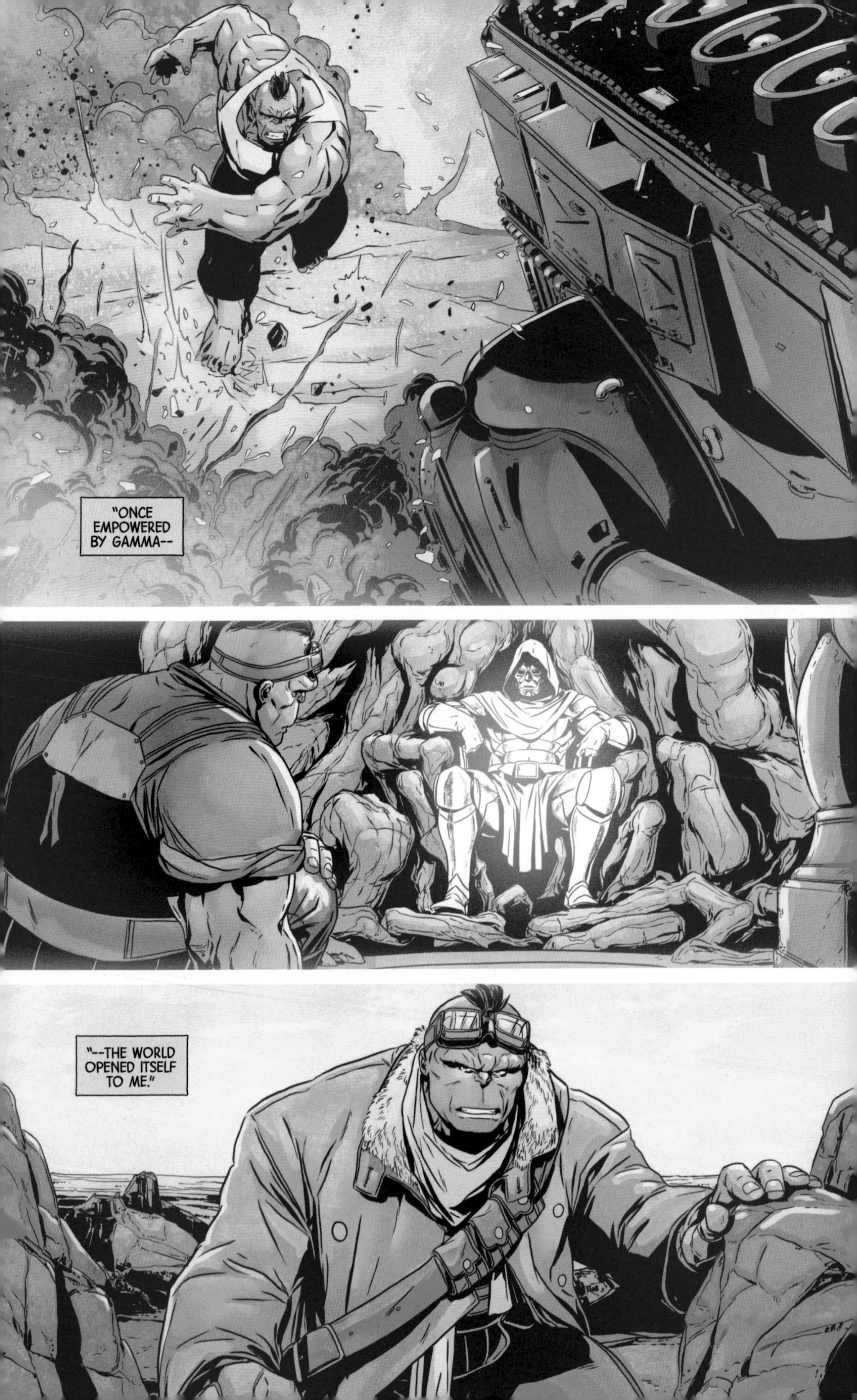
"ONCE EMPOWERED BY GAMMA--
"--THE WORLD OPENED ITSELF TO ME."

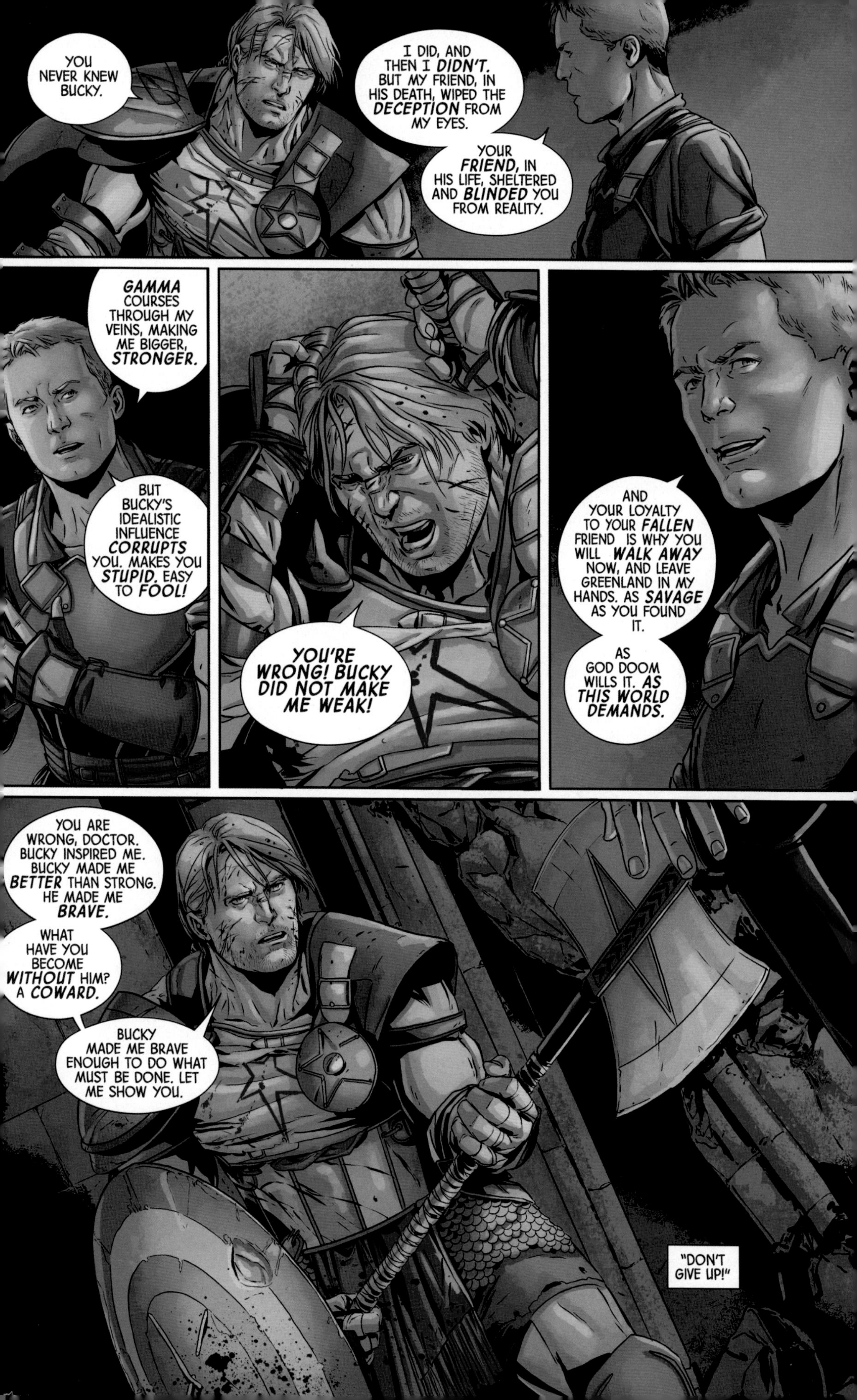
YOU NEVER KNEW BUCKY.
I DID, AND THEN I DIDN'T. BUT MY FRIEND, IN HIS DEATH, WIPED THE DECEPTION FROM MY EYES.
YOUR FRIEND, IN HIS LIFE, SHELTERED AND BLINDED YOU FROM REALITY.
GAMMA COURSES THROUGH MY VEINS, MAKING ME BIGGER, STRONGER.
BUT BUCKY'S IDEALISTIC INFLUENCE CORRUPTS YOU. MAKES YOU STUPID. EASY TO FOOL!
YOU'RE WRONG! BUCKY DID NOT MAKE ME WEAK!
AND YOUR LOYALTY TO YOUR FALLEN FRIEND IS WHY YOU WILL WALK AWAY NOW, AND LEAVE GREENLAND IN MY HANDS. AS SAVAGE AS YOU FOUND IT.
AS GOD DOOM WILLS IT. AS THIS WORLD DEMANDS.
YOU ARE WRONG, DOCTOR. BUCKY INSPIRED ME. BUCKY MADE ME BETTER THAN STRONG. HE MADE ME BRAVE.
WHAT HAVE YOU BECOME WITHOUT HIM? A COWARD.
BUCKY MADE ME BRAVE ENOUGH TO DO WHAT MUST BE DONE. LET ME SHOW YOU.
"DON'T GIVE UP!"

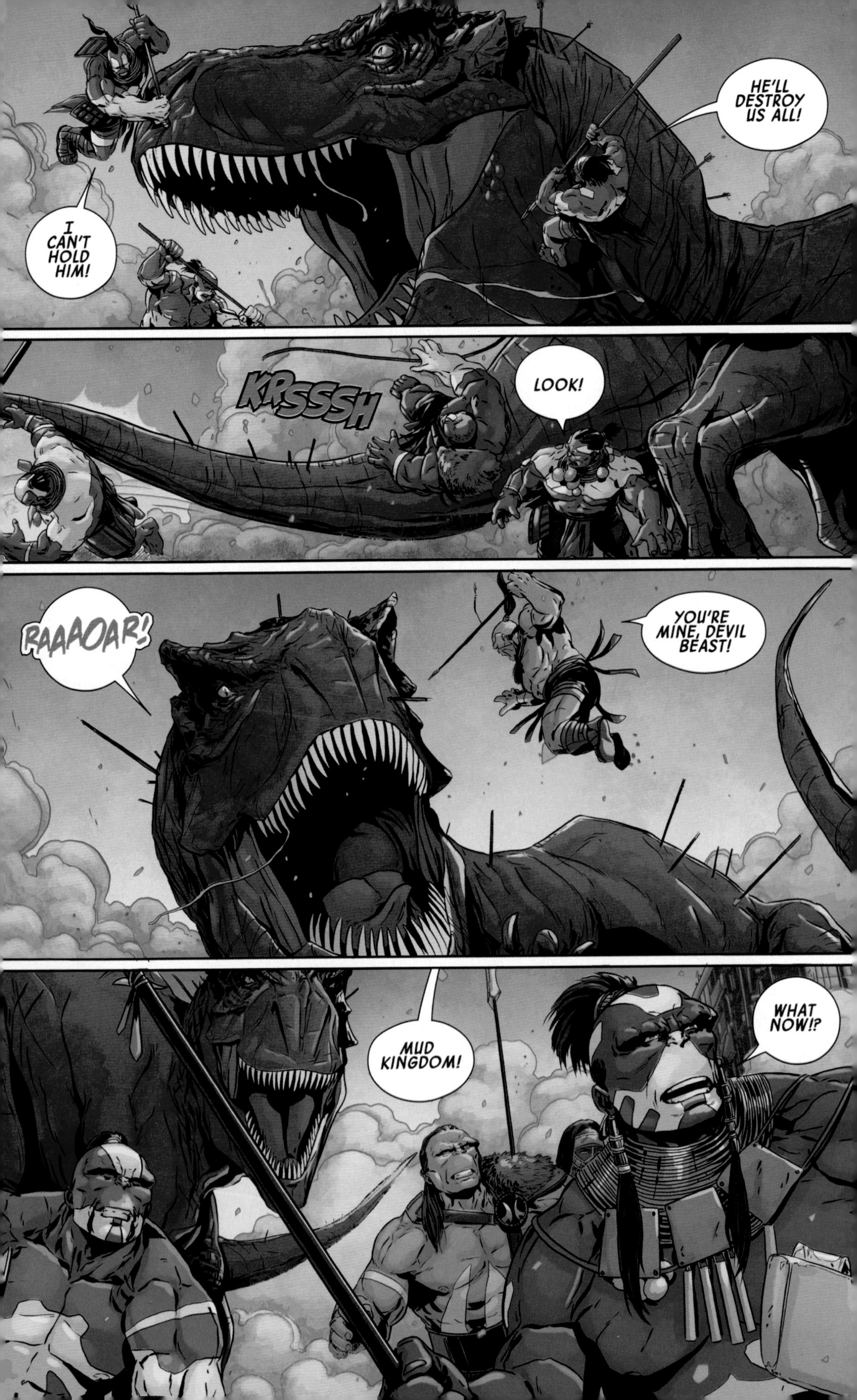
HE'LL DESTROY US ALL!
I CAN'T HOLD HIM!
KRSSSH
LOOK!
RAAAOAR!
YOU'RE MINE, DEVIL BEAST!
MUD KINGDOM!
WHAT NOW!?

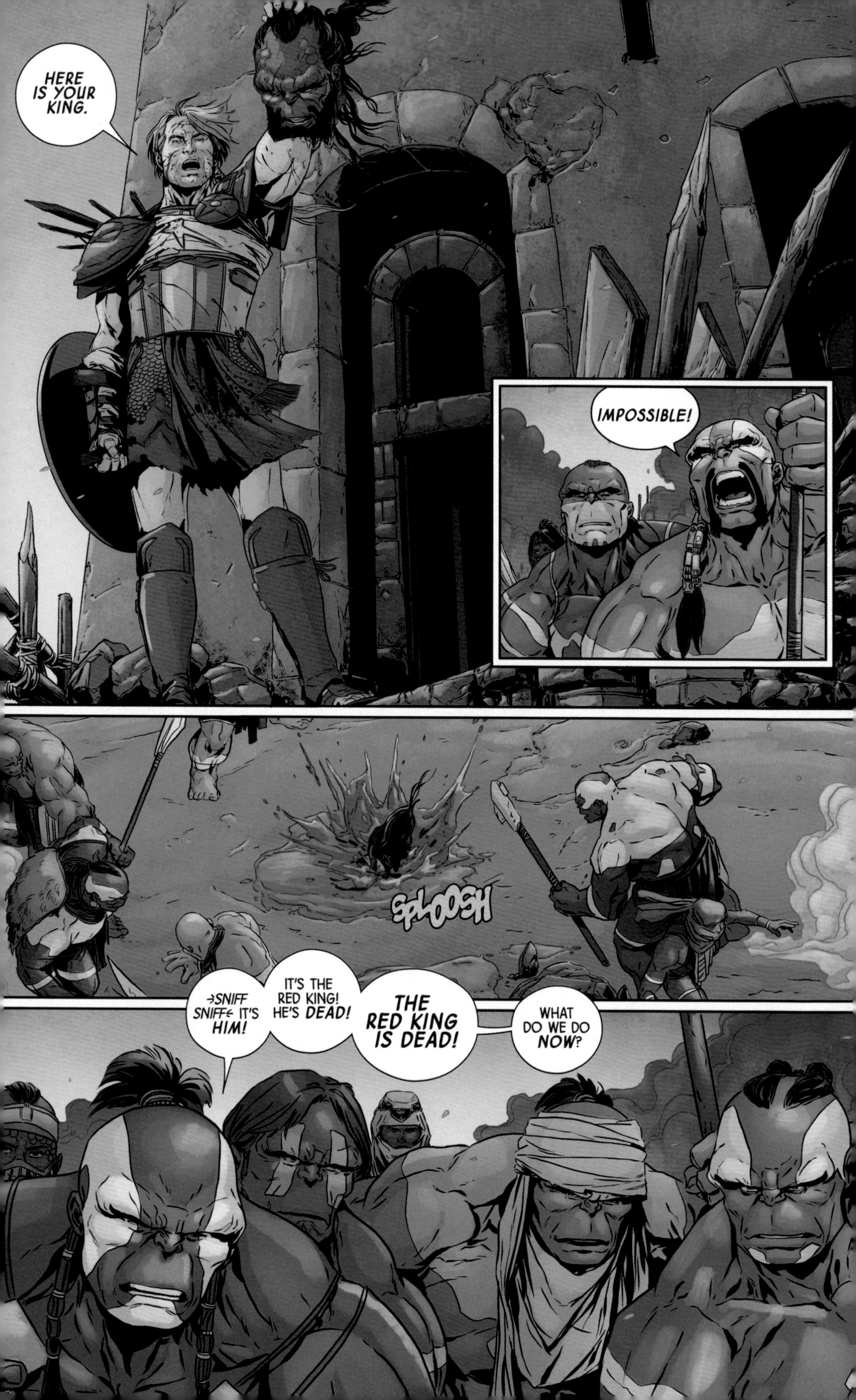
HERE IS YOUR KING.
IMPOSSIBLE!
SPLOOSH
→SNIFF SNIFF← IT'S HIM!
IT'S THE RED KING! HE'S DEAD!
THE RED KING IS DEAD!
WHAT DO WE DO NOW?

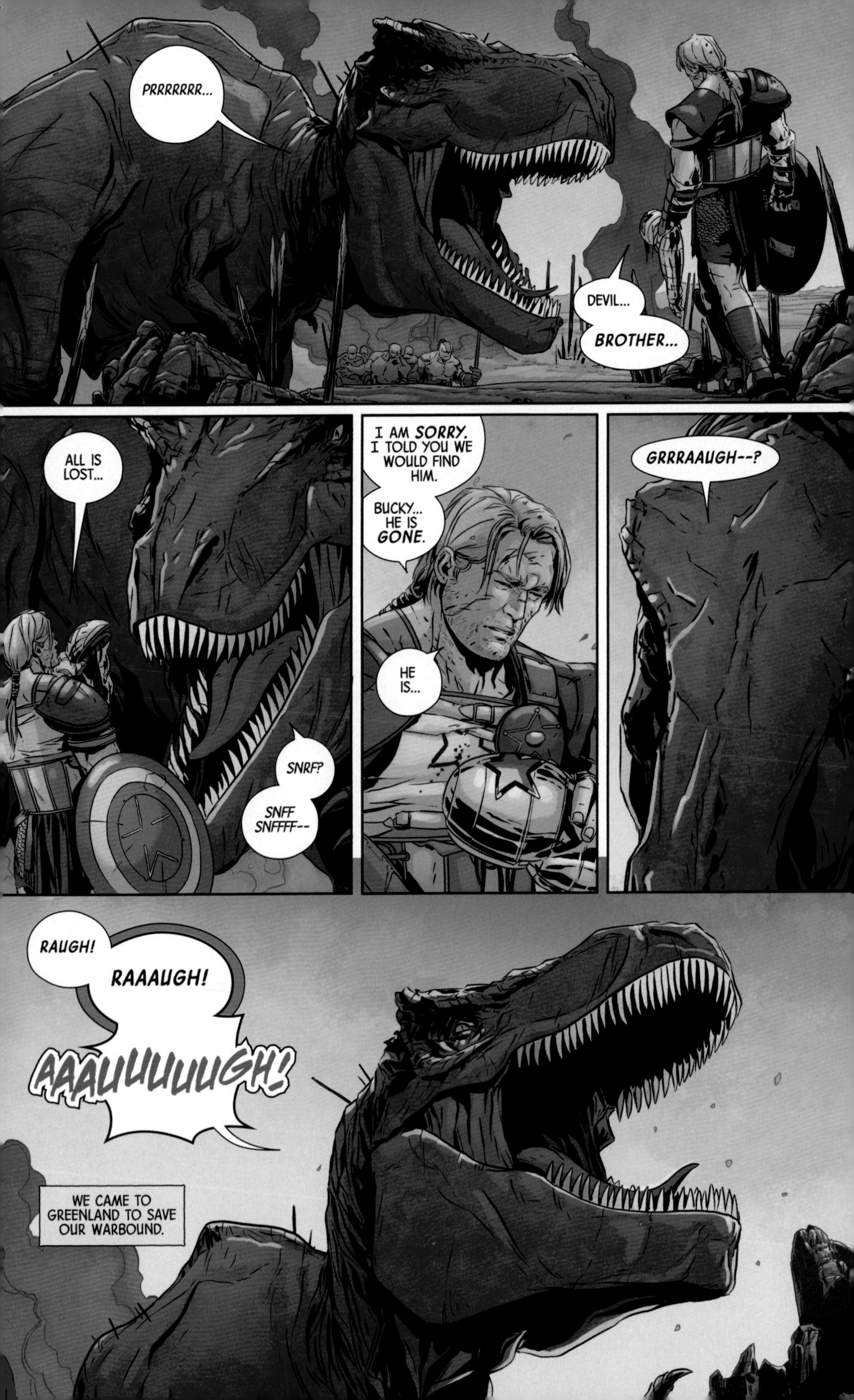
PRRRRRRR...
DEVIL...
BROTHER...
ALL IS LOST...
SNRF?
SNFF SNFFFF--
I AM SORRY. I TOLD YOU WE WOULD FIND HIM.
BUCKY... HE IS GONE.
HE IS...
GRRRAAUGH--?
RAUGH!
RAAAUGH!
AAAUUUUUUGH!
WE CAME TO GREENLAND TO SAVE OUR WARBOUND.

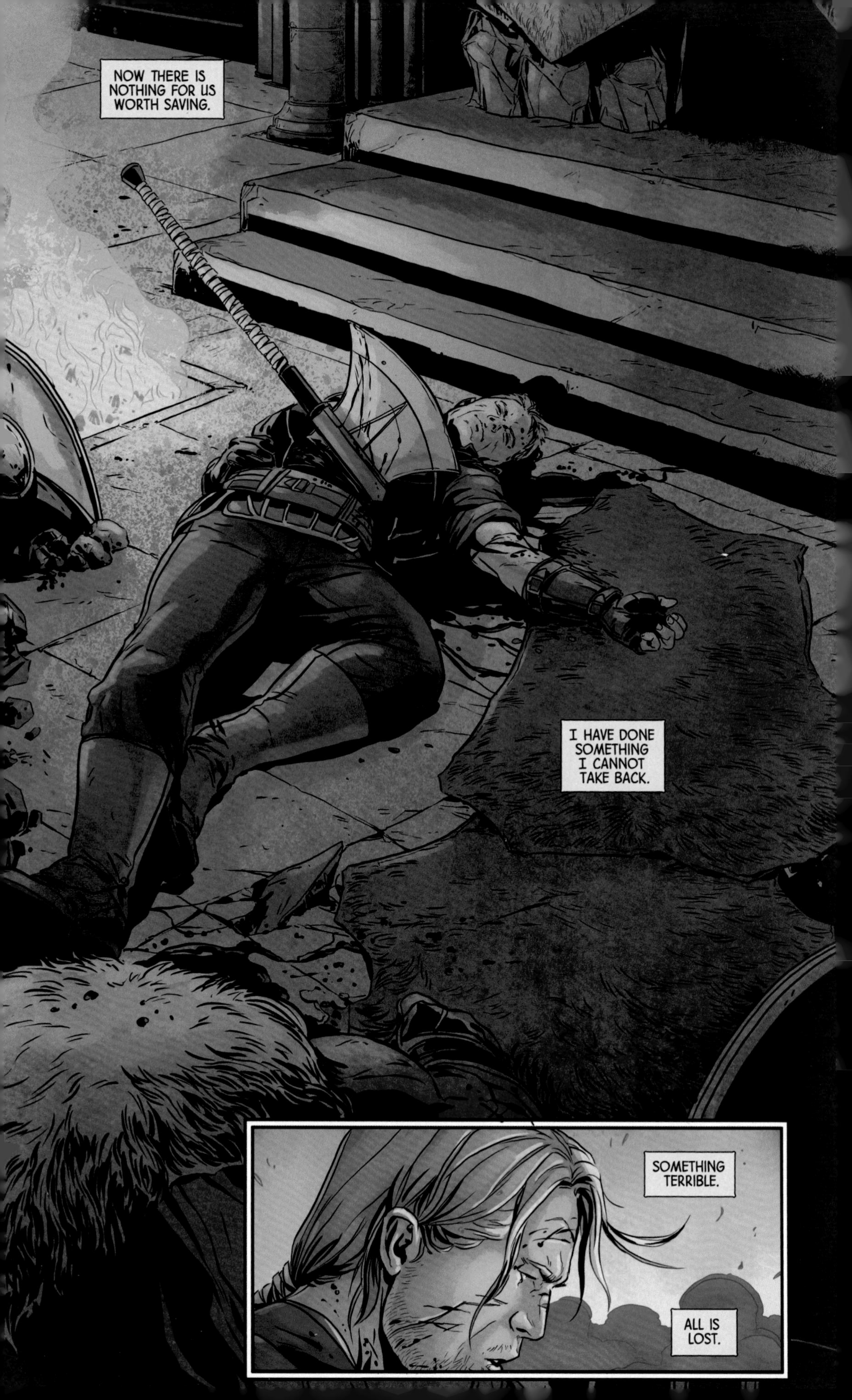
NOW THERE IS NOTHING FOR US WORTH SAVING.
I HAVE DONE SOMETHING I CANNOT TAKE BACK.
SOMETHING TERRIBLE.
ALL IS LOST.

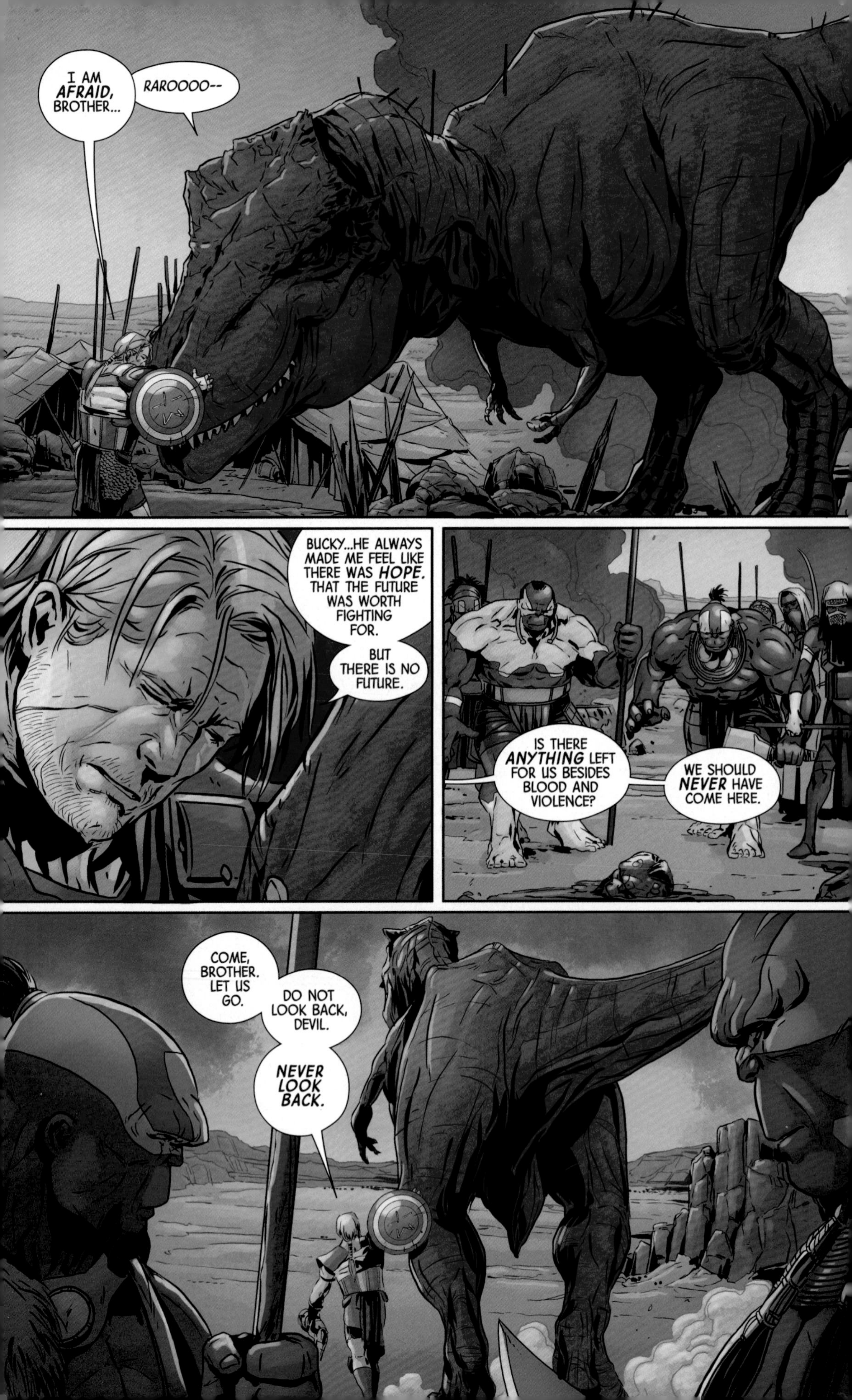
I AM AFRAID, BROTHER...
RAROOOO--
BUCKY...HE ALWAYS MADE ME FEEL LIKE THERE WAS HOPE. THAT THE FUTURE WAS WORTH FIGHTING FOR.
BUT THERE IS NO FUTURE.
IS THERE ANYTHING LEFT FOR US BESIDES BLOOD AND VIOLENCE?
WE SHOULD NEVER HAVE COME HERE.
COME, BROTHER. LET US GO.
DO NOT LOOK BACK, DEVIL.
NEVER LOOK BACK.

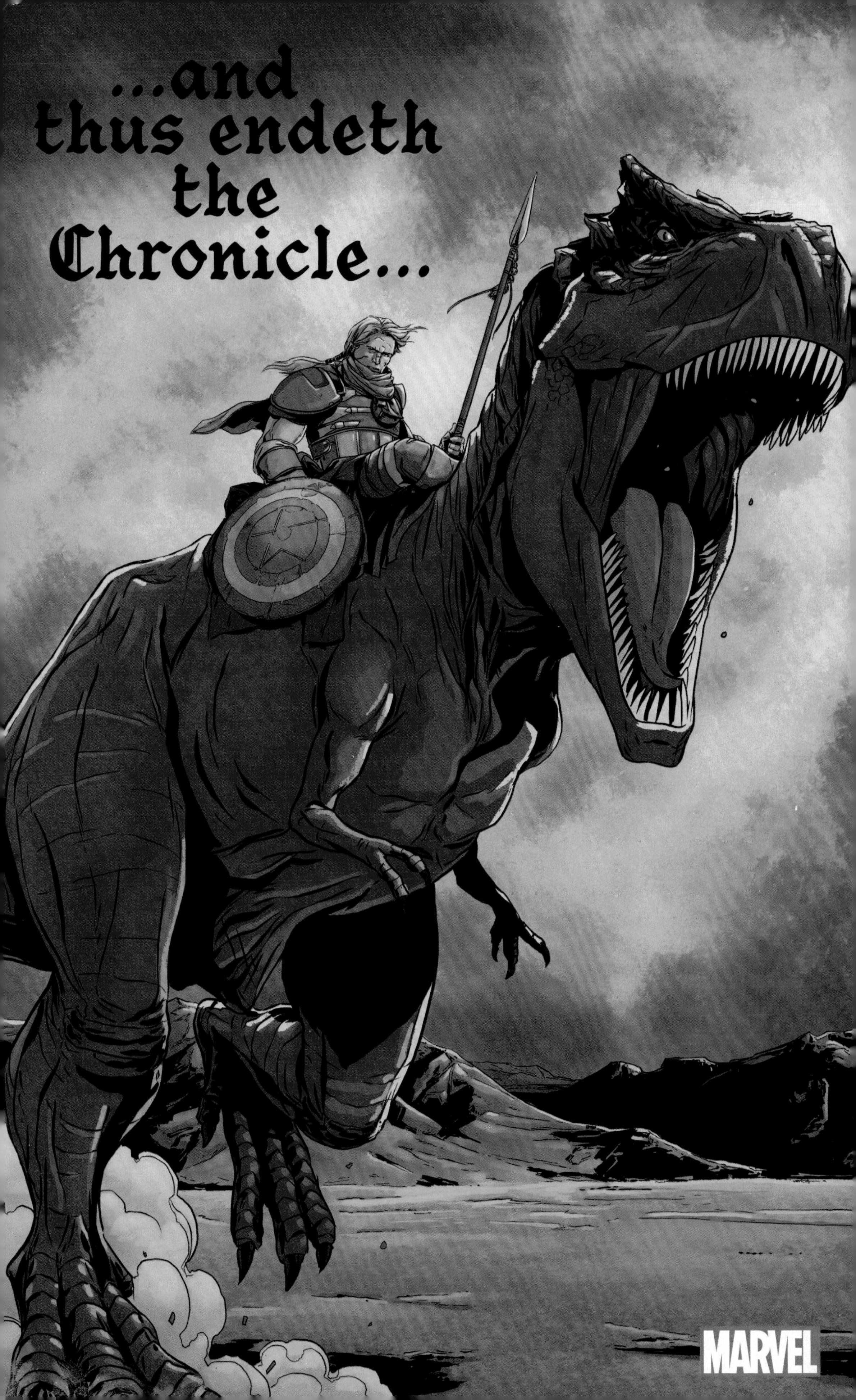

...and
thus endeth
the
Chronicle...
MARVEL

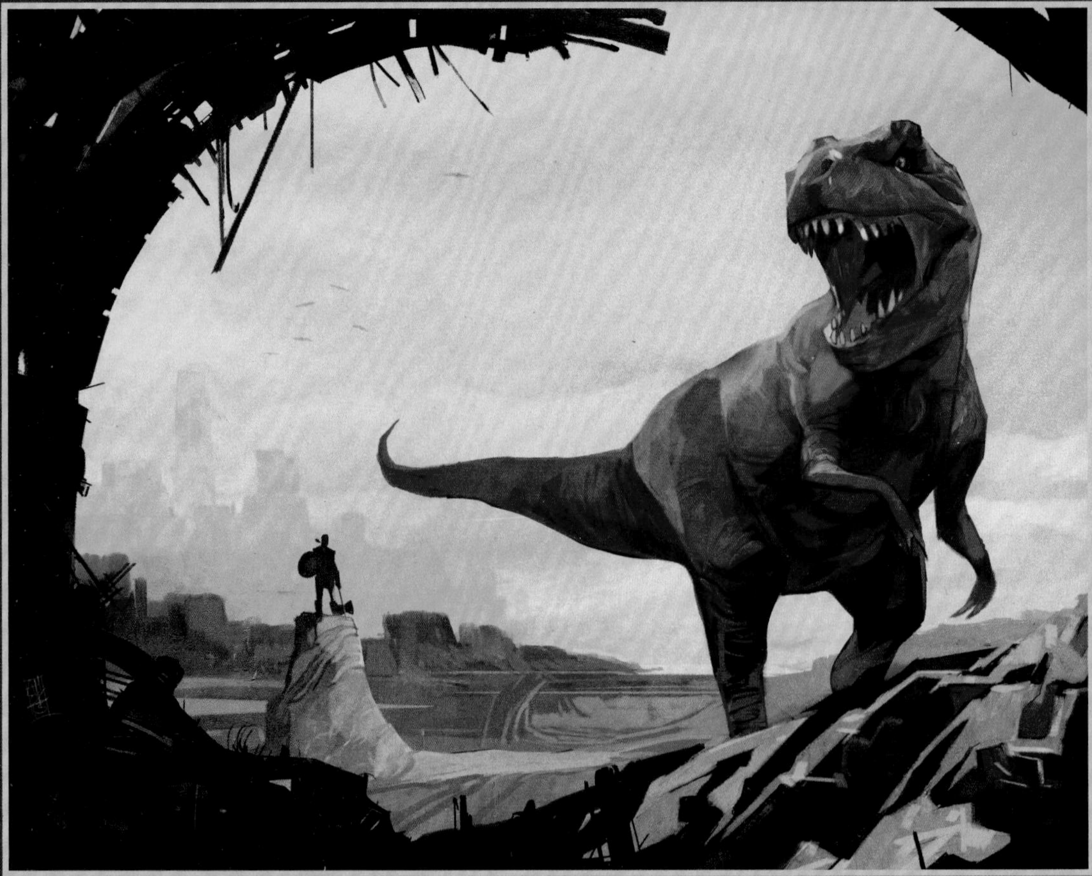

#3 LANDSCAPE VARIANT BY ALEX MALEEV

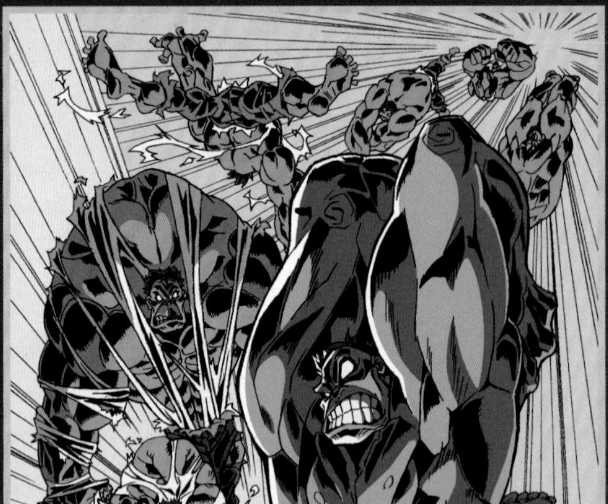

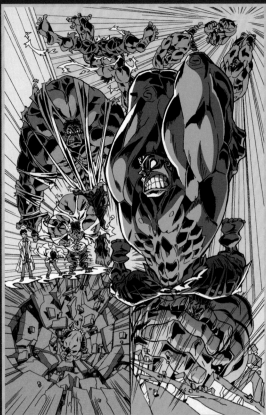

#4 MANGA VARIANT BY
HIROYUKI IMAISHI & GURIHIRU